PIERRE PRADERVAND

messages
of life from Death Row

Disclaimer

Roger McGowen has had no say whatsoever in, or control over, the writing of this book, except in agreeing that excerpts of some of his letters be published. He derives no financial benefits from its publication. The information contained in the book has been put together from various sources, including published research on the death penalty and court transcripts. The opinions expressed in this book (except those in Roger McGowen's letters) are solely those of the author and of the informal, international support group assisting in Roger McGowen's defence, and any errors or inaccuracies are their responsibility and theirs alone.

This is a completely revised, adapted, and expanded version of the book
Messages de vie du couloir de la mort published in 2003 by Editions Jouvence,
B.P. 7, 74161 St-Julien en Genevois, France

ISBN 9780954932657

Published in the UK by Cygnus Books, PO Box 15, Llandeilo, SA19 6YX
www.cygnus-books.co.uk

Printed and bound in the United Kingdom by
Cambrian Printers, Aberystwyth, Wales
www.cambrian-printers.co.uk

TABLE OF CONTENTS

Table of Illustrations

FOREWORD
By Christiane Singer

Reader, be warned!

The impact of this book is unavoidable, the shock it causes profound and lasting. First comes the discovery of that desolate place where the world comes to end: the daily life of the buried-alive who are the Texas death row inmates of today. The isolation, the brutality, the endless screaming all night long compounded by an entire penitentiary institution devoted to tightening the stranglehold. Experts in inhumanity inventing ways to increase suffering -- a legalized, state-sponsored regime that is designed to ensure the continuous degradation and humiliation of the prisoners.

And then, from that demonic hell emerges that which could never be conceived, nor imagined, nor dreamed:

A consciousness.
A fragile beacon of truth.
The finest pinnacle of human tenderness.
His name: Roger McGowen.

This incandescent document is the result of his correspondence with Pierre Pradervand. An Epictetus manuscript for the 21st century. The sublime and gentle Phrygian slave, born 50 years B.C., who, in the middle of the worst brutality of servitude, invents the most radical freedom -- that which no chains, no shackles can restrain -- reappears two thousand years later in a Texas House of Death. In the meantime, Epictetus has met Jesus-Christ, another gentle soul, another mad man, and his *amor fati** has been magnified by an *amor dei et homini**, a fervent invitation to never confuse the worst in men with their ferocity only – to dare look further, further, and further yet into the divine seed that is the foundation of their being.

Yes, I agree! What Roger tells us goes beyond our usual limits. One is entitled to hesitate, to disbelieve, to look for the flaws... Isn't Roger getting high on love just as others get high on hatred? No. Because to get high would mean to dodge, to escape the awareness of an unbearable destiny and the paranoia that it generates. Well, what we find here is precisely the opposite: the love radiating from those letters is born of *the clear awareness of what is* – an awareness that is lived through and through and faces life head-on- it is not an ordinary rapture for escaping a savage reality! Such love goes beyond that deadly zone to emerge into a space unknown – a space the existence of which nothing could have allowed us to foresee.

A space without illusion, which does not take sides pro or con, and of a light so intense that the eyes of the flesh cannot endure it. When touched by it, rage and indignation melt away, every argument loses its substance; there isn't anybody to convince of anything anymore. From now on, the floodgates of compassion are open and everything runs over.

Rare are the souls able to effect such a radical change. Rare those who have lived through hatred, despair, and indignation, and have emerged into that secret garden one used to name with a solar word today obsolete: holiness. But, as the poet Matsu Basho says, the green color of the pine tree is neither modern nor ancient.

Holiness is that invisible force that keeps the world together since its creation. It is the deliberate choice a man makes to be whole (*heilig*, holy), to welcome good and bad, injustice and justice, cruelty as well as kindness, illness and health alike – to welcome and to embrace the entirety of what is – without condition, without restriction, to hold against his heart this scandalous and sublime world as one would rock a sleeping monster.

In a cell of six by nine feet, where light trickles through a six-inch opening, Roger, Black American incarcerated for murder, sentenced to death and innocent, teaches us freedom.

———

* *amor fati*, love and acceptance of one's destiny; *amor dei et homini*, love of God and man [note of transl.]

Christiane Singer is the French author of about twenty books, all published by Albin-Michel (Paris). "Notes of a Hypocrite" has been published by Hodder & Stoughton (London).

PREFACE

In 1997, I met a woman from Zürich, Switzerland, who was corresponding with a prisoner on death row in Texas. The inmate, Roger McGowen, had an active execution date, and the woman hoped I could help her prevent the irrevocable deed. The story she told me was so moving that I started corresponding with Roger myself. At the same time, the courts intervened, and he received a stay of execution pending further appeals.

With each new letter, my relationship with Roger grew, increasing in beauty and depth. He came to occupy a place in my thoughts more meaningful than anyone else's, except that of my wife's, Elly. Roger became a major source of inspiration for me. Today, after more than a decade of correspondence and annual visits, I can honestly say that few people have exercised such an influence on my life. Roger's letters were too beautiful to keep for myself. They belong to the spiritual heritage of humanity.

One day when the death penalty will have been banished from the whole planet – *and that day is certain to come* – our descendants will be astonished to learn that there was a time **when human beings were put to death**! They will be stunned to hear of the barbaric and degrading conditions in which death row inmates would spend 20 to 30 or more years of their lives waiting to be executed. And even more shocking, they will discover that due to a very poorly functioning judicial system, *innocent* people were put to death.

There is a flipside to the astonishing dehumanizing practice of capital punishment: the equally astonishing discovery that every now and then a death row inmate rises far beyond what could be expected of anyone caught in such an environment and becomes a symbol of hope for us all. Men and women who, at the start, were ordinary humans (even former criminals like Karla Faye Tucker) have grown in prison to levels of spiritual understanding many of us will not reach during our life on earth.

One of the powerful messages in the following pages -- one that I have discussed at length with Roger and which he insists I must emphasize -- is that he does not consider himself to be an exceptional person. To put him on a pedestal is to put his spiritual equanimity and strength beyond the reach of ordinary people like you and me. It provides a convenient excuse for snuggling into our comfort zones where we need not challenge ourselves to grow. Like many of us, Roger goes through bouts of depression, deep anger, and once, after a terrible lockdown, he felt hatred, something he had not had to deal with for many years. But he moves through those states and eventually regains his equanimity.

I believe Roger is right when he says he is not different from you or me. This means that we too can achieve what he has achieved, that we too can learn to love unconditionally, to forgive the seemingly unforgivable, to bless others daily, and to express gratitude again and again -- even in circumstances as hellish as Death row. Roger's story, from behind prison walls, is disturbing and confrontational. The following pages are not for the faint of heart!

I suggest, dear reader, that as you find your way through these pages, you listen to the silence between the words. Imagine that you are sitting opposite Roger in his 60-square-foot cell. There are no chairs. He has installed you, his guest of honor, on the bed. He sits on the floor. Picturing this scene will enable you to understand the kind of life experience that makes his words possible and gives them the weight they carry.

Among the many messages you can hear, the following strike me as especially important:

- Love is the fundamental law of the universe, the reply to every situation, our reason for existing, the essence of what we are. Love is easy – hate is the difficult role to play.

- Everything that happens in life is an opportunity to learn. Life is a school of higher learning.

- We can refuse to be victims and take total responsibility for our lives. Even happiness is a *choice* to be made, whatever the circumstances of one's existence.

- God, infinite Love, provides a field of infinite possibilities so each of us can create a life that is perfect for us.

- Everyone creates their own reality essentially through their way of looking at, and interpreting, events, people, and situations.

This can explain why some find peace, even on death row, while others, enjoying every possible social and material advantage, decide to commit suicide. *What we see, what we hear, what we feel is entirely "created," i.e. colored by our consciousness,* and has no other reality than the reality we choose to give it. In other words, **consciousness is all**. It is like a pair of colored glasses through which we filter – create – our existence. Quantum physics has made us aware that the very presence of the observer changes the behavior of particles. Replace "particles" with prison "guards" or "officials," and you will get Roger's message.

There is a Zen story that Gary Zukav tells in his book on modern physics, *The Dancing Wu-Li Masters*. Nan-In, a Zen master of the Meiji period in Japan (end of 19th century), welcomes a university professor who has come to inquire about Zen. As is usual in the Japanese tradition, Nan-In begins by serving tea to his honored guest. When the cup is full, Nan-In continues pouring. The cup starts overflowing. A growing look of puzzlement lightens the guest's eyes as Nan-In keeps pouring, and the cup keeps overflowing. Finally, the professor shouts, "What are you doing? Can't you see it is spilling everywhere?!" Nan-In replies, "You are like this cup of tea -- full of preconceived ideas and concepts concerning Zen. How can I teach you anything if you don't empty your teacup first?"

It is to be hoped that some of Roger's affirmations will prod you to empty a few teacups. Please accept this opportunity to question some of your assumptions, however treasured, instead of keeping your cup of preconceived ideas unnecessarily full. For instance, Roger writes that love is so easy and demands no effort, whereas hate goes against the grain. He claims that hate is not part of our true nature and harms both mind and body. Rational Cartesian minds might revolt at such a statement. And it is true that if we see ourselves only as poor mortals, it is often almost impossible to love and all too easy to hate. But if we see ourselves as children of the Universe, as sons and daughters of the Master of Works (to use an expression from the *Bhagavad-Gita*, one of the great sacred books of India), and we accept that love is the *ultimate essence of our being* and the invisible space in which we move spiritually (as opposed to geographically and physically), then Roger's expression is less startling and may even be accepted as an exciting hypothesis that merits testing in everyday life.

With this in mind, I encourage you to *listen* to these pages as if Roger were sitting opposite you and talking directly to you. Out of this listening, an understanding may well come forth that will unveil for you undreamed-of vistas.

When I first visited Roger in April 1999, he was at the Ellis One Unit in Huntsville, Texas. At the time, I didn't realize that it was a relatively humane place compared to the stark, dehumanizing harshness of his present abode, the Allan Polunsky Unit in Livingston, Texas, where inmates have no physical contact with each other and are almost permanently in solitary confinement. Nonetheless, upon leaving the prison confines I prayed for the strength to never complain about anything in my life again, ever. I believe I can say it is one of the rare promises to myself I have been able to keep!

The Dalai Lama once said that no one is born under an unlucky star; some people simply don't know how to read the heavens. Well, whenever for a fleeting moment I am tempted to complain about something, I immediately think about Roger, and the temptation fades.

It might be useful to explain that, on a spiritual level, Roger is essentially self-taught. He is a universal spiritual thinker who does not belong to any specific religion or denomination -- although he would be the first one to acknowledge the profound influence the Bible has had (and still has) on him, thanks to his devout Baptist mother. He has read broadly and eclectically in the spiritual field, and thinkers as varied as Eckhart Tolle (*The Power of Now*), Neale Donald Walsh (*Conversations with God*), and Mary Baker Eddy (*Science and Health with Key to the Scriptures*) have had a significant impact on his development. He has also been a student of yoga. Some of his correspondents have (unsuccessfully) tried to convert him but he has always remained an independent thinker.

The following pages show the profound attachment that can develop between inmates and their correspondents. Such ties constitute quite literally a lifeline *and are often the only thing that enables an inmate to keep his or her sanity*. Roger spent years on death row before receiving his first visitor.

The idea of writing this book came to me quite naturally after corresponding a few years with Roger. Uplifted by the ideas and resilience conveyed through his letters, I decided that I could not keep to myself what this man was sharing with me. It belonged to the spiritual heritage of humanity. I was fortunate to have a very exceptional Swiss publisher, Jacques Maire, founder and director of *Editions Jouvence*, who immediately accepted my proposal for a book composed in a way that breaks with convention.

The resulting French edition of the book, like the present English version, featured Roger's letters on the right-hand pages and my corroborating narrative on the left-hand pages. The narrative is a compilation of information concerning the American judicial system and life on death row along with highlighted quotes from Roger or other inspirational texts that relate to some aspect of his life. For the information given on many of those pages, I have relied heavily on a website widely viewed as the very best Internet site on the death penalty: www. deathpenaltyinfo.org. Posted by the Death Penalty Information Center (DPIC) this comprehensive site is superbly organized, easy to navigate, and constantly updated. Moreover, it is a model of clarity.

I have made very minor changes in Roger's letters--slight adjustments in punctuation, wording and grammar for the sake of clarity. Also, to avoid the document being replete with dots, I have dropped the dots commonly used to indicate that a passage has been skipped. The letters featured here constitute extracts from a voluminous correspondence. While the selection is *necessarily* subjective, I have tried to present as honestly as possible the Roger I have come to know over the years through our correspondence and our face-to-face visits (two four-hour sessions once a year), This edition includes letters written by Roger in the years since the publication of the original French version (where letters stop in February, 2003) as well as a few letters from him that were spontaneously shared by some of his other correspondents (mostly members of an international group created in 2006 to support an effort to reopen his case). Letters **not** preceded by the mention of the recipient's name were addressed to me.

To protect identities I have replaced most names with initials and avoided specific professional titles, preferring the use of neutral terms such as "the administration," "person in charge" and "officials," etc.

Roger has become a source of unique spiritual inspiration for me. For instance, no one has ever helped me as much as he has to overcome the temptation to feel a victim. Since coming to know this rare soul, complaint has practically disappeared from my life. How could I, who am so privileged in so many ways, still find little niches in my life to stuff with dissatisfaction or bitterness, when my friend placed in the nightmare of Death row still manages to rejoice, to bless and thank his Creator?

For death row is anything but a rose garden, and death row in Texas is acknowledged as one of the toughest in the United States. Only Oklahoma, where death row is underground and inmates never see the natural sunlight or feel a gust of wind, is more physically punishing and inhumane. As evidenced in the pages ahead, the incredible inhumanity of the death row system actually represents the sort of "cruel and unusual" form of punishment forbidden by the United States Constitution.

Death row inmates in Texas are in almost permanent solitary confinement and never have the possibility of embracing another inmate or a visitor, even in passing. They are submitted to what is called "sensory deprivation," i.e. a life in grayish surroundings, without contact with wind, rain or sun (other than brief and occasional moments in a small courtyard exercise area). For individuals so cut off from the world having a correspondent can literally be a matter of life and death. Beyond helping sustain the will to live, it can make the difference between remaining sane and succumbing to insanity.

For those who spend years without receiving a single visit, but also for those who do have people who come to see them, a correspondent or pen pal can become *the most important relationship in their life*-especially when the period of detention spans two or three *decades* without light at the end of the tunnel.

Hundreds of death row inmates throughout the United States are yearning for pen friends. It is rather sad that many inmates find correspondents only in Europe. I can only hope that these pages will inspire Americans of good will – of whom there are so, so many, as my yearly visits to the States over a period of 40 years have shown me – to start corresponding with death row inmates.

In his letters, Roger mentions frequently that most of the officers (prison guards) are decent people, just earning their living doing a very tough job. This is an important point. It is the very *system* of death row and high-security prisons itself that is so inhumane. Also, a few sadistic officers or one harsh warden or major can transform the place into a living hell, however decent the rank and file may be. Please keep this in mind as you read these letters.

At the same time, it must also be stressed that most death row inmates are in prison for crimes they admit having committed. Some of those crimes are horrendous, especially those against children, and my heart goes out to the victims and their families. I specifically remember one case where an inmate on a US death row was ostracized by other inmates because the crime he had committed was so utterly gruesome. I have grandchildren who are the greatest joy in my life. If their lives were terminated, like that of some of the children described on victims' websites, I do not know how I would react. I can well imagine the emotional urge for vengeance, even though I do not believe vengeance has ever healed any conflict situation or anyone of pain. I'm convinced there is a better, more effective way -- as the members of victims associations *against* the death penalty show. But I think it important at the beginning of this book to state that I cannot emphasize too strongly how deeply I feel for and with families who have lost members in the cruelest of circumstances.

This book can be read in different ways. One would be to read all Roger's letters first, and to then read the left-hand pages. Some readers of the French and Dutch editions chose to do it the other way around. And yet others read both together, which may be the most logical approach.

The response to the original French edition of this book has been amazing (see the website: www.rogermcgowen.org). Roger was overwhelmed with letters from readers who come from every walk of life. Some sent incredibly generous donations for his defense fund. Among the contributors, an unemployed electrician with very modest resources wrote me a five-page letter explaining how the book had changed his life, and enclosed a check for $2,500. Classrooms of schoolchildren began writing to Roger, and whole congregations in monasteries started saying prayers and masses for him. Today, Roger is "carried" by the prayers of many people in many countries.

"*The winds of grace are always blowing, but you have to raise the sail,*" the Indian teacher Ramakrishna once stated. Roger raised his, *even though it appeared there was no wind to move it.* Yet, this very act of faith caused his sail to fill and start moving his boat forward. And now, many others have started sailing in the wake of Roger's boat, named unconditional love and forgiveness. One day we will all get there.

It is humanity's ultimate spiritual destiny to replace hate and indifference with love, all forms of want with the demonstration of infinite abundance, and societies based on competition with relationships that are *all* in the win-win mode (including man's relationship with nature). In the meantime, dear reader, climb aboard Roger's boat for a few hours and let your sail be filled with the winds of grace.

———

ACKNOWLEDGEMENTS

I wish to thank Garance Jaquet, Ron and Robin Radford, Mirjam Conrad, Conor Perry, Monica Pejovic, and Humberto Normey, members of Roger's international support group, for a very thorough reading of the initial manuscript, and my American writer friend Bunny McBride for carefully pruning the manuscript and substantially improving it. I also wish to thank all the members of the support group from eight countries for their steady support of Roger's cause.

For her utterly tireless efforts, my thanks to Evelyne Giordani, the volunteer chairwoman of the Swiss *Lifespark* network, whose hundreds of members correspond with death row inmates in the United States. She is one of a vast army of volunteers around the world who work in areas of great social concern. Most work quietly in the background unheralded by the media. Yet, without their contributions, the world would come to a grinding halt in a matter of days. The *Lifespark News* Evelyne so ably edits has been my main source of information on the US legal system and death row for years.

My thanks also to John Rizzo and the layout and design teams at BookSurge for their help in publishing this English edition of the book.

Above all, I wish to thank the many readers of the French and Dutch editions of this book from the handicapped person who sent $12 to the anonymous donor of $9,000. Their immense generosity enabled us to finally hire Roger's present lawyer.

Pierre Pradervand, Geneva, Switzerland, info@vivreautrement.ch

———

BACKGROUND INFORMATION
ON ROGER'S YOUTH AND TRIAL

Roger McGowen, the seventh of ten children, was born on December 23, 1963 in the 5th Ward, then one of the worst ghettos of Houston, Texas. His parents, Mary and James McGowen, divorced when he was still a child. He spent most of his youth in the 5th Ward with his mother, a profoundly devout Baptist, but for a few years during adolescence he lived in the 3rd Ward with his father. The 3rd Ward neighborhood was less tough and more structured, and Roger keeps a luminous memory of his years there. Schools were slightly better, the streets tidier, people more open. His step-mother, Ernestine, encouraged him in his school work, and he formed a strong attachment to his half-brother Terry. In 1982, just before Roger's 18th birthday, an armed robber killed his father who was only 42 years old.

Roger always remained in very close contact with his mother who communicated her lively faith to her son. In a brief, ten-page autobiographical document, Roger described her in a manner that shows the profound impact she had on him:

"My mother was a lady who believed strongly in God and looked for the good in everyone. She taught us the value of life, and also the heartache of pain, which comes from suffering. She was the strongest person I ever knew in my life, and she remained that way till she was called home to God. Many of the lessons she taught me have remained with me till this very day. But at the time, when she was imparting her wisdom to me, I had no use for it. I was young and thought that I knew everything, only to learn that when I thought I understood, I only misunderstood.

So often we take the wisdom of our elders for granted, not realizing that we have not even begun to encounter half the things which they have experienced, the experiences that will eventually make or break us, as one says. My mother would tell me:"Roger, wisdom does not come from age, it comes from experience. It comes from countless encounters with the things that life will show us, give us, or take away from us.

It would be years before I would realize what she was talking about. But today, even though she now rests in her grave, I call upon her wisdom to sustain me and guide me through the perils of a sometimes cold world."

Life in the ghetto was hard. By age ten, Roger was working outside school with his uncle Jimmy, who had a large, 18-wheel truck. Later, Roger found a job in a restaurant. "When I was nine-ten years old I was purchasing clothes for my sister Rhonda," he recalls.

Roger's elder brother Charles was, as Roger puts it, his "idol." To grasp what happened later, when Roger was accused of murder, it is important to understand their almost symbiotic relationship, which Roger explains like this:

"My eldest brother was well known around our neighborhood. He was known for not being one to mess with, and being his little brother, I was privileged not to be messed with either, unless you wanted to deal with Charles.

Man, could he fight. I saw him fight a guy one day for beating up one of his friends. It wasn't really a fight. He hit the guy, and the guy hit the ground. But in other fights I watched him weave and bob and slip punches. I thought he could whip Mohammed Ali, the then heavyweight champion of the world.

He and I were very close. I would try and follow him and his friends. He would see me and run me back home. But sometimes I would follow them from a distance, without them knowing. I tried to walk like him, talk like him, practically become him. He was my idol then. He was great. He used to talk to me and tell me things about him and his friends and swear me to secrecy. I thought I was carrying a real top secret and was ready to defend it with my life, if need be. Thank God it never came to that."

Charles had brushes with the police early in life. In his teenage years he was even charged with murder, but as he was still an adolescent, he was sent to a juvenile facility.

Shortly before Roger's mother passed on, she was taken to the hospital where she stayed quite a few days in a coma. In a letter dated March 6, 2005, Roger gave me the following details of this experience which would play such a crucial role in his life:

"While I was visiting her in the hospital, she came out of her coma. She was speaking very incoherently. She would start talking about one thing, then right in the middle about something else. She realized it too, and started smiling. She said to me, 'Roger, I don't want to die, but I feel there's nothing between me and God. I'm young, I have a lot to live for, but I'm at peace. If I don't make it, look after your brother. You are strong and always have been, and you've had it good. Your brother hasn't. He can't go back to prison. You are the backbone of the family. Take care of them.' One of the nurses came into the room, and saw me talking to her, and realized she had come out of her coma. She rushed me from the room and that was the last conversation I had with my mother."

At the time of the crime which he was accused of committing (1986), Roger was 22 years old and worked full-time. He was caring for his sisters who lived on the other side of town. He would stop by regularly to inquire about their wellbeing, bring them food, and make sure their bills were paid.

Among his mother's ten children, Roger was the only one who had a car, and he shared it generously. One day, Charles and Roger's cousin Kerwin (who was then living with Roger) went to a bar in Roger's car, intending to rob the place. From what we understand of the situation, Kerwin went in first to examine the place, then came out and told Charles to perform the robbery. But the owner, Marion Panzer, pulled out her gun and apparently shot Charles in the leg, who then fired impulsively, presumably in self-defense, and killed her. Charles told Roger he was involved in the crime, which Roger by then had heard about. Later, the police came to Roger's apartment to question him.

Because of his mother's request just before her death that he protect Charles, Roger accepted the blame in lieu of his brother. One of the police detectives questioning Roger had assured him that, as he had no criminal record and was not a felon, he would only get a "slap on the wrist," and certainly did not risk the death penalty. As Roger saw it, nothing tied him to the crime, and he felt certain his innocence would become evident, especially since he had an alibi. He only hoped that by sacrificing himself he could show his brother how much he loved him, and that this would lead Charles to break with delinquency and change his way of life.

The detectives took Roger's confession in a manner that is now being condemned—typing it out for him and then getting him to sign it. This method of taking statements has played a major role in cases involving false confessions. Many states have now mandated that the statements of the accused be video-taped to prevent false confessions and subsequent convictions. The Houston Police Department had the ability to video-tape their interrogation of Roger but failed to do so.

It is important to realize that false confessions lead to many wrongful convictions. For example, it is known that of the 242 post-conviction DNA exonerations to date (September, 2009) for severe crimes in the USA, including 17 men who served on death row, a full 25% had been wrongly convicted on the basis of a false confession and self-incriminating statements.

Soon after Roger's arrest, police shot and killed Charles during an attempted robbery. Hearing this news was one of the cruelest experiences in Roger's life: his beloved brother for whom he had taken the blame – which ultimately came with a penalty of death – had died. All of a sudden, Roger's sacrifice seemed completely devoid of any sense.

As is usually the case with indigent capital defendants, Roger had a state-appointed attorney who visited him only once very briefly before his appearance in front of the judge. This lawyer, a known alcoholic, was later chastised repeatedly by the Texas Bar Association for his poor performance. When the State of Texas finally set stricter minimum standards for the appointment of capital counsel to indigent defendants in 2001, he was unable to qualify. In 2004, the Texas Bar Association put him on a (partially-probated) three-year suspension. But in the meantime, Roger – and at least fifteen others represented by this particular attorney – have been sentenced to death (more than ten have been executed so far).

The entire trial was marred by major judicial and constitutional errors. The lawyer prepared his plea solely on the basis of the police report. At different times during the trial of his client, he fell asleep. He never bothered to even make a single phone call to check Roger's alibi. All in all, his defense was simply pathetic.

It is not uncommon in the United States for prosecuting attorneys to seek inmates willing to give incriminating testimony against a defendant. Such people are called jail "snitches" and there is an unspoken agreement that if a snitch agrees to testify against a defendant, he will receive a substantial sentence reduction. The agreements – if written – almost always call for truthful testimony in exchange for favorable treatment in their own cases – usually relating to their sentence. For inmates desperate to get help on their own sentence, though, it generates a tremendous motive to create evidence, even if false, against the target of the case. Testimony (usually false) by snitches contributed to wrongful convictions in 16% of cases of post-conviction DNA exonerations in the United States.

In many Texas jurisdictions at the time of Roger's trial, these "agreements" were not written down, were often made in secret, and were hidden from the court and the defendant. Because they were kept secret from everyone but the state and the "snitch," they became known as "wink and nod" agreements. Alas, this happened with Roger's case. The District Attorney contacted an inmate who had known Roger as a young adolescent. The inmate, N.R.W., invented some 1500 armed robberies purportedly committed with Roger over a two-and-a-half-year period, at a time when Roger had been working full-time! As Roger told me:

"In one instance, N.W.R. said he and I robbed this old man who was a security guard at a supermarket. The prosecutor contacted the man and had him testify for the prosecution against me. N. said I had the knife and I was going to kill the man. But when the elderly gentleman took the stand, he said it wasn't me! He said it was N. and someone else."

Also, there is a signed affidavit by N.R.W. stating that the Assistant District Attorney (ADA) handling the case had been given information before the trial that Charles had committed the murder, but the ADA failed to disclose that fact to the defense lawyer representing Roger. This constitutes a *major* constitutional violation. Furthermore, also in violation of the Constitution and Texas law, the presiding judge refused to instruct the jury about the difference between voluntary homicide and voluntary homicide with premeditation.

Roger's attorney also neglected to protest against serious breaches in the jury's behaviour. Those alone should have justified a new trial. A few examples:

- In their deliberation room, the jurors had access to newspaper articles presenting a highly biased view of the crime, in which the police falsely claimed that Roger had committed about 50 armed robberies. Roger's lawyer made an inadequate challenge to this misconduct and the court failed to insure that Roger had a jury that was free of the resultant taint against him.

- One of the jurors, herself a lawyer, confirmed under oath that the jury foreman, a former policeman, had unlawfully introduced information during the jury deliberations that had not been presented in court; that information greatly influenced the jury's decision in favor of the death penalty for Roger.

- Various members of the jury were not in favor of the death penalty for Roger, but because of the strong personality of the former policeman who presented himself as an expert and was highly biased throughout the trial, they finally gave in. Yet, Texas law states that "the presence of one partial juror on the jury destroys the impartiality of the body and renders it partial."

- Whereas the jury initially voted eleven to one (11 to 1) for life imprisonment instead of the death penalty, the judge presented information which erroneously implied that if Roger were sentenced to life in prison, he would end up spending only a third of the time in jail before being released. This untruthful information also contributed to the jurors switching their position in favor of the death penalty for Roger.

This list comprises only a very few of the grave irregularities that marred the trial. Finally, it should also be stressed that the sentencing system under which Roger was condemned to death has now been repudiated by the Texas legislature. However, unfairly, the changes were not made retroactive and apply only to cases tried on or after September, 2005.

Roger appealed the judgment and was given a second state-appointed lawyer – a man who did not bother to contact him for well over four years. Finally, Roger managed to reach him by phone. (In his first prison, the Ellis One Unit in Huntsville, inmates could make two phone calls a year. This is no longer possible in the Allan Polunsky Unit in Livingston where all Texas death row inmates are presently held.) Roger's initial relief about making contact vanished when the lawyer informed him that he had decided not to take the case, because one of the policemen on the case was a close friend of his! Roger asked him why he had needed over four years to come to that conclusion…

Things seemed more promising with Roger's next state-appointed lawyer, who came to see him on death row. However, upon meeting Roger, he asked him point blank, without so much as a greeting, "Why did you kill her?" Roger politely told him he did not need a lawyer who had already made up his mind concerning his supposed guilt and declined his services.

And so it goes in a system that makes it possible for inmates to spend more than 30 years on death row without being executed. Is this not one of the most unusual and cruel forms of punishment ever to exist in a civilized country? Roger, now 45 years old, has been in prison since the age of 22 (he spent about a year in the county jail before the trial).

It is important to constantly remind yourself, as you read the following letters, that their author has been an inmate since 1987 in one of the worst death row penitentiaries of the USA, and he knows he is there simply because his most elementary constitutional rights have been trampled on – in a country claiming to be the world leader in the field of human rights.

Thanks to a correspondent living in Switzerland, a group of friends in that country got together and gathered funds to hire a private lawyer. He presented a Writ of Habeas Corpus, the legal document demanding a new trial, in the Court of Criminal Appeals, State of Texas, and in the District Court of Harris County, Texas (which has had many more death sentences and executions than any other US county, and more than any US state outside of Texas).

In 2005, at long last, the Court of Criminal Appeals asked the judge sitting on the case to reactivate it. Then that judge withdrew from the case and another one was appointed. At the same time, Roger's private lawyer left Texas. Roger was given a new state-appointed attorney without having even been consulted. The following summer, that lawyer also moved to another state. By that time (January, 2006), I had established an international defense committee comprised of about 12 individuals who correspond closely with Roger. That fall we hired a private lawyer, who is now working diligently toward a new and fair trial for Roger.

For more information about Roger, and for the latest news about his case, see www.rogermcgowen.org

———

"I believe in my heart that one day I will walk out of here. I have never thought otherwise."

(Roger McGowen, June 6, 2004)

A drawing by Roger for a correspondent

Roger's letters from the Ellis One Unit

These early letters were written from the Ellis One Unit in Huntsville, where Texas death row inmates were imprisoned until March, 2000. At Ellis inmates shared cells, there was a large recreation area where they could meet each other every day and they had the much treasured right to undertake "piddling" – inmate jargon for the handicraft activities that helped many of them maintain sanity in the wretched world of death row.

1990

To Conor, Ireland. (Conor was one of Roger's first correspondents and the first person to start visiting him.)
I was married for three-and-a-half years, and I have a son. He turned seven recently. I have not seen him since I have been here, and that's over three years. It breaks my heart just to speak his name. My hobby now is exercising and reading. I also make objects from matchsticks and toothpicks – jewelry boxes and picture frames -whenever I find the materials.

I did not really know what loneliness was until I came here. Sometimes you want to reach out and touch someone, share your feeling with someone, but then when you reach out there is no one there. It is impossible to get help here in the US. When they have an execution, people gather outside what we call death house and chant: "Kill 'em, kill'em" *(December 16, 1990)*

1991

To Conor
This is the first time I have spoken in two weeks. Well, I'm not exactly speaking to you, but to me it's the closest I've come to. I was lonely and have been for some time until I received your letter. I don't know, sometimes I start remembering my family, maybe I'm feeling sorry for myself, but I long to be embraced by loving arms, I long for a smile.

Where is the soft soothing voice that used to be there when you thought it was all over, that said "It's going to be all right, don't you worry" and through some game of fate, it dawns on me: It's over, you're alone now, all alone. It hurts like hell. I never knew I could hurt so much, so deeply. *(September 25, 1991)*

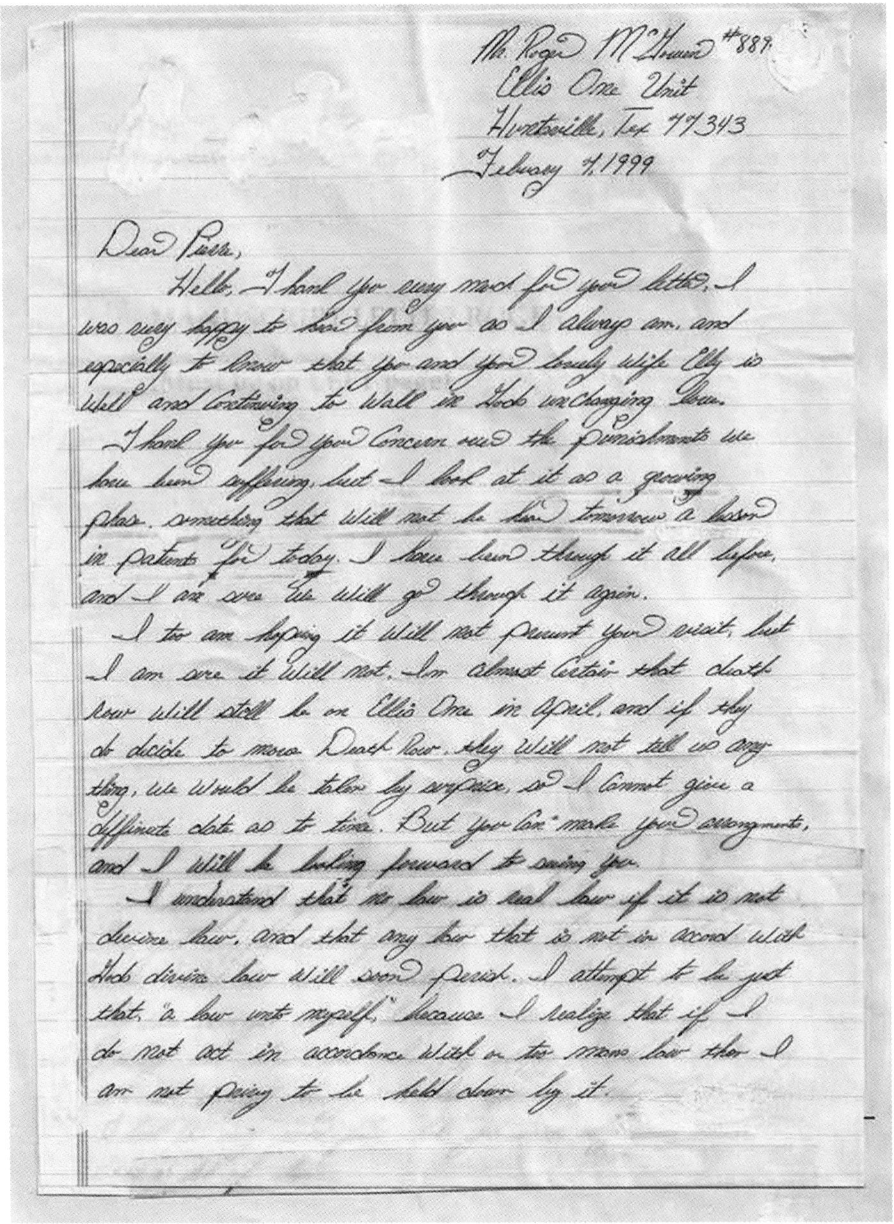

Mr. Roger McGowen #889
Ellis One Unit
Huntsville, Tex 77343
February 4, 1999

Dear Pierre,

Hello, Thank you very much for your letter, I was very happy to hear from you as I always am, and especially to know that you and your lovely wife Elly is well and continuing to walk in God's unchanging peace.

Thank you for your concern over the punishments we have been suffering, but I look at it as a growing phase, something that will not be here tomorrow, a lesson in patience for today. I have been through it all before, and I am sure we will go through it again.

I too am hoping it will not prevent your visit, but I am sure it will not, I'm almost certain that death row will still be on Ellis One in April, and if they do decide to move Death Row, they will not tell us anything, we would be taken by surprise, so I cannot give a definite date as to time. But you can make your arrangements, and I will be looking forward to seeing you.

I understand that no law is real law if it is not divine law, and that any law that is not in accord with God's divine law will soon perish. I attempt to be just that, "a law unto myself," because I realize that if I do not act in accordance with the same law then I am not going to be held down by it.

A handwritten letter from Roger

1993

To Conor

The heat has gotten unbearable and the executions have gotten so out of hand that it is hard for one to think straight. They executed two very good friends of mine. They were brothers, the Harris brothers, Curtis and Danny. Curtis the younger brother was executed on the first of July, and then they turned around and executed Danny on the 30th of July, one day before his 31st birthday. He wrote me a letter and I received it the very next day after his death. I was so touched that through all his suffering and all his heartache after losing a brother then facing death himself, he could take the time and write to me to say goodbye. The day before yesterday they executed another inmate I knew well.

Conor, I had to make a change in my life. I had been on lockdown for three years, looking at the same sights, hearing the same racist remarks every day, trying to assist people but all the time ending up by being used because you showed a little love, a little kindness to someone which [here] is considered being weak. I could no longer take it. The manager of the garment factory came and asked me if I would get back on the work program. I decided that if I did not get a change soon I would go crazy so I wrote him and told him why not. So that is where I write you from. I have a lot of trees to look at. They are so beautiful it is intoxicating. When I first saw them I could not take my eyes off them, they were so lovely that I wanted to cry. All of this I have been missing. I felt grass for the first time since I have been here. *(August 7, 1993)*

1996

To Conor

Hello, how are you and your family? I pray that you are all well.

Man, you are the cool guy for putting up with me this long. You have much patience, Conor. I hope everything is going well with you. Thank you very much for being my friend. You have helped more than you could ever know, you were there when I was down, you went through it all. Thank you, you are a true friend. *(April 14, 1996)*

When truth comes from the mouth of babes

"Our governor is a physician, a minister, runs on a pro-life platform, and signs a death-penalty warrant for Ralph Baze. What's wrong with this picture? How can someone be pro-life and pro-death at the same time?

My daughter, now grown, asked me when she was five years old why someone on the news was executed. I explained that he had killed someone.

She looked at me and asked: 'If they are killing him for killing someone, who is going to kill them for killing him?'

That had a long-lasting, profound impact on me. I do not know Ralph Baze or anyone else on death row. What I do know is that killing is wrong on any level."

(Pat Bush, Letter to the editor, *Journal-Courier*, Louisville, Kentucky, August, 2007, quoted in *Lifespark newsletter*, No 34, 2007)

1997

To Pierre, Switzerland. (Roger and I began corresponding in 1997. As noted in the introduction, all letters in this book were written to me, unless identified otherwise).

There are over 30 execution dates set for the next three months here in Texas. The atmosphere is filled with the stench of death. Many men try to ignore the coming storm, hoping their name will not come up too soon, but in the end they all do. My cellmate was just moved two weeks ago, because he is being prepared for demise. He is a 36-year-old child. He has never had a mother. His father tried to raise him, but with work and booze it was impossible, so he raised himself the best he knew how, and that means on the street. He cannot read or write, his comprehension is almost non-existent, he has the mind of a child. I tried to teach him how to read and write. It was very difficult, but he tried.

The last few days before he was moved we spent time in the cell together. He could not sleep, and I did not sleep, knowing he wanted to talk. Those were the hardest talks I have ever had. It was like trying to explain to a child why people had to die. He wanted to know what was going to happen to him. Would someone there try to stop them? What could I tell him? What could I do? So I remained silent. I listened to him for a week before he was moved to the death cell. It is possible that before you get this letter he will be dead.

He will die alone – his father passed on two months ago from a stroke. I told him that he had a very long, lonely walk ahead of him, and that there was nothing I could say to change that, Pierre. What would you have said to a man who was looking at his last sunrise and sunset, who would never again feel the rain or the sand between his toes? I thought that I could say something to comfort him, but in the end, everything that I said were only words, nothing more, and he must still walk that last yard alone. *(April 4, 1997)*

My friend has passed on, and with him went several more: I talked to each of them, minutes before they were taken to their final destination, and I found myself struggling to find the words to comfort them and at the same time say my farewell. This is one of the most difficult times I have had besides saying goodbye to my mother before she left for her journey.

I believe we can change people and situations through love and prayer. The power of love and prayer is something we think we understand, but we really do not. When I was a child growing up, my mother would always tell me:" Never pray for yourself, Roger. Always pray for others, and then your prayers will be answered." And I have never forgotten that lesson.

Lethal injection – a form of torture?

"The infliction of unnecessary pain in putting people to death is a form of torture. Lethal injection poses a substantial threat of unbearable pain and cruel and pro-tracted death. The very slightest error in the administration of one of the three drugs used can leave the prisoner "conscious but paralyzed, a sentient witness to his own slow asphyxiation" (Court of Appeals in *Chaney v. Heckler*).

The three drugs used are:

1) sodium thiopental, widely known as "Pentothal" (an anesthetic that puts the inmate to sleep)
2) pancuronium bromide, tubucarine chloride, or succinylcholine (muscle relaxants that paralyze the voluntary muscles, but have no impact of any sort on the awareness and sensations of the inmate)
3) potassium chloride (not used in every state), which interrupts the electrical signaling necessary to the heart function and causes great pain. This combination of drugs seems to have caused some inmates to suffer excruciatingly painful deaths. If this is true, it undoubtedly constitutes a particularly unacceptable and barbaric form of cruel and unusual punishment.

The fact that chemicals inducing general anesthesia can cause unbearable pain when administered incorrectly is corroborated by the experience of an eye surgery patient, Carol Weihrer, who describes what happened during her eye operation:

"I experienced what has come to be known as Anesthesia Awareness, in which I was able to think… lu-cidly, hear, perceive and feel everything that was going on during the surgery, but I was unable to move. It burnt like the fires of hell. It was the most terrifying, torturous experience that you can imagine. The experience was worse than death"(Affidavit of C. Weihrer in *Texas v. Jesus Flores*, 877,994A).

In other words, this drug misleads witnesses to believe they are seeing someone being gently "put to sleep," when in fact the person being executed may well be undergoing ravaging pain amounting to extreme torture.

One of the leading medical magazines in the world, *The Lancet* (365,1412-1414, 2005), suggests that a full 43 percent of inmates might still be conscious when the potassium chloride rips through their veins in its mission of heart arrest, and a leading science magazine, *Nature*, called on scientists and MDs to refuse any participation in such ex-ecutions. If terrible accidents such as the one described above can happen in hospital settings with qualified personnel, what might be happening with often poorly trained prison medical technicians or nurses?

(continued p. 18)

My cellmate now is a young man. He is only 22, but he has a chip on his shoulder bigger than Texas. I do not know how or why he got it. I only know that he does. He thinks that every time someone says something of him, it is a threat against his manhood. Many times I have had to talk him out of trouble. He wants me to do everything for him: write, read to him, feed him, clean up after him, and every other unimaginable thing you can think of. He is one of the laziest people I have ever seen. Last night, we were able to go to the [prison] store to purchase things. After we came back from the store, he was sitting in the cell with a frown on his face like he was really mad. I told him that when I came to the cell, I expected a smile on his face, otherwise he could leave it until lock-up time. He looked at me and says: "You didn't get me anything from the store?" I said. "Did you ask me?" He says nothing, so I go back and get him an ice cream. He took it and left, never saying thanks or anything.

I have been praying for this kid ever since he has been in the cell with me, and I believe that as long as I do not give up on him, he can overcome whatever problems are disturbing him. But he must at least be willing to change. He shows no inclinations of even wanting to change, but I will continue to pray for him, because prayer is all that is left for this kid. You can pray for him as well. His name is James. *(July 9, 1997)*

I was very happy to receive your letter with the "peace sticker" from your wife's foundation. [This sticker says in six languages: "My home is a place of peace"]. It has already gone up on my door. They can pull it off. But the symbolism of it remains.

I'm sorry to inform you that the first articles you sent me were destroyed by the officials during a major shakedown [complete search of cell] for a shank [knife]. Whenever they have major shakedowns, they first lock every one up, and begin to destroy everything in sight. They do not ask what you would prefer to keep or throw out. They throw it all out. The articles were on a board that I had fixed on the wall. It was ripped off and thrown out. I am so sorry. *(October 7, 1997)*

There have been many executions since we last corresponded. Yet I am here, and that counts for something. Things are looking as good as they ever were. I believe that God has sustained me for a reason. I do not believe in luck. I believe this concept is used by man to keep him from giving God His proper dues. But all dues and praises go unto Him.

I try to give each person I meet the joy, patience, understanding, and honesty that God has given to me.

Thank you for your inspiration and friendship. I'm sorry this letter is not longer – please understand that my old arm must redevelop itself. [Roger's typewriter broke down]. Take care, and God's praises be formed on your lips and in your heart, and His mercy surround you. *(October 14, 1997)*

Lethal injection (continued)

In 2006, Arkansas, California, Florida, Kentucky, Louisiana, Maryland, Missouri, and South Dakota temporarily halted all executions. A year later, all States declared a moratorium on executions by lethal injection, pending a ruling by the US Supreme Court about the constitutionality of the method. On April 16, 2008, the Supreme Court ruled that execution by lethal injection does not constitute a "cruel and unusual punishment" and is therefore not in violation of the US Constitution. A few weeks later, some States resumed executing inmates by lethal injection.

Since 1981, 19 states, including Texas, have made it illegal to euthanize animals by using sedatives combined with a neuromuscular blocking agent. Further, a report by the American Medical Veterinary Association (AMVA), the leading professional association of veterinarians, prohibits the use of such drugs in the practice of euthanasia. It is especially interesting that Texas enacted a legislation mandating "humane" methods for putting animals to death, specifically recognizing that the use of these chemicals is totally inappropriate and inhumane for euthanizing pets.

Apparently, Texas inmates do not qualify for the degree of compassion shown toward animals.

This form of execution, long hailed by its supporters as superior to previous methods, is so flawed that it falls far below veterinary standards for euthanizing sick animals. Whereas the AMVA calls for the highest level of training and qualification for personnel euthanizing animals, researchers who analyzed execution procedures in Texas and Virginia (which together execute close to half of those put to death in the USA) discovered that the executioners–usually emergency medical technicians or medical military personnel– *had no training in anesthesia*. No records were kept about sedation doses nor were any checks made after the execution to ensure a "proper" death.

Not surprisingly, the American Medical Association has ethical guidelines forbidding doctors to take part in executions as such participation violates medical ethics.

(Source: most of the information from this page comes from the article, *"The Extraordinary Execution of Billy Vickers, the Banality of Death, and the Demise of Post-Conviction Review,"* by David R. Dow, Jim Marcus, Morris Moon, Jared Tyler, and Gregory Wiercioch, in *13 William & Mary Bill of Rights Journal* 305-521 (2004). Professor Dow is one of the leading US authorities on the death penalty. His book, *Executed on a Technicality – Lethal Injustice on America's Death Row*, Beacon Press, 2005, is "must" reading for anyone concerned with this topic. See also www.rogermcgowen.org)

1998

Many of the guys here look at each other with a certain forbearance. It's as if everyone knows that some will not be here to welcome the next year in. Many know that their appeals are almost up, and life is getting shorter. I try to think that way sometimes, Pierre, but I can't bring myself to think of myself as dead yet.

I had been trying hard to raise money to hire a certain lawyer considered the best appeals lawyer in Texas. He already got three people off death row. Since I could not hire him, I let my friend D. R. know about him and helped him write some very good introductory letters [to this lawyer]. D. was able to find help and hire the lawyer. The lawyer has secured his freedom, and now D. is going home. Sometimes I feel: "Why, Lord, couldn't it have been me, given all the work I did?" Is that wrong? Yet I am happy D. is going home, because it gives everyone else hope that they can do the same. I realize that God has given us all certain work that we must do before we claim our glory. I just wish my job was a lot clearer. I am sure that my calling is to help others, because that is all I do, that is what I like to do, Pierre. But sometimes I get confused and need some guidance. *(January 10, 1998)*

In this next letter dated March 29, 1998, Roger tells how he was placed in solitary confinement as a result of a ploy to get him off the wing where he resided, his presence being a hindrance to certain illegal activities masterminded by some inmates. For the same reason, he lost his most precious belongings – the handicraft tools he used to fashion exquisite boxes, the result of years of practice. After "piddling" daily for nine years, he writes, "What a blow to wake up and realize there is nothing, man." A blow indeed, for creative work is a major source of stability and sanity in such an environment.

How are you and your beautiful wife? I hope and pray that God's blessings stay upon you and sustain you for as long as you wish. God is truly wonderful. He gives us untold blessings, including some that we cannot see, nor ever understand.

Texas Death Row: the only one without TV

In the Ellis One Unit in Huntsville (where Texas death row inmates were kept until the year 2000 and where Roger spent his first 13 years in prison), inmates were often housed two to a cell and could meet and talk in the courtyard with other inmates for a while every day. Moreover, prison regulations allowed them to engage in all sorts of handicraft activities. (Roger, for instance, made beautiful little carved jewelry boxes, truly exquisite). Death row inmates at the Ellis One Unit also had access to TV and could make occasional phone calls. These are *major* factors in keeping basic mental health and balance, especially for the many poorly educated inmates who don't have the skills to benefit from reading or writing.

When transferred to the new Allan Polunsky Unit in Livingston in 2000 death row inmates found themselves totally segregated from any direct contact with other inmates, without the possibility of "piddling" (all kinds of creative activities except drawing), and without access to TV. Moreover, they could no longer make or receive phone calls to or from anyone.

Inmates in the Allan Polunsky Unit can keep the following items in their cells – but only if they have the money to buy them: radios, fans, hot pots, typewriters (usually of such poor quality that they break down regularly and have to be replaced at high cost), authorized religious materials (the only "authorized" religions on death row are Christianity, Islam, and Judaism), legal materials, mail, limited art supplies, and a very small number of books along with a few games – most notably chess and checkers (inmates play by numbering the positions on the boards and shouting the moves to each other).

Can you imagine, dear reader, living 22 out of 24 hours confined in a 6 x 9 feet-cell, years on end (and 24/7 during lockdowns) - with three cold meals a day during lockdowns? If you are barely literate and have few inner resources to draw upon, you have no distractions whatsoever except for a poorly functioning radio (if you're among the fortunate prisoners who have one). Day after day, 365 days a year (for Roger that amounts to 7,800 days by 2009, for some of his friends, like R.C. or M.D. who have spent 33 years on death row, more than 11,300) with the same poor food and for some inmates never a visitor, never a letter.

In 2004 the Texas Department of Criminal Justice, in response to a request from the American Civil Liberties Union demanding TV for death row replied that "the issue was not open for debate." This is not the opinion of the highest court in the land. The US Supreme Court stated in 2002 (*Atkins v. Virginia*) that "evolving standards of decency" were best reflected in the various relevant laws enacted throughout the country and characterized state legislation as "the clearest and most reliable objective evidence of contemporary values."

Yes, I was placed in solitary confinement for a while. It seems that when we sometimes attempt to do the right thing, we all too often do the wrong things, and we suffer from our mistakes, as I have. I thought long and hard about the situation, and I often asked myself if what I did was right, but my judgment was clouded. But when I received your letter and found your piece about integrity, the clouds subsided and my vision was somewhat more clear. I did what I thought was right at the time, and did not know that the person who was supposed to be my friend was in fact abusing the very friendship that I had entrusted him with. In the end, I only grew stronger by his betrayal instead of weaker.

But it goes deeper than that. I found out that the aim was to get me off the wing, because some people wanted to take over the wing, and they did not feel they could do it while I was still there. Since I left the wing, many officers have come to tell me they did not believe it [the illegal object someone put in Roger's cell] was mine, and that since I left the wing, there have been many fights and trouble. But God works in mysterious ways, brother Pierre.

On top of that, I lost all my piddling equipment. When I was placed in solitary, my property was taken from me and sent to the property room where only general population inmates run everything.[1] They cleaned me out, Pierre. Many of the things they took were things that I had made over the years to assist me with my crafts, things that you could only make after years of working and realizing that they would make your job easier. They also stole all my craft material, my coffee pot, much of my typing supplies. It would take me several years to acquire again the things that I had.

I stay up as late as I can now, so that I can sleep most of the day away, because I dread waking up and not having my hobby there. I have been getting very depressed. Your letter helped me a great deal.

So now I am trying to fight off my depression and move on. I do not know how I will ever replace all I lost.[2] They will not allow us to order anymore, and even if they did, it would cost so much.

I am truly paying for that one mistake, but it was a lesson, and that is all that life is, a series of lessons that we must learn before we can become complete and one with God again. However, this time I was able to hold on to all your articles. I guess the people who stole my things were not looking for enlightenment at the time of their theft, so they chose to leave them – thank God!

---

1   General population are the inmates who are not on death row.
2   Roger never did recover his piddling instruments. In the Allan Polunsky Unit in Livingston, where all death row inmates of Texas are currently held, piddling is forbidden, despite the fact that this prohibition goes against the prison rules which stipulate that inmates have a right to do manual work.

Integrity

Integrity is a quality of being. It is holding on to what you know to be your highest sense of truth and vision at all times, whatever the cost. It is resonating with that deepest fiber of your being which urges you to peacefully but firmly hold your ground whatever the supposed prestige or authority of the person opposing you – not out of stubbornness, but prompted by the quiet daring of that inner urge in you which says, *"This above all, to thine own self be true..."*

It means following your highest sense of right at all times, whatever the consequences, however lonely the path and however loud the jeers and mockery of the crowd and philistines.

Integrity is about "speaking truth to power" as the old Quaker saying goes, when silence would be easier or more advantageous to your interests. It is holding on to the power of truth when everyone around you is accepting compromises and pretending "it really doesn't matter." It is standing firm and undaunted when others disappear into the underground shelters for their fears and timidity.

Integrity is an ongoing refusal to water down your inner sense of truthfulness even to satisfy, appease or gain the approval of a loved one.

Above all, integrity means refusing to cheat with *yourself*, lie to *yourself*, or abide in the doubtful shadow of half truths. You can cheat and lie to others and be forgiven. You can slip and fall and even know defeat and you can rise again. But when you lie to yourself, who is to forgive you? After *that* kind of defeat or fall, who will pick you up? And even if you indulge in the supreme absurdity and ultimate sin of deceiving yourself, will not even your inner strength shirk the companionship of one who is scuttling their own ship? Then only grace can save you.

Deceiving oneself kills that inner discernment which is the basis of true discrimination and worthwhile choice. Consciously eluding what one knows to be true or lying to oneself is the sin against the divine essence we were created to emanate – the one Spirit, which "beareth witness unto our spirit" that we are truly the children of God.

Integrity is a state of being reflecting unbroken wholeness, complete soundness of mind, a quality of sterling authenticity. It carries with itself a sense of impeccable entireness, "of having no part or element taken away or wanting." Integrity is totally genuine, unmarred by compromise, undiluted by approximation, founded in law, always upright because it is the backbone of Principle. All this, yet integrity is never rigid. (Source: Pierre Pradervand, *The Gentle Art of Blessing*, Personhood Press, Fawnskin, CA, 2003, p.55, Cygnus Books, Llandeilo, Great Britain, 2010 and Beyond Words/Simon and Schuster, 2009).

I try to live my life in favor with God and myself. I try to keep in mind that we are all bound by the same cords of life, and that to exist we must come into unity with one another and realize that no man lives just for himself, that every living thing is bound by a cord to every other living thing.

I am very happy to see that Elly continues upon her course chosen by God, and I know that it is a blessing to live with someone with such love and determination for all mankind. It is very rare to even meet in one's life someone so filled with the spirit, let alone marry them. You are very much loved in God's eyes as in mine.

Man, I love your piece on integrity. It helps me get through the days now, it helps me to understand what I face and why. And I do it with my head held high. I may not have any of my tools and I may not recover them, but I can go on and rebuild.

As long as I don't lie to myself, as long as I stand on truth, I am all right. And with friends like yourself and L., if my life was to end today, my only regret would be that I did not meet you sooner. Please know that my prayers for you, your wife and friends are very sincere.

I pray that God in his infinite wisdom never frowns upon you, and continues to strengthen you for the work you must do. Thank you, my friend Pierre, you help me to stay free, free in my heart, mind and soul. *(March 29, 1998)*

Being true to one's self in this place is like trying to tame a rattlesnake because one is confronted with so much. It is a wonder more people have not gone mad. I guess that has been one of my biggest problems, staying true to myself, because you meet so many people here, so many diverse backgrounds and different beliefs, that in order to fit in you almost have to convert to something other than what you are to stay popular.

Being true to myself is not something I have to work on, that is the most natural thing there is to me, because I had to confront myself years ago, and I like what I have become. Someone told me that some of the guys here did not like me, and I asked him why. And he said: "Because you walk with your head held high all the time, you do not talk much, and all the officers respect you."

I never thought much about it until he told me that, and I guess after that I became a little self-conscious, and after a while I found myself trying to walk with my head not so high, and began looking to see who was staring at me! But after I prayed about it, I realized that is was nothing to be ashamed of, that in fact it was something to be proud of, because all the years that I have been here, I have still retained the respect that I have for myself. So whenever a situation arises, and I am confronted with it, I ask myself, how would the outcome affect not only me, but also my friends?

The Jesus prayer

The Jesus prayer, also called the prayer of the heart by some Church Fathers, is a short prayer that one repeats in the course of the day, sometimes for hours at a time. It has been very widely used in the Eastern Orthodox and Catholic churches. The words have varied across time and space, but the most common ones are, "Lord Jesus Christ, Son of God, have mercy upon me a sinner." Those who use this prayer consider it to be one of the most profound and mystical prayers, and for many believers it is a cornerstone of their spiritual practice.

Most probably, the Jesus Prayer originated in the Egyptian desert, home to the Christian monastic tradition (St. Anthony, St. John Cassian). An inscription of it has been found in the ruins of a Christian cell in the Egyptian desert. Its practice dates from the fifth century, perhaps earlier. Although some have compared this prayer to a Hindu mantra, its orthodox users feel uneasy with the comparison. Even if the "mechanics" of mantra and prayer are similar, the theology behind the two practices is very different. For a Hindu, the power of the mantra is in great part due to the fact that it was specially selected for a disciple by his guru, whereas for the orthodox believer, the power of the Jesus Prayer is due to the invocation of the Son of God (or the Holy Trinity in some versions).[3] The power of the practice is beautifully expressed in a story told by Leo Tolstoy, summarized below.

The Three Hermits, by Leo Tolstoy

Tolstoy tells the story of a Russian bishop who was travelling on the White Sea:

On the boat, the bishop heard a passenger talk about three hermits who lived on a small island. He expressed the desire to visit them, and in those days, the wish of a bishop was practically an order, so the captain stopped the boat when they neared the island, and lowered a rowing boat with a couple of sailors to take the bishop to the island.

After being greeted by the hermits, the bishop asked them how they prayed. "We pray in this way," the hermits replied. "Three are ye, three are we, have mercy on us." The bishop told them that they had evidently heard something about the Holy Trinity, but that it was not the right way to pray. So, he proceeded to teach them the Lord's Prayer. It turned out to be an incredibly laborious process. The hermits were hardly brilliant intellectuals, and the bishop spent hours repeating and repeating the prayer, sentence after sentence, until at last his three students of the day had learned the prayer by heart.

---

3   For an excellent, brief presentation of the Jesus prayer, see http://en.wikipedia.org/wiki/Jesus_Prayer

(continued p.26)

You are so correct, everyone, regardless of stature, is at their highest level of consciousness – and most never realize it. I believe that everyone's consciousness was meant to evolve to the highest level, to reach the pinnacle of perfected being. But when we begin to lean on our own understanding, then we stunt our growth and development.

Whenever I see white racists, I somewhat feel sorry for them, because I realize how lost they are. They are always talking about what is theirs, that everyone else should leave America, and that theirs is the only true race. I do not hate them, because I have hated enough at one time. Hatred eats at everything that is man, not parts, but all of him. It leaves you empty inside, as if some unseen powerful force turned you upside down, and emptied your soul onto the ground. I don't think I could ever hate anyone. It did too much to me, while doing nothing to the person it was directed at.

I try to read everything you send me. I have just finished reading "Yesterday, Today and Tomorrow." As I was reading, I realized just how much I was trying to live the days that had passed, and not those yet to come. For instance with my piddling equipment, I want things to be like they were before my things were taken, but they will never be like that again. Yet I am neglecting the time that I have today by thinking of what was, and of the way I want things to be, forgetting that my presence is all that I am for now, and forever to come. That was a great lesson for today.

I would like to have a picture of you and Elly if I may. It does me good to look into the eyes of my friends when I write. It is like sitting down and having a conversation. *(May 24, 1998)*

Thank you for the copy of [the first chapter from] Science and Health[4] on prayer. It is very interesting. It is correct when it speaks of "the silent prayer that is not unknown to God." I agree wholeheartedly that one does not have to constantly pray out loud and gather a crowd for God to hear their request. I believe in praying constantly. I read a book called The Jesus Prayer. It tells believers that they should constantly keep the name of Jesus on their minds and repeat it at least a hundred times a day, to just keep repeating it, and after a while, it will always be on one's mind, without any conscious effort.

---

4   *Science and Health with Key to the Scriptures* by Mary Baker Eddy, a book on spiritual healing presenting a unique non-dual vision of Christianity, has been an important resource for Roger since the end of the 1990s. For more information, see: www.spirituality.com

The Three Hermits (continued)

It was night time when the bishop left, a beautiful moon was shining on the water, and he was satisfied, grateful that he had taught those poor hermits how to at least pray properly.

Once on the boat, not feeling sleepy, he decided to stay on the deck to enjoy the moonlight sparkling on the waves. Suddenly, he saw a shimmering white light dancing on the water. Intrigued, he went to the helmsman and asked him what it might be. The helmsman abruptly let go of the helm with a cry of terror: the light was the three hermits catching up with the boat on the sea. They were not even moving their feet, they were simply gliding on the surface. They arrived alongside the boat, saying to the bishop, who by now was surrounded by a crowd of pilgrims: "We have forgotten your teaching, servant of God ... teach us again."

The bishop crossed himself, and leaning over the ship's side, said: "Your own prayer will reach the Lord, men of God. It is not for me to teach you. Pray for us sinners."

Mary Baker Eddy once wrote *"A deep sincerity is sure of success, for God takes care of it. Sincerity is more important than form."*

Number of inmates in American prisons

The United States prison population soared from less than 300,000 in 1980 to over two million in 2009. The USA, home to four percent of the world's population, houses one-quarter of the world prison population – i.e. five times the world average. In 2004, 738 people were locked up for every 100,000 residents, with the rate increasing steadily from year to year. In 2007, one of every 135 US residents was in prison. *Prisons and jails are adding more than 1000 inmates per week.* Sixty-two percent of people in local jails have not been convicted. Louisiana and Georgia have over one percent of their residents in jail. Around twelve percent of African Americans in the 25-29 age group are in jail. One of the most amazing paradoxes is that *whereas overall crime rates have been going down, incarceration rates continue increasing.*

The building of prisons in the USA has exploded in recent years, especially with the privatization of many prisons. At the start of this decade, 500-inmates penitentiary facilities were being built at the rate of one per week.

Prisoners represent the "ideal" docile work population: no vacations, no social security or other similar expenses, no labor unions, no absenteeism, and purely symbolical salaries – if any. In privately-run prisons, inmates receive as little as 17 cents an hour and a maximum of 50 cents. At least 37 states have legalized the contracting of private labor by private corporations that operate inside prisons, and companies involved represent the cream of US corporate companies: IBM, Boeing, Motorola, Microsoft, AT&T, Dell, Honeywell, Hewlett-Packard, Revlon, Macy's, and Pierre Cardin, to name but a few. Oregon State representative Kevin Mannix urged Nike to cut its production in Indonesia and bring it to Oregon, commenting that there would be no transportation costs for the goods and that *"we're offering you competitive prison labor here."* Some companies have actually closed down operations in the Third World and relocated in US prisons. An inmate can generate 30 to 60 thousand dollars in a year.

The Correctional Corporation of America (CCA), one of the largest private prison owners, saw its profits double annually from 1996 to 2001. GEO Group (formerly The Wackenhut Corporation) is a prison multinational running jails all round the world. Together, they control 75 per cent of the US private prison population. Operating costs are constantly lowered, thanks to high-tech innovations which allow a minimal number of guards for a maximum number of prisoners, such as the CCA prison in Lawrenceville, Virginia, where five guards on day shifts and two on night shifts control 750 inmates. (Source: Death penalty Information Center and other Internet sites)

(continued p. 30)

[Science and Health] is correct when it says that self-sacrifice combined with prayer is the most crucial. I like what I have read so far in that chapter. It states: "God is Love. Can we ask Him to be more?" How can we ask Him to be anything more? God is really my life. Nothing is done, or could be done, without the power and force that is God. He gives us what we need, not what we want. I will continue to pray, hope and believe, but I do it knowing that in the end all lies in God's hands. Jesus said: "Greater is he that is in me than he that is in the world." Christ is the way, the truth and the life. He is my strong fortress, and even death cannot blow down the foundation He has given me. It is only another path that must be explored.

I understand now why Elly is so beautiful and spiritual as you state so often. To run something of that magnitude is almost overwhelming for one person. I see that most of the women involved are those living in the rural areas of small towns and villages. I bet they make tremendous contributions to their communities, even if never recognized for doing so. It is good that someone has designated a day just to honor them. So it is good to have someone stand up for these children and these women and be the voice that whispers to them in the middle of the night, when all else has failed, and says: "It is all right, someone cares, someone is doing something for you." Your wife is a very special person. I have never met her, but from what you tell me, she is an angel.[5] *(July 16, 1998)*

It is so hot here you would not believe it. At the moment it feels like well over 100 degrees. Last Thursday, a guy four doors down from me was found dead in one of the small cells that we are housed in. His name was Emile Duhamel. He was 52-years old and had no reason being here on death row. He had the mind of a twelve-year old, mentally impaired child; he couldn't even spell his own name. He had been here fourteen years. Fourteen years he lived in this prison, not really understanding what was happening to him, never really complaining about anything (if he did, I never heard him). He died from an apparent heatstroke. The prison officials will never admit it though, because if they did, they would be open to a suit for negligence. He lived here for fourteen years and he never had a fan![6] *(July 16, 1998)*

---

5   The Women's World Summit Foundation founded and run by Elly is a not-for-profit, international NGO. It has a variety of world programs including a prize rewarding creative rural women at the grass roots, and the World Day for the Prevention of Abuse against Children. For more information, see www.woman.ch. What has been especially moving is to see the compassion Roger, who has so many immediate problems to face, feels for the most downtrodden in the Third World whom his love embraces.

6   Temperatures in the region have been known to soar well over 110 Fahrenheit. When you live in a cement cell with the sun beating on cement walls and a window opening no taller than a coffee cup, the heat can become unbearable.

Number of inmates in American prisons (continued)
A striking comparison

Increase of per capita spending for high school and college level education in Texas, 1980-2000: **37 percent.**

Increase of expenditure for prisons in Texas, 1980-2000: **401 percent.**

(Source: *YES, A Journal of Positive Futures*, Winter 2003, p.11)

A blessing for the inmates and guards of a prison

I bless this place of detention that, despite locked doors and bars, its inmates may discover the freedom within.

I bless the inmates:

-in their desire and ability to forgive, including themselves when needed

-in their steadfastness, hope, and patience when days drag on

-in their ability to summon from the depths of their true selves the supreme power to return good for evil

-in their unwavering trust in divine justice, which ultimately wins and rights all wrongs, including those of a human penal system full of imperfections and outright abuses

-in their capacity to find bodily rest and peace despite the strain of prison conditions, and, for many, their starved sexuality.

I bless the guards in their desire to treat inmates as fellow human beings, to look through the penal label to the soul hungering for brotherhood and sisterhood, to be generous rather than mean, and to apply the spirit of the rules rather than the letter.

I bless the inmates, that they may unite with that space of integrity deep within them – a space that has never been touched by error, fear, hate, darkness or lack of any sort, and rekindle the flame of their true being, which always remains pure, generous, and upright.

I bless all the prison personnel in their ability to do a challenging job in a spirit of service and deep compassion.

(Source: *The Gentle Art of Blessing*, op cit. p.270)

I love the part of your book entitled "A blessing for inmates and guards of a prison," because it gives the prisoners something to hold on to. It allows them to see men through all of man's inhumanity, through all the degrading and humiliating conditions they face, [and to realize] there is a part of them that wants to bless, that needs to bless everyone, including those who treat them the worst, because only good can conquer evil, and in their true selves, their supreme selves, there is goodness.

I like it very much. It is refreshing. Many inmates want to hate the officers and officials alike for the conditions they find themselves in, but we cannot repay evil with evil. The blessings show one how to look above and beyond our human imperfections, and once we see past these, then we can move on and forgive those who wrong us, and ask those whom we have wronged for their blessings.

I have seen many men find peace behind these walls, the peace they never knew while free, a peace that is so pure and perfect that once they have found it, they would rather be confined with that peace than free without it.

Finally, as you bless the citizens, you bless the conditions that were created by them. Dr. Martin Luther King Jr. said: "Justice denied one is justice denied all." I heard them talking on the news about construction being approved of several new prisons. The people were applauding as if this were an accomplishment. But prisons are indications of a society's failures, not its accomplishments. Every time a society locks a person behind bars, part of that society is exposed, and a piece of every person in that society is locked away with the condemned. It is said that no man is born unto himself [alone], that every living thing is bound by cords to every other living thing, and every time I do something to harm you, I harm myself. And when I do something to uplift you, I uplift not only myself, but the society I live in.

I like those blessings very much, Pierre. I am going to put a frame around them, and put them on my wall inside my cell. Many officers come by and read the things we put up.

Prayer and goodness have never let any man down. Many of the inmates look for reasons to hate the officials who hold them here, and sometimes it is so hard not to.

> *"They can only imprison me if I consent,*
> *and my consent I do not give.*
> *I am free as long as God is in me, and I in Him."*
>
> (Roger McGowen, August 31, 1998)

For example, for the last two months it has been very hot, in the 100s (Fahrenheit). The kitchen sends us iced tea and punch to drink along with our meals, and the juice barrels are filled with ice. The officers will come in and take all the ice from the barrels, and leave the juice sitting in the heat for over an hour before they pass it on to us, and by then it has become very warm. When we asked them why they did this, they told us that if they cannot have ice, while they are at work, then we can't have any either. And many days pass when we are confined to these cells in all this heat without anything cold to drink, unless we get a cold drink from the unit store, and that is only once a week.

Yet I can't find it in my heart to hate them for what they do. I only pray for them. Your blessings help one to understand that only good comes from good – there is no other way.

I know that all things are possible to God, including walking away from this place. I do a great deal of dreaming and hoping, because I realize that as long as my heart and soul are free, my spirit will soar. They can only imprison me if I consent, and my consent I do not give. I have walked away from this place time and time again. I am free as long as God is in me, and I in Him.

It is a wonderful thing to be loved, and know it, and everyone is loved, and everyone should know it. We were loved before we came, and nothing can separate us from the divine love that God has given us. We are all one, aren't we?

Thank you for believing in me. You give me strength to believe in myself, and to believe in the goodness of mankind. I have always believed that God is in everything, and that everything is in God.

Please give my love and greetings to your beautiful wife Elly, and I also send you hugs from Huntsville. Take care, and know that I love you too. *(August 31, 1998)*

Love – the ultimate cause, substance and law of all

"In love for man, we gain a true sense of Love as God; and in no other way can we reach this spiritual sense, and rise – and still rise – to things most essential and divine."

"The little that I have accomplished has all been done through love – self-forgetful, patient, unfaltering tenderness."

"Know, then, that you possess sovereign power to think and act rightly, and that nothing can dispossess you of this heritage and trespass on Love."

"At all times, and in all circumstances, overcome evil with good. Know thyself and God will supply the wisdom and the occasion for a victory over evil. Clad in the panoply of Love, human hatred cannot reach you."

(These quotations are all from the writings of Mary Baker Eddy, founder of Christian Science. Roger has found great support and vision in her key work, *Science and Health with Key to the Scriptures*, which he still studies regularly.)

The introduction to your book [The Gentle Art of Blessing] you sent me is very beautiful. I like it the way you make it sound so simple. Most people feel that if things are not complicated, then it is not worth the effort put into it. But blessings are the easiest things there are to give. Like you, I believe that love is unconditional. You cannot love today and hate tomorrow, or love one and hate the other.

There are guys here who wonder why I never argue with the officers, or why I sometimes meditate for long hours at a time. When I am through with my meditation, I do not speak for hours, even days. I have explained to them many times that I have to go inside, that it is my way of escaping, of healing myself, because so many times I want to let off at the officers, and I want to let off at some of the inmates for allowing themselves to be lured into the officers' trap. But instead I go inside myself, because that is where the heart really is, and it is where my strength lies. So I try my best to remember that I do not only have to think for myself, but for those I encounter who are not in the right frame of mind to think for themselves.

I try to learn from every little thing that happens to me. For instance, one of my friends is always talking about the fact that I do not kill the spiders on the wall, the roaches that crawl over the floor, or the crickets that make so much noise in the middle of the night in the corner of the cell. I do not kill them because the same force that supplied me with my life also supplies them with theirs. Everything was placed here for a reason. I allow the insects to have their space, and I have mine. But I learn from the insects. I watch them, how hard they work to stay alive and to exist, and I get strength from the heart that they exhibit.

We are all that love is and ever will be. People think they have to work at loving, but love needs no work, it only needs to be allowed to love, and it will be complete. Yes, "love reflects itself as love, because we are all that love is." Love is the substance of all that we are. Love is so very simple to give, to show, and to accept. Why is it so hard for people to understand that? I will from this day repeat every day in my spiritual preparation for the day "Love is my only possible response to any event, person, encounter, aggression, situation, joy or fear that crosses my way, because love, which created me, is what I am."

This place can make the most religious person hang his head in wonder, but it is also a place of higher learning. It teaches you patience, it teaches you humility, it teaches you love, it teaches you sorrow, heartache and pain. And it teaches you the greatest gift: that you have the patience to show humility and love to all, because in the end love is what really matters, everything else dulls in comparison. *(September 30, 1998)*

My identity: # 889

"My name is Roger Wayne McGowen. Until I came here, I never realized or thought much about numbers, but being here has reduced not only myself, but all the men here with me, to simple numbers, numbers that send a sense of doom and dread into the heart of every man I spend my waking hours with. Because the numbers I speak of are the numbers of death. My death number is #889. At first I believed this number was just to keep track of me while I was here inside the system (prison). But after having a guard ask me "What is your death number," I realized that this number was more than a tracking device as I had perceived it, but in fact a number which the system uses in its efforts to reduce me to nothingness, uses to steal the identity of every inmate in the system. . . Nothing is more frightening than when a man loses his identity. As an African-American [this loss] is twofold to me: first, believing myself to be like everyone else in this great State of America, this land of the free, the home of the brave, what a very rude awakening I had after finding I was born with two strikes against me: being Black and being Poor. And then finding that the system was not going to give me another swing at the ball, and that I had to do whatever it took to regain my identity from the thieves who wished to take me into nothingness along with all my other fellow brothers. . . Each time I think of the number #889 I get a feeling that these numbers themselves can tell a story, a story of heartache and pain, disappointment and gloom. . . Several times I almost fell into believing that maybe it was destiny, maybe I should accept my fate. But numbers lie as well as people, so why should I believe them, fall prey to them?"

(From an undated brief autobiographical document by Roger. Elsewhere, Roger refers to his TDCJ number-Texas Department of Criminal Justice- which is the same)

On December 23, I will have my birthday. I will be 35 years old, Pierre. Time has really flown. Sometimes I wonder how any of us survive without the grace of God. I guess I will sit back as I do every Christmas and thank God for allowing me to see another year, and say a prayer for all of the many guys who are no longer here to say one for themselves.

Thank you so much for the [quotations from the] Scriptures. They really did help me. You know, we all need reminding of why we were placed here today. At times we all lose our way, and our objectives become unclear and that is when we need reminding that we all have a purpose and that we are all special. You have constantly given me inspiration, and your friendship and compassion have never wavered. Your letter is the first letter that I have received in over four weeks, and I was kind of letting it get to me. But I received your letter and I realized that nothing is really what it seems, especially when one is dealing with God.

God has been very good to me, Pierre. I may not have physical freedom, but I have an inner peace and love that even death cannot kill. I would rather be imprisoned with God than free without Him. I ask myself: "Why has God brought me this?"

I am searching desperately for an answer, and you have given me part of it. We were all placed [here] so that God's glory could be manifest through us. We are all small pieces in a large puzzle, and the puzzle will never be completed until we all realize our place in God's plan and come together as one, joining one piece to the next, until we make God's perfect peace! I know and believe God has a plan for me.

The Kingdom of God does live within each of us, and our heaven is where we chose to make it. *(November 30, 1998)*

1999

Thank you for your concern about the punishments we have been suffering.[7] I look at it as a growing phase, something that will not be here tomorrow, and a lesson in patience for today. I have been through it all before, and I am sure we will go through it all again.

I understand that no law is real law if it is not divine law, and that any law that is not in accord with divine law will soon perish. I attempt to be "a law unto myself." I get my strength from realizing that divine law is the only law. *(February 7, 1999)*

---

7   An exceptionally tough lockdown was imposed on death row – then in Huntsville - following an attempted escape on November 27, 1998, during which one of the inmates fleeing managed to hide in the neighboring marshes (where he finally drowned).

> *"God is great.*
> *He has never given me*
> *a weight*
> *I could not carry."*
>
> (Roger McGowen, November 30, 1998)

In April 1999, I visited Roger at Ellis One Unit in Huntsville for the first time.

I really did enjoy our visit. I was very moved and think about our visit every day. I think I came away a better person for it. It prepared me for what was to come, because at the moment we are going through some very difficult times here, being treated very badly by the administration. (When I say we, I mean death row [inmates]).

They have torn our cells apart repeatedly, throwing away our property. They allow us to buy items from the unit store, then they change the rules and tell us we are not allowed to have them, and send the officers to destroy our cells looking for them.

I do not think it would be a very good idea at the moment to have an interview with your journalist friend. Things are kind of bad here at the moment, and I am trying very hard to deal with the officials here. They are attempting to take away our communication privileges with the media and ways of getting our stories out. I am sure the interview would have gone very well, but at the moment things here are going very badly, and I am using every ounce of strength I have to remain civil while my rights are being trampled on. But through it all, I try to do it keeping my head high.

I find it very difficult to complain about things when there are people who are free and still chained by misery, desolation, and despair. I cannot complain, even going through what I am going through, I cannot complain. I can only deal with it the best I can and attempt to keep them from taking my spirit away. God is great, He has never given me a weight I could not carry. I try to keep in mind that there are people out there who love me, who wish the best for me, and are fighting to set me free. The love they have for me and the love I have for them lifts me out of despair and sets me on solid hope. I feel that love whenever I receive one of your letters, Pierre. I can feel your love for me across the oceans, and that love makes me fight harder. Thank you.

I had to throw many of my books away, because I had no place to store them. They give us very small boxes and we have to place all of our personal property in those boxes, and whatever does not fit in it is thrown away, so I lost many of my books. At the moment the entire prison is in chaos, everyone is mean and vile to each other, including the officers. I have not had time to read or write in quite a while. I am sure everything will calm down soon, but at the moment they are bad. *(May 28, 1999)*

The gassing of D.T.

A friend living on the same pod (unit within the prison, a group of usually about 64 inmates) as the inmate described below tells about an event that happened on November
2, 2004, after officers discovered the inmate had committed suicide (names withheld).
The information was received through the *Lifespark* network of Switzerland. Roger was
not involved in any way.

*"When I got to my cell from the shower, he said he needed his reading books back and gave me mine
back. So we did that. Then he said "I'll holler at you later." When the officers brought last chow
[meal] at around 5:30 p.m., he wouldn't respond. When the officers in the picket cut off the over-
riding cell lights, the two women officers screamed loudly and took off running. It only took a few
seconds to have at least 40-50 officers there...*

*They ran up to the door and saw him hung up. I could hear a woman say "Look at his tongue." Then
Lt. X said "Spray him." What??? All the inmates went off. Because they sprayed him with gas! He
could still have been alive. Why spray him with gas? They had no right to spray D. with gas. With the
chance he could still be alive, they should have opened the cell door and with all the reinforcements
got to him. But this is what they did. They sprayed him with gas two or three times and walked away
from his door. To wait for gas masks. Dammit, he could still have been alive! Why?! All the inmates
were mad. We cursed [the officers] and begged them to go in there and get D. They just cursed back.
Finally, when they got him out, it was too late.*

*I lost all composure. I spat on an officer in front of my door four or five times. I was screaming
at them for the lack of respect for D's life. They could have saved him. But they sprayed gas. I was
emotionally crazy! I went all the way off. They took D. out and came back and gassed me three times
and suited up a five to seven man team to come in my cell and force me out."*

To Mirjam, Switzerland. (Mirjam started corresponding with Roger in 1998. Portions of the following letter she received from Roger describe methods used by inmates to commit suicide that are so terrible I have omitted one of them.)

Suicide is a selfish thing, because the person who is attempting the act is not thinking of those left to grieve. But you have to be in the shoes of the person committing the act to truly understand. Believe me, Mirjam, I know that pain can cut so deep it would take others lifetimes before they could even imagine how deep it goes. I feel it every day, and it is by the grace of God that I have kept standing so long. You ask if I have ever known anyone to commit suicide. I wish to God that I did not, but unfortunately I did.

Now remember, the cells are not high enough for anyone to hang themselves in, and besides there is nothing to tie anything to. We do have a shelf going the width of the cell in the very front, but it is only 6.5 feet high and there is nothing to jump from or stand on. However, this guy named J. G. tied his sheet to the door and the shelf and made a noose. He then got down on the floor, on his knees and stuck his head in the noose. Then he proceeded to lean into the noose and strangle himself. At any time, all he had to do was get up from the floor and it would have been over. His hands were not tied. But instead, he leaned into the rope until he strangled himself to death!! Can you imagine the pain he had to be experiencing to take his own life that way?

Another guy here paid another inmate to strangle him to death in the recreation yard!! And they were best friends. He strangled him to death through a fence.

Another guy, right after I had finished having a normal conversation with him... (description withheld).

Yet another one waited late one night and tried to kill himself by cutting off his penis.

So the answer to your question is: yes, I have witnessed acts that would make the ordinary person go insane. But I know what kind of pressure these men were under. I myself have felt the same pressure, but I do not think that I would commit such an act. But one never knows. There is a very thin line between insanity and sanity. There are many guys who give up and just drop their appeals, opting to allow the state to kill them, afraid of doing it themselves. But either way, the pain and the torment does not lessen.

I am fine myself, trying to stay healthy and at the same time to keep my sanity. Neither is a very easy job here, but I do the best I can with what I have and with good friends such as yourself it gets easier. I know that I am not alone. Thank you for thinking of me when you did. That means a lot to me. Thank you lady. *(May 30, 1999)*

Cruel and unusual punishment

The 8th Amendment to the United States Constitution forbids cruel and unusual punishment, and the rules of International Law abide by the same principle, as stated in the
quotes below:

"No one shall be subjected to torture or to cruel, inhuman or degrading punishment or treatment"
(The International Covenant on Civil and Political Rights).

*"All prisoners shall be treated with the respect due to their inherent dignity and value as human
beings"* (United Nations, Minimum Basic Principles for the Treatment of Prisoners).

A psychologist, assessing the impact of the American Secure Housing Units (SHU),
or "supermax" prisons, wrote of Pelican Bay's SHU in California that it was "inflicting
unprecedented levels of psychological trauma on the prisoners" that were tantamount
to "psychological torture." Dr. Stuart Grassian, a specialist who evaluated the psychological impact of a series of supermax prisons concluded that solitary confinement can
cause symptoms such as perceptual distortions and hallucinations, massive free-floating
anxiety, acute states of confusion, violent or self-destructive outbursts, overt paranoia
and panic attacks, etc.

An American Friends Service Committee (AFSC) report notes that the level of desperation reached by some inmates in Secure Housing Units can be such that some revert
to extreme levels of self-mutilation or even smear themselves with their own feces. In
2004, a 74-year old man, J.B. Hubbard, was executed in Alabama for a crime committed in 1977. At times, he forgot who he was, due to attacks of dementia. One 89-year
old inmate was debilitated by deafness, arthritis, and heart disease. Ruchelle Magee in
California lived twenty years in extreme isolation. Ojore Nuru Lutalo has been thirteen years in total isolation in New Jersey without even having been charged with an
infraction.

In some supermax prisons, inmates cannot even see or hear another human being unless the administration decides they can, and the AFSC report mentions "physical torture, such as forced cell extractions, strap downs, hog tying, beating after restraint, and
provocation of violence between prisoners. . . Human rights monitors throughout the
country increasingly hear about the use of torture devices – pepper spray, mace, stun
belts, head masks and even restraint chairs and beds described as having holes for void-
ing bodily wastes when prisoners are tied down for days on end. One person reported
being strapped down in a restraint chair for twenty-one days."

(continued p.46)

Pierre, I cannot bring myself to hate anyone. I can't lie to you and tell you that I do not get frustrated and upset sometimes. Sometimes I want it all to just end. I do not care how, just end. I sometimes lose the urge to write, sometimes I get tired of answering questions, I just get tired of it all. Then when I think I am at the end of the rope, God sends me strength to keep me standing, to keep loving, and to keep me strong. He knows just what I need, and He knows when I need it.

There is really not much to tell at the moment, besides it being very hot. We are under lockdown again. Someone from another prison has escaped, jumped the wall right in front of the officers at noon, and now they have everyone locked down. We are not allowed any recreation, so we just sit in these very hot cells 24 hours a day. The frustration and despair mount. Many guys are talking of dropping their appeals right now, and to be honest, Pierre, I really can't blame them. There is no life here, it is only wasting away, and there is nothing left to contribute. So why fight something – death – that will only bring peace and freedom? I have not come to these conclusions myself, and pray I never will. But I am getting tired, Pierre, I mean a deep down tiredness that I thought I would never feel. I look out from behind the bars and see a whole world out there, a world that is filled with God's works and wonders, a world that reminds me the life we are living here is not life at all.

I do not want you to think I have lost my faith or that I feel like giving up. On the contrary, I want to fight with all my heart. I am just telling you what I see, what I hear, and sometimes what I feel. So please, you can rest assured knowing that I am fine. As I said earlier, I am just a little tired.

Please pray for me and ask God to strengthen me and give me the courage to stand and fight when everyone has abandoned the field. I know this letter is not very good, but I will not be false with you. I will write and tell you the truth at all times. Sometimes I will stumble a little, but I will never fall, because God's arms keep me up. I am only human like everyone else, and things do get to me. I just have to work through them. *(June 28, 1999)*

I write to quite a few people who are always trying their best to convert me to what they believe. They send me materials to read and lessons to study. I have studied quite a few different religions, and I keep coming back to what I believe. I hear guys arguing and fighting over the runs [open recreation spaces on the prison grounds] all day about whose religion is the best. The Christian argues with the Moslem, telling him that if you do not believe in Jesus, you are going to hell.

Cruel and unusual punishment (continued)

The AFSC report concludes: "The US ratified the International Convention Against Torture in 1994 but does not comply, continuing to use punitive violence and brutality in control unit facilities."

(Source: *Solitary Confinement Torture in the US*, by Bonnie Kerness, American Friends Service Committee, Philadelphia, fall 1998.

See also http://www.sonic.net/~doretk/ArchiveARCHIVE/Prison/prissues.html)

Walk in my shoes, reader friend: a death row inmate tells

Imagine spending year after year with your own death hanging in front of your nose. After having been rescheduled several times, your execution date has finally been set. You're escorted to the Death House. The strap-down team is ready to take you to the gurney, when the execution is abruptly called off - part of the relentless emotional roller-coaster of a death sentence. Some inmates have experienced this three to four times.

You live in almost permanent confinement in a tiny cell which would drive an animal crazy or so apathetic it would let itself die. Sometimes, you are days without leaving this space, with only three cold sandwiches for meals. Your toilet can be clogged for days and you live in your own stink. The food is appalling, totally unappetizing – once you even found residues of a rat in it. Health support is extremely poor, and you and several other inmates believe a new drug was tested on you as it left you all desperately sick.

Your cell can pass from near-freezing in winter to unbearably hot in summer. One of your neighbors died of a heatstroke. Wind and sunshine are words of the past (and in Oklahoma, where death row is underground, even normal daylight has been banned). Strip searches are routine, sometimes in front of female guards. Chemical sprays and gassing are frequent in many situations of even slight tension, as are physical and mental abuse by some of the staff. You have no TV, cannot make or receive a phone call (Texas), and do not have the slightest physical contact with another human being, apart from an occasional brushing of hands with a guard when handcuffed. Your environment alternates between periods of intense noise with some mentally insane inmates screaming and screeching, and a loneliness so thick, so heavy you could slice it with a knife. It generates in you a profound anguish, but religious services which could help are non-existent: why offer the help of religion to someone who is not going *to* hell but *lives* there?

You are in a situation of enforced idleness for years: no handicrafts or other morale-generating activities. Even work for 17cents an hour would be a gift. But no, that is only for the prison's general population. Because you are supposed to die, there is not the slightest attempt to rehabilitate you; penology goals of the prison system do not extend beyond incapacitation and punishment.

Living in an invariably gray environment without color or stimulation has a deadening effect on your soul. You have not had a visitor for three years. Correspondence with your family has been decreasing steadily, and after eighteen years, you can understand this.

Time continues to drag on and on and on . . . . day after day, week after week, month after month, year after year, and yes, decade after decade. Finally, in total desperation, you write to your state-appointed lawyer whom you met once, four years ago, that you are dropping your appeal. Death almost seems friendly for one who barely survives the living torture of death row.

The Moslem argues that Jesus was a prophet, but that Mohammed was the last prophet, and that Islam is the true religion and the oldest. Then you have your Catholics and Protestants, and even Jehovah's Witnesses. I believe that every man has the right to worship God in his own way, and that if what you believe in makes you a better person, then you are one of God's children. I do not believe that I have to be of a certain religion to be saved.

I listen to these guys here, claiming they are right, talking out loud so that everyone can hear what they are saying and find favor with them and believe that they are the children of the true God. And thirty minutes later, they are calling each other names and cursing, and God is all but forgotten. I am getting frustrated with religion, but not with God and Jesus.

I meditate daily. I know that I was created to worship God. Every day I try to keep in mind that I am a part of God, and God is a part of me, and that as He is in me, I am in Him. I love God with all my mind, body, soul, and strength, and I know that every quality that God has, I have also, because I was made in his image and after His likeness. And I meditate on that every day. It keeps me strong, mentally alive, and spiritually focused.

Actually, as bad as things get, I still cannot bring myself to complain, because when I am watching the news or reading the papers, I am always seeing people who are less fortunate than I am. I found myself really saddened by the J. F. Kennedy, Jr. tragedy. Because here is a man who, it seemed, had everything, still taken away in the prime of life. I see people every day on television digging in trash cans to feed themselves.[8] I see people living under bridges in one of the greatest countries in the world. What is there really for me to complain about? Of course, I wish I had my freedom, but to tell you the truth, Pierre, I would rather be in prison with Jesus than be free without him. *(August 2, 1999)*

Spirituality means to me that every person has to seek out his or her own religious experience and seek God's face by their own means. We all find religion in different things, different places, different ways. It is a path I believe in my heart that every man, woman, and child will have to walk one day, and what they find on that path will be between them and God. The path of enlightenment is not just for a select few, but for all who choose to seek it. Religion has been used to justify some of the most atrocious acts ever committed by man, but it has also produced some very great spiritual leaders. It cuts like a two-edged sword, but in the end the result is always the same: It is what we believe that makes us what we are.

---

8   This was in the Ellis One Unit of Huntsville where inmates still could watch TV in the evening.

Botched executions

This is possibly the most distressing section in the entire book and the facts it presents are hard. When one is attempting to convey honestly the scope of the death row system, it is impossible to skip what amounts to extreme torture of the most heinous sort. After all, the death penalty *does end on the gurney*, and how that end takes place is of significance. What follows is a brief selection from dozens of pages dedicated to this theme on the Death Penalty Information Center (DPIC) website.

Stephen McCoy (lethal injection, Texas, May 24, 1989). He had such a violent physical reaction to the drugs (heaving chest, gasping, choking, back arching off the gurney, etc) that one of the male witnesses fainted. The Texas Attorney General admitted the inmate *"seemed to have a somewhat stronger reaction,"* adding, *"the drugs might have been administered in a heavier dose or more rapidly."*

Jesse Joseph Tafero (husband of Sunny Ray Jacobs, electrocution, Florida, May 4, 1990). During the execution, six-inch flames erupted from Tafero's head and three jolts of power were required to stop his breathing. State officials claimed that the botched execution was caused by *"inadvertent human error"* - the inappropriate substitution of a [cheaper] synthetic sponge for a natural sponge that had been used in previous executions. They attempted to support this theory by sticking a part of a synthetic sponge into a common household toaster and observed that it smoldered and caught fire.

Allen Lee Davis (electrocution, Florida, July 8, 1999). Commenting on this particularly horrible execution, Florida Supreme Court Justice Leander Shaw commented that *"the color photos of Davis depict a man who for all appearances. . . was brutally tortured to death by the citizens of Florida."* (The details are so horrific that we have omitted them here.) Justice Shaw also called the botched execution of Jesse Tafero and that of Pedro Medina (not reported here), *"barbaric spectacles"* and *"acts more befitting a violent murderer than a civilized state."*

Angel Diaz (lethal injection, Florida, December 13, 2006). After the first injection was administered, Mr. Diaz continued to move and was squinting and grimacing as he tried to mouth words. A second dose was administered and 34 minutes passed before Mr. Diaz was declared dead. Two days after the execution, Governor Jeb Bush suspended all executions in the state and appointed a commission *"to consider the humanity and constitutionality of lethal injections."*

(Source: www.deathpenaltyinfo.org/article.php?scid=8&did=478 Spring, 2007)

I have a friend here, his name is William Prince David, and he has been on death row for 22 years!!! He is going to be executed Friday, 10th of September. He is only 40 years old. He has spent more time on death row than free. And now they are going to kill him!! In any other country of the civilized world, that would have been enough time to convince any fact-finding jury that he would have served his time and paid his debt to society. But not in the USA. We will miss him - he really is a classy guy. He was very young and came from the poorest part of the city of Houston. Keep him in your prayers.

It is amazing how you love your wife. I only wish that somewhere, sometime in this lifetime I could know a love so true and so strong. God indeed blessed you, and it shows every time you speak of her. Give her my greetings and blessings. I have included her in my letters and in my prayers, because she is your other half. If I write to you without including her, it seems that my letters are incomplete, only half done.

I love you and Elly, Pierre. Never doubt that. *(September 6, 1999)*

You would not imagine how hard a time we are having here. It is ridiculous actually. They took our fingernail files, so we can't cut or clean our fingernails any more. They won't give us mirrors to shave with, yet they want us to shave. Last month, the hottest month of the year with temperatures of 113 degrees, they turned the air conditioning off, and I swear I felt like I was going to suffocate.

I have drowned myself in religion for so long that it does not seem to help me any more. But do not get me wrong. I still believe wholeheartedly in God and my faith is as strong as ever. But the same people who are doing these things to us use the same Bible to justify their misuses of us, and they use it to justify the killings they are doing. It is very hard after awhile to continue to take comfort in the same book, if you know what I mean. But I will hold on and continue asking God for guidance. If it is meant for me to come back to the Bible, then I will come. But I believe that certain things happen for a reason. *(September 16, 1999)*

Recidivism is high, here in America, because the prison system provides no counseling to the prisoners. Most times, they are just thrown in jail and treated very badly. The guards get away with unimaginable tortures and treatments, and any form of resistance is met with harsh discipline. So, the prisoner is filled with so much hate and anger when he is released, that he strikes out at the first person who crosses his path. Also, many of the guys who are in prison were victims of abuse when they were children.

> *"Lord, don't move my mountain,*
> *But give me the strength to climb.*
> *And Lord, don't take away my stumbling blocks,*
> *But lead me all around."*
>
> (from the favorite hymn of Roger's mother, written by Mahalia Jackson)

The following passage is one of the most important in Roger's correspondence. It shows a change in his perspective – a shift from seeing himself as a total victim in an unjust system into someone who assumes the full responsibility for his life. Being responsible does not mean that he caused the situation he is in, but that he is capable of responding with intelligence, creativity, and love to any situation that presents itself to him. He suggests that while we are all victims of certain circumstances in some way, what counts is how we choose to react – objectively, one may be a victim of a given situation (i.e. being in prison due to a court trial that was a total travesty of authentic justice), yet subjectively one may choose to respond in a responsible manner. This is one of the keys to Roger's inner strength. It explains why he continues to grow in a system that is intentionally designed to punish, crush, and humiliate.

I believe that everyone is responsible for his or her life. At one point I thought I was a victim, and I actually started to feel like one, blaming everyone else for my problems. But I realized that I had to take responsibility for my actions and that doing so was the only way I could ever stop feeling like I did. Every day I hear people complaining because they thought that something that was supposed to go one way instead went another, or because they had to work an extra hour or two!! People always complain about what they do not have; they very seldom stop and thank God for the blessings they do have. People claim that they love life, but how can they love life when they do not know how to live?

Every single day of my life, I find something to thank God for. When it is cold and the guys are complaining about it and do not want to get out of bed in the morning, I roll out of bed onto the floor and start doing my push ups. All the time I am thanking God that I am still able to feel and know what it is like to be cold, because a lot of the guys that were here last year complaining about the cold weather are not here any more to complain this year. Every day and every thing in it is a blessing to me, Pierre. We are responsible for everything that enters our lives, because the things that we allow into our lives are the very things that shape our lives. We can allow those things to be of heaven or of hell – but it is our choice. *(August 2, 1999)*

In an earlier letter to Roger, I mentioned the astonishing story of a Jewish lawyer from the Warsaw ghetto, told by George R. Ritchie, MD, in his book Return From Tomorrow. *Ritchie explains how he arrived with the American army, in which he served, at a Nazi concentration camp near Wuppertal, to help the newly liberated prisoners. He recounts the horror of seeing those emaciated people who were hardly more than ambling zombies. Yet, in their midst, he discovered a lawyer from the Warsaw ghetto in perfect health. The Jewish lawyer, with whom Ritchie worked daily for a while, had been in that extermination camp since 1939. He was an unexplainable human and medical miracle: how could he survive six years of extermination camp and manage to stay in such good health and high spirits?*

One day, he opened himself up to Ritchie, explaining that when the Nazis marched on to his street in 1939, they lined up everyone from the apartment building (except him, as he spoke German), including his wife and five children, and gunned them down in cold blood.

Thank you, Roger

I received the following from a reader of the French edition of this book:

"After having read the book and consulted Roger's website, life took on an entirely new dimension for me. I now understand better what it means to bless my neighbor and I feel pleasure doing it.

Each time I am tempted to criticize or to feel dissatisfied, I think of Roger, and it is as if he were calling me to set me straight again.

Every day I think of him and ask God to help Roger accomplish what he requests of divine Love. I feel everyone should know his story - mankind would make a giant step forward.

As soon as I awaken, I start blessing my day and thank God for His goodness towards me and mine. I used to do it before, but now I include Roger and the world, and I do it with greater intensity and with much more love. So now, thanks to Roger and you, I have the impression of being a new Florence. The first shocks I felt when reading the book have been transformed into waves of love, which I hope to radiate as well as I can."Florence (Switzerland)

"I had to decide then," he explained to Ritchie, "whether to let myself hate the soldiers who had done this. It was an easy decision, really. I was a lawyer. In my practice, I had seen too often what hate can do to people's minds and bodies. Hate had just killed the six people who mattered most to me in the world. I decided then that I would spend the rest of my life – whether it was a few days or many years – loving every person I came in contact with."

Since then, the new medical science of psycho-neuro-immunology has proved that expressing love reinforces the immune system! That could, at least partially, explain the truly remarkable resilience of the Jewish lawyer. (This story, with a scientific explanation, can also be found in the best seller of Dr. Bernie Siegel, Love, Medicine and Miracles).

Love is a very powerful source. It is something that lifts and mends and holds together the very fabric of our beliefs. I am sure that we are all capable of such acts of love because we have God in us, and Jesus said, greater is He that is in us, than he that is in the world. Many times we are asked to do just that, here on death row, because many times our friends are killed by the state. The very officers that we see each day are those who drive them to their destination with death, and come back laughing as if it were all a joke.

I had an officer just this morning tell me that we were animals!! I simply smiled at him. I could have gone off and started calling him everything but a child of God. But instead, I just looked at him and told him that he made me very sad, and then I walked off. I try very much to show love every day, to everyone, Pierre. But I am only human, and I can tell you that it is not easy. But I will do my best, and I will strive to remember that I represent the highest authority anywhere, and that is God's. *(October 19, 1999)*

Loving all is a challenge of the most difficult kind, because here we are faced with the cruelty of officers and inmates alike. Often, in the blink of an eye, you can lose a friend you have known for years, over something like a radio played too loud or a stare in the wrong direction that lasted too long.

So you must not only be able, but also ready to forgive just as fast, and to allow love to guide your judgments all the time.

Restoring an inmate to health so as to better execute him

Lifespark is a network of Switzerland residents who correspond with US death row in-mates. In their October, 2000 _Lifespark Newsletter_ issue, Texas death row inmate C. N. tells the story of inmate David Long who, the night before his execution, swallowed a large amount of antidepressants he had hidden in his cell, preferring to take his own life rather than being legally "homicided." Guards found him still alive. He was rushed off to hospital. The next day, day of his execution, none of the doctors wanted to let him leave the hospital, given his critical situation.

Prison officers transported him in an ambulance, with oxygen mask on and all the rest, to be executed a few hours later in Huntsville. (_Lifespark_ Newsletter, October, 2000)

Sometimes – when God is merciful enough to allow me to see another day – I ask myself, Why? And before the words can get out of my mouth, I know why: so that each and every day, God's glory can shine not only through myself but through all of us who claim to walk in His light. Every day that I wake up in good health and sound mind is a testament to His greatness and His mercy. I am thankful that I am still able to praise His name after so many years and so much pain, but I praise Him the most for the wonderful friends that He has allowed to come into my life. Thank you for being my friends, you and Elly.

I told Roger that I was sharing his August 2, 1999 letter on refusing to be a victim with the participants of my courses, workshops, etc, and that it deeply moved many people. Referring to this, he wrote:

This is the greatest present that I can ever receive – to know that something I have written is helping others. I guess that is what we are all really striving for: to be of inspiration to others.

Death watch cell is the cell where inmates are placed days before they are scheduled to be executed. The other day, one of the guys who had been placed there was very sick and he had a heart attack while he slept. This was Monday, and he was scheduled to be executed on Wednesday. They rushed him to the hospital so that they could save his life and have him back for his scheduled appointment with the executioner. I often ask myself: are they doing this because they feel it is their job to do so, or are they doing it because they have no compassion for human life? It was a very sad thing.

In my preceding letter, I gave Roger details about the Prize for Creativity in Rural Life created by Elly's foundation, which celebrates the poorest of the poor, the rural women of the Third World (see www.woman.ch). Here, he refers to it:

I am sure that all of these women are very courageous and deserve so much more, but to just be recognized for the efforts that they have made for the betterment of human-kind is probably all they really want. You know, I was just thinking that if we were still able to piddle, I could over the months build some very beautiful boxes, handmade and crafted, as presents for some of the winners. But they stopped us from doing this.

I wish to God that maybe just one day God will bless me to attend one of Elly's prize ceremonies, and one of your workshops. I am sure the little woman you spoke of [one of the laureates of the prize] could feel the love that was present in that room for her. The heart is a remarkable thing, Pierre, it can pick up signals from miles away without a word being spoken. Many times when I receive letters from you or L, I am moved to tears, so I know what you mean.

"I know that when you try your best
to do your best
under all circumstances,
God is watching, and He will reward you.
I look around and see
how blessed I really am
and I want to cry."

(Roger McGowen, December 27, 1999)

There is no such thing as rehabilitation in the vocabulary of the people who make the decisions that eventually lead to the rules and regulations governing penal institutions. Now they are renting out prison labor to private corporations. They can go to a prison and get their product made for nothing, and there are no regulations placed on them.

Being here in prison is not like the media or the politicians would have most people believe. Here we have to buy everything that we get. They have stopped giving us soap now, and the food is so terrible that in the last year and a half twelve death row inmates have been diagnosed with diabetes. I do not have any money this year, but it is all right, I can do without, because I realize that even here on death row, there is always someone who is worse off than I, and I am always looking for that person to give him half of what God has blessed me with. *(December 7, 1999)*

Roger's birthday is on December 23. I quoted one of his letters in the Christmas message Elly and I send to all our friends with our handmade Christmas card. Roger wrote the following after receiving his:

MERRY CHRISTMAS AND HAPPY NEW YEAR! Thank you very much for your wonderful card and greetings. I was very touched when I opened your letter and read my words in your Christmas message. You did not have to send me money. I was very content to spend Christmas as I was. I had everything that I needed. Your gift is very much appreciated, and you know what I am going to do with it? I am going to use it to buy something for one of the new guys who just got here and cannot buy anything for himself. A lot of the time new inmates need soap and deodorant and writing materials. I will use it for them. As it was sent to me as a gift, I will make it a gift.

I had a good Christmas, Pierre. All the guys on the wing with me got together and sang "happy birthday." It was very loud, and they passed around a card and everyone signed it for me. Even the officers brought extra food on both shifts. This was the best Christmas I ever had here yet. However, all the time I could not help but feel so sad for all my friends that were no longer here this year to share in my happiness. I know that when you try your best to do your best under all circumstances, God is watching, and He will reward you. I look around and see how blessed I really am and I want to cry.

The card you sent me arrived on the 24th of December. But I was not allowed to receive it, because it was home made. The mail room lady did let me read a little bit of it, that is how I know about the money that you and some of your friends sent, but she did not have time to allow me to read the entire card. I am sorry. They have very strict rules. Before the escape,[9] they did not enforce them as they do now.

---

9   The escape attempt by a group of inmates mentioned above, which resulted in the transfer of all death row inmates from the Ellis One Unit in Huntsville to the then Terrell Unit (later renamed Allan Polunsky Unit) in Livingston, Texas.

Note: the high cost of full-color prints has prohibited us from printing the drawings in their original form. You can see them on Roger's web site www.rogermcgowen.org

I just wanted to say to you and Elly that I have come to think of you as family, and I love you guys very much.

I pray that the approaching year will bring with it a craving for truth, knowledge and understanding, because when we have them, Love is always present as well, and without Love, nothing that is, could have been. *(December 27, 1999)*

2000

I may not be free in body, but I am free in mind, and when we meet again, regardless of where I am at the time, it will be with the mind and heart of a free man, because as long as God is in my life, I will never be bound. I believe that this year will bring with it new hopes, and with that a long awaited physical freedom.

My birthday was one of the most wonderful days I have had since being here. There are truly some wonderful people here. God does not care where one is when He sends His blessings, as long as one recognizes them when they come. And He blessed me by surrounding me with lovable men with remarkable hearts that can look beyond the walls that confine them, into the hearts of everyone around them, and bring out the God that they know is there. I will never forget that day, as long as I live.

I know exactly what you mean about little children, so much beauty and wonder in their eyes, so much adventure, so many things to explore. It is not the large things that I miss – I know I have told you that before. But it is the small things that people take for granted, such as the smile of a child, the smell of a newborn baby, the way a child's eyes light up when he/she discovers something new. Just to know that someone is depending on you, or to know that person loves you just because you are there, not because of what you have on, but because it is the nature of a child to trust. I love children so much. Just think – I have not held a baby in my arms for almost 14 years! *(January 25, 2000)*

Inmate Nanon Williams describes the stark and shattering solitude of death row

"Polunsky Unit is not just another prison to house death row inmates, but a place of permanent solitary. Not solitary-like, but complete and total isolation.

As a result of being in permanent solitary, most men here are beginning to suffer from sensory deprivation. . . ., a breakdown and loss of one's senses (touch, taste, hearing, sight, and smell).When the body receives no stimulation,. . . . a deep depression sets in, resulting in the inability to control moods. I am not a psychiatrist and cannot list all the effects this is having on men here, but I can tell you from experience that it is altering the minds of men, literally killing them. . . .

The souls of these men are gone. They are alive, but they are not living. Some of the men sink into deep depressions and never recover. Others slowly become more aggressive like a tortured, beaten, and starved lion.What will happen when this lion is released from its cage? Is it fair to say it would act rational? No! It will act irrational, finding refuge in the anger it feels. . . .

Though some feel a destructive rage, others have enough internal fortitude to recognize that show-ing any act of violence will not help or improve our conditions. Consequently, any attempt at physi-cal or mental preservation triggers the use of unnecessary. . . . force by prison guards. It is excessive force to the point of crippling and killing prisoners. Just the other day, another man was gassed and beaten beyond recognition; all while handcuffed and shackled. The administering guards laughed as they bragged about who did the most damage. All of this "excessive force" inflicted on a man who was helpless and otherwise harmless.THIS IS BARBARIC! This must be investigated and stopped.

The prisoners here release bouts of displeasure through shouts, screams, snarling, gnashing of teeth, and sounds so foreign one wonders if it's a show of masculinity or insanity. . . .

Since being transferred here [to the Allan Polunsky Unit in Livingston], things have changed dra-matically.We are "dead men walking"— not living, just existing. . . .

As a civilized society, we pride ourselves on the ability to act rationally when the world around us is irrationalWhat is taking place here is not only irrational, but inhumane and horrifying. Animals in a zoo are required more space than what we are allowed, more food and better treatment.There are laws in effect that protect animals from cruelty. There are laws to protect us, but they are not enforced. . . ."

(Source: Nanon Williams quoted on: www.fdp.dk/uk/cond/cond-23.php)

ROGER'S LETTERS FROM THE ALLAN B. POLUNSKY UNIT IN LIVINGSTON

In early March 2000, Roger and the other death row inmates were transferred from the Ellis One Unit in Huntsville to a high security prison – the Charles T. Terrell Unit in Livingston (later renamed Allan B. Polunsky Unit). There, prisoners have no physical contact with each other and little contact with the guards. They have no daylight except a small slit in the wall, close to the ceiling, just high enough to put a coffee mug, and no control over the lighting in their own cells. The little outside exercise they have, one-two hours, five times a week, takes place in a small cage, roughly the size of a cell, in the prison yard, with an open ceiling, enough to see the sky, but not much more. During lockdowns, which are frequent and can last weeks, they are confined in their cells 24 hours a day.

When I visited Roger in June, 2002, he had not had a single warm meal since moving to the Livingston prison. Cold meals were the norm and, very occasionally, a dish that had remained barely lukewarm during its long trip from the kitchen. At the beginning of his time there, the silence weighed heavily on him, like a coffin pall – as he explains below. But for some inmates, the silence and especially the solitude were so unbearable that they started yelling at the top of their voices and shaking the bars of their doors all day long. Then the prison wing became an insane asylum of screams and expletives exploding like mortar fire.

2000

We were moved here on the second day of March with our hands chained to our ankles and placed on a bus for the hour long ride. Since we have been here [16 days at this point], we have not had a single warm meal. I believe they cook the food the day before serving it.

The solitude here is sometimes like a wall. I can sometimes swear that if I take another step, I will walk into a wall of silence. The solitude acts as a trigger that sets off an emotional switch inside your subconscious that projects all your fears, all the things that you ever ran from, onto a screen in front of your mind. There you have to confront all the demons that you have run from for so long. Either you confront them, or you go mad. Last night a man on a pod a couple of doors down attempted to kill himself because he could not look his demons in the face. We all have them, whether we believe we do or not. He tried to face his demons without God standing by his side, and that we cannot do. We have to arm ourselves with the shield of truth and the sword of righteousness that only God can provide us with. To do otherwise is madness itself.

The entire prison system in Texas is under a statewide lockdown, and no one seems to know why. For three days we have been eating peanut butter sandwiches and cold pancakes and occasionally a mackerel sandwich. No showers. It is the worst place I have been here on the planet. The only upside to this place are the officers. They are much more courteous than at Ellis.

The Case of Odell Barnes

During the 1990s, the case of Roger's close friend Odell Barnes became a "cause célèbre," illustrating the injustice that can result from a hasty prosecution marked by a botched police investigation, an incompetent defense attorney, and a judge and prosecutor elected by a population in its majority pro-death penalty. The key elements of that case:

1. Barnes was arrested for the murder of his friend Helen Bass (killed in her house in Wichita Falls in November 1989) on the basis of Robert Brooks' *testimony*, which was riddled with holes. For instance, Brooks claimed to have seen Barnes at 10:30 p.m., yet Ms. Bass arrived at 11:30. Also, Brooks admitted that at the time of this sighting, he was wearing tinted glasses and the street lighting was poor. Moreover, he was just driving by and hardly knew Barnes – yet he was able to identify him from a distance of 40 yards. Initially, Brooks stated he was alone in the car, when in fact his sister was with him and he had told her the man was NOT Barnes.

2. Police noted numerous *blood splashes* widely spread all over the room, with only two minute bloodstains of that same blood on Barnes' clothes; had Barnes been the murderer, the blood would have been all over his clothes. More disturbing is the fact that an independent forensic expert, Kevin Ballard, M.D., testified that those two minute bloodstains could not have come from natural bleeding, as they contained a preservative used to conserve blood in test tubes. This suggests the blood on Barnes' clothes was planted (by the police?)

3. *Fingerprint*: Barnes' fingerprint was found on a lamp in the victim's house (which Barnes had visited many times before Police claimed the lamp was recently acquired (hence the fingerprint could not have been left from an earlier "social" visit), yet Ms. Bass's own son, Cory Bass, said the lamp had been there at least five years. Quite a few other fingerprints were found on the premises, but the police made no effort to compare them to those of other potential suspects.

4. *Shoeprint*: police claimed that the kicked-in door of the house held the print of a shoe belonging to Barnes. Yet, an expert who examined the door and Barnes' shoes concluded that thousands of shoes were capable of making a similar print.

(continued p.66)

But I still feel very blessed, Pierre. I am blessed that I am in good health, mentally and physically. I have a roof over the head and a clean place to sleep. Regardless of where I am or of the conditions that are confronting me at the time, I try always to remember that there are many people all over the world who are free and yet who do not have what I have. I am blessed to be able to recognize the blessings that I have, so that I will not complain about the things that I do not have.

Odell Barnes was a very good friend of mine. We were very close. I gave him my typewriter. He and I spent many nights talking about all kinds of things. He was a very intelligent young man, one that could make you laugh on a dime. We would often sit and talk about his case. He was certain that he would be exonerated. Several times he told me that he was innocent, and I believed him. It was important for him to have me believe that he was innocent, and I believed it. I knew he was going home. But I guess God had other plans for him, plans that no one saw but God. And now he is gone from this plane. But he will forever be in my heart and on my mind.

I do not know what to say about Texas. Whatever it is I choose to say about Texas, I would only be repeating something that has been said before. You can't hurt the devil's feelings by talking about him. A great tragedy will befall Texas soon for all the atrocities they commit against their own citizens. As much as I want to say something very bad about them, I can't, because there are too many people involved, and already too much hurt for me to add to it. But I do cry inside, and wonder when an end will come, one way or another. But once again, only God can answer that.

I believe that we are all one, that we are all one with everything and with everyone, and everyone and everything is one with us. There is no you or I or me – all is us. That is why when we see things that are not right, we hurt, because what is being done to one is being done to us all. We are all children of God, and we are God because we are a part of God. When we harm one another, we are only harming ourselves. All that is, is God. He is everything, and everything is Him. When we meditate, we tap into where we come from for just a moment, and we feel what we really are, and that is love, because love is everything, love is God.[10] Yes, we are all and we are nothing. Jesus had to die and become nothing to become something. *(March 18, 2000)*

---

10   In this key passage, Roger explains his fundamental non-dualism, or philosophy of Oneness, which is a great source of strength to him. The great majority of the world's religions and spiritual teachings (including traditional Christianity, Judaism, and Islam) are dualist. All things go in pairs: God and man, good and evil, heaven and hell, man and woman, spirit and matter, life and death, the past and present, or present and future, salvation and damnation, etc. In the non-dualist tradition, or philosophy of oneness, all is one. It is superbly summarized in Jesus' statements: "I and my father are one" and "My son, thou art always with me, and all that I have is thine."

The Case Of Odell Barnes (continued)

5. *State witnesses*: in a sworn testimony, the former girlfriend of Pat Williams, a known drug dealer (and key witness claiming to have seen Barnes with a gun that *could* have been used during the crime), said Williams had made a deal with the District Attorney that if he agreed to testify against Barnes, he would not go to jail for a serious drug offense of which he was guilty. Another witness, Johnnie Ray Humphries, went to the home of Marquita Mackay in the company of two other men. Armed with guns and covered with blood, they demanded clean shirts, and Humphries threatened Mackay, saying, "I'll kill you like I killed Helen Bass."

These are just a few of the inconsistencies in the prosecution against Odell Barnes. But the main factor is that *Barnes had no motive whatsoever* to kill his friend.

(Source: http://www.ccadp.org/odellbarnes.htm For the prosecution's standpoint, see www.prodeathpenalty.com/Pending/00/mar00.htm)

HAND DRAWING OF ROGERS' CELL
at Polunsky Unit

BY ROGER

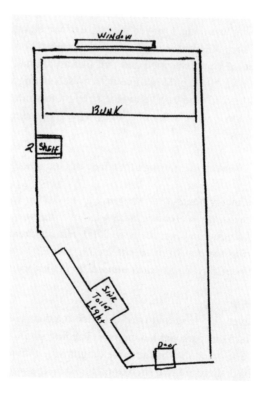

Hello, my wonderful friend. How are you, you and your beautiful wife Elly? As I look up to the ceiling at the sun coming in through the small window and reflecting on the walls in the cell that I occupy, I can't help but hope and pray that your life is as sunny and bright as that sun, because that is how my day is every time I receive a letter from you. Thank you, my friend, for remembering me in your prayers.

The trials that we went through [being transferred from the old prison at Ellis One to the new unit of Terrell, now Allan Polunsky] will remain with me forever. I can still feel the shackles that bound my hands and feet together as the officers stood outside and laughed and made fun of us as we were being loaded into the buses that would take us to our destination. And yet even now, as I look back, my heart can hold no hatred, no animosity for what was done. I prayed the entire trip over, only asking God to keep me from hating, to keep me from seeing through the same eyes that despise me. I could live with the shame of being shackled and tied like an animal, for being humiliated and reduced to nothing, but I could not live with myself hating those that hate me for the sake of hating. I asked God to give me the strength to smile, though I was crying inside, and the courage to walk with my head held high, even though I was bound and shackled ankle to wrist.

What was meant to weaken me, through the grace of God made me strong.

Roger wrote the following passages in response to my asking him to describe his cell and daily routine. Evidently, his routine had varied over the thirteen years of detention he had served at that point in time, the year 2000. His apparently innocuous remark about sleeping during the day so as to not see the sunrise says volumes about how heavy the mental strain must be for most inmates to be just waiting to die, year after year after year.

We have a bunk seven feet long and two feet wide. Under the bunks there are three shelves for us to place our personal belongings. The first shelf is about one foot wide and two feet long. The other shelf is the same length with a divider in the middle. On the far wall in the back there are two shelves mounted on the wall. The bottom shelf is one foot wide and about a foot and a half long, just big enough to place a typewriter. The second one is shorter, not very big at all. On the same side we have our toilet and sink, joined together with the sink on top, in a stainless steel combo. Above the toilet is the light, mounted into the wall behind very thick Plexiglas. It is about a foot wide and four feet tall, and when it is on it lights up the entire cell. We have a button set into the wall that controls the light (on/off, no dimmer). But the officers also have control of the lights from the control picket, and they can turn them on when you are sleeping so that the officer on the run can see inside your cell. They turn them on regularly, and you can't turn them off.

Texas justice and the death penalty: major flaws

The Texas Defender Service, TDS, (www.texasdefender.org) is one of a handful of private organizations performing a much needed public service in the field of justice. Established in 1995 by experienced death penalty attorneys of Texas, this nonprofit organization, apart from authoring some of the most outstanding research in the death penalty field in Texas, is active in three areas: 1) direct representation of (usually poor) death penalty inmates; 2) consulting, training, case-tracking, and policy reform at the post-conviction level; and 3) the same, at the trial level.

In 2000, TDS released its carefully documented study, *A State of Denial: Texas Justice and the Death Penalty*. The report revealed major flaws in the system, including:

Official misconduct The study documents a disturbingly high number of trials (84) in which a Texas prosecutor or police officer *deliberately* presented false or misleading testimony, voluntarily concealed, lost or *even destroyed* evidence that exonerated the accused, or used notoriously unreliable evidence from a jailhouse "snitch." In many cases, this was the *primary* evidence used to obtain a conviction.

In other cases presented in the TDS report, police and prosecutors resisted scientific examination of various clues, manipulated the testimony of witnesses, and even used threats against defendants or their families to obtain forced confessions. *"In the overwhelming majority of these cases, the misconduct* [by police and prosecutors] *that sent these men to death row only came to light years after the trial."*

Fooling the jury with disreputable experts In 21 cases, an expert psychiatrist testified with *"absolute certainty that the defendant would be a danger in the future."* It is scientifically incorrect to state with absolute certainty that someone will be a future danger. Such a statement, while having no scientific credibility, exerts undue influence on a jury concerned about the possible ramifications of a defendant's eventual release. Furthermore, a weak defense attorney might not challenge such a statement. Prosecutors cleverly build up the supposedly "scientific" nature of psychiatry in a manner that easily fools juries, from which anyone against the death penalty has been carefully eliminated. In 36 cases, the state relied upon the most unreliable of forensic evidence – hair comparison. This kind of "proof" has fallen into disrepute among all conscientious forensic scientists, and it demonstrates the amazing power of manipulation of some prosecutors.

The overwhelming weight of race Outright racism in the administration of justice in Texas has been officially recognized and condemned by no lesser an authority than the US Supreme Court, e.g. in the case of Thomas Miller-El, thanks to the careful documentation prepared by the TDS, which showed how African Americans had been systematically "weeded" (the word is especially appropriate here) from the jury."

(continued p. 72)

It is hard to give you an exact daily schedule, because it differs. I mean I do not do the same thing every day. But normally, I sleep during the day and stay up at night. Most of the guys do the same. I guess it makes the day go by faster, and you do not have to see the sun coming through the window to remind you of what you are missing. But let me see now. Today is Tuesday. It is about 10.04 a.m. and I just came in from recreation about 30 minutes ago. I have been up for about a day-and-a-half, because I have been finding it very difficult to sleep. Sometimes it is very noisy here, and sometimes very quiet. I am trying to see how best to answer your question. It is hard, because I have no set patterns.

Let us start at 1 a.m., because that is when I start exercising. I attempted to go to sleep the day before yesterday at about 5 p.m. and could not. So I got up and decided to type. I typed a few letters and it became too noisy, so I had to put the typewriter away and try to read. I tried to read but I could not concentrate, so I tried to go to sleep again, and lay there on my bunk for almost an hour, and still could not get any sleep. So about 7 p.m. the officer came around doing a wing count. The officer in the control picket turns your light on, and the officer on the run comes and asks your name and Texas Department of Criminal Justice number, and I answer 000889. He or she then moves on to the next person.

Then I get up and turn on the radio to listen to some soothing music, but the reception is so bad, and I can't pick any radio station, so I cut the radio off. I lay back down on the bunk and wait for the mail to be passed out. I do not have any, apart from a newspaper, The New York Times,[11] to which my friend M. subscribed for me. So I start to read the newspaper, even if it is two or three days late. I begin to feel sleepy, so I lie down, hoping that this time sleep will not elude me. But I can only sleep for a few of hours and I wake up at 12.30 a.m. So I roll out of my bunk and begin to pray. At about 1 a.m., I begin to exercise. Today is the day that I do my stomach workout, so I start by doing crunches. I do 250 crunches and 100 roll crunches. When I am through with my crunches, I do 500 jumping jacks.

By the time I am finished, the nurse is coming by to give me my insulin shots. The officers will come to my cell and tell me it is time for my shots, so they shake me down and I back up to the pan hole that is cut into the center of the door about two feet from the floor. I stick my arms [through the opening] so that I can be handcuffed, and once I am handcuffed, the officer in the control picket opens the door. I step out, and the nurse gives me a shot. I then step back into the cell, the control officer closes the door and I back to the door again, scoot down and stick my hands through the opening and the officer takes my handcuffs off.[12]

---

11   The subscription was later terminated.
12   Every single time an inmate leaves the cell, the same ritual is performed. They can never walk around outside their cells without being handcuffed.

Texas justice (continued)

While a 1998 study indicates that 23 percent of all Texas murder victims were black men, only 0.4 percent of those executed since the reinstatement of the death penalty were condemned to die for killing a black man. Conversely, white women represented 0.8 percent of murder victims statewide, but 34.2 percent of those executed since reinstatement were sentenced to die for killing a white woman. Non-whites are for the most part excluded from the process of assessing a punishment that is disproportionately visited upon them. *African-Americans are the least likely to serve on capital juries, but the most likely to be condemned to die.*

Another TDS study, *Lethal Indifference* (Houston, 2002) relays the story of Clarence Brandley - a black man wrongly convicted of sexually assaulting and murdering a female student while employed as high-school janitor in Montgomery County, Texas. When the police arrived, they interviewed Brandley and the white janitor, who were on staff duty at the time. The police officer conducting the interview said to Brandley, *"One of the two of you is going to hang for this. Since you're the nigger, you're elected."* During the trial, the state sponsored perjured testimony and deliberately withheld evidence that would have exonerated Brandley. Brandley's conviction was finally overturned after further misconduct on the part of the state was revealed.

Abysmally poor representation: you get what you pay for The poor level of legal representation by state-appointed attorneys in some cases is beyond belief: lawyers who sleep during the trial (Roger's case) or arrive drunk to the court, lawyers who have no experience whatsoever with the death penalty process and are forced to stay on the case despite their own protests, lawyers who are extremely poorly paid (in some cases, less than $12.00 per hour) and have no funds to pay experts… This dismal list could cover pages. Two specific examples from TDS' *State of Denial* report: defendant *"Joe Lee Guy was represented at trial by an attorney who ingested cocaine on the way to trial and consumed alcohol during court breaks. Guy's state habeas attorneys failed to investigate the misconduct — which means those facts may never be considered by either state or federal court."* In the case of Leonard Rojas, a Hispanic man sentenced to death in 1996 and too poor to afford a lawyer to represent him for his state level *habeas corpus* appeal, the Texas Court of Criminal Appeals appointed a lawyer who had never handled such an appeal, had been sanctioned several times for neglecting clients, *and was under treatment for serious mental illness.*

These are not occasional occurrences, as defenders of the status quo contend. The TDS studies painstakingly document one tragic and unavoidable conclusion: these are *regular* patterns in the administration of justice in Texas.

> *"More often than we want to recognize,*
> *some innocent defendants have been convicted*
> *and sentenced to death."*
> (US Supreme Court Justice Sandra Day O'Connor)

Then I start cleaning up my cell and get prepared for breakfast. They serve breakfast at about 3.40 a.m. and I get a diet tray. It is the worst food you could imagine: egg whites, and not many of them, a spoonful of boiled potatoes, a piece of white bread and milk, and that is all there is to it.

Once I have eaten I will wait until the shift change which is around 6 a.m. That is the time we go outside in the morning. We are placed in small cages with only a toilet and a table and the kind of exercise mattress you find in school gyms. That is where you stay for an hour. All the recreation rooms are diagonal from one another, so if another prisoner is out at the same time, you can speak to him.

The exercise room, actually, it is not outside. It [simply] has no roof. You cannot feel the wind blowing, nor does the sun shine into it, and you are only allowed one hour.

Once we are finished with "recreation," we are brought back into our cells, to wait all day long until the next shift arrives – about seven hours later - before we shower. We can shower every day if we so choose.

So, while waiting for the shift to change, I will pray and read a little from the Bible and Science and Health and then pray again. When the second shift officers come on, they will normally wait and escort the nurse around the wings so that she can administer the insulin [shots] to the diabetics, which takes about 30 minutes. Once they have finished escorting the nurse, they begin the showers, which are situated at the very end of the runs. They are no bigger than the average clothes closet, and you can barely turn around in them. After we have showered, we are led back to our cells to await the evening meal, which for diabetics consists of boiled white noodles with a few scraps of hamburger meat sprinkled over the top, two slices of white bread and whatever vegetables they can find in the kitchen. After they have fed the chow, I will say my prayers and lie down to rest.

Normally I will do that by tossing and turning, because I have difficulty sleeping, but I attempt to anyway, until I get tired and decide to get up and try my hand at reading or something. But there really is no set pattern here like there was at Ellis Unit.

There is no physical contact whatsoever with anyone except the officers when they are escorting you. The food has gotten worse, if you can believe that. I have not had a hot meal since I have been here [March 2000]. They do not have a kitchen in the building where we are housed, so they have to ship the food from the main building to our building, and by the time it gets here, it is cold and it is served that way.

The Delma Banks case: when Texas overshoots

In a March 9, 2004 editorial, the *Dallas Morning News* called for a death penalty moratorium in Texas, saying that "*the fact that public servants played fast and loose with the law should
outrage the most ardent death-penalty advocates.*"The editorial came in response to the case of
Delma Banks, Jr., who spent 23 years on death row due to deliberately rigged, malicious
testimony by two witnesses who lied from A to Z in front of the District Attorney who
was aware of, and actually encouraged, their perjury. Newspapers across the country covered the story, including *The Boston Globe* and *The Christian Science Monitor*, quoted below:

"*The Supreme Court delivered a stern critique of Texas's conduct in a high-profile death penalty
case yesterday, ruling unanimously that the state had wrongfully sentenced a man who came within
10 minutes of being executed last year.*

*By a vote of 7-2, the court ruled that prosecutors violated the constitutional rights of Delma Banks
Jr. by withholding information that his defense lawyers could have used to discredit a key prosecution witness during his 1980 sentencing hearing.*

*By a vote of 9-0, the court also ruled that Banks should be allowed to appeal his murder convic-
tion, because prosecutors may have improperly withheld information during the phase of the trial
in which jurors found him guilty of killing 16-year-old Richard Whitehead — a crime he denies
committing. Banks is African-American;Whitehead was white, as were all 12 jurors.*

"*As a result of the twin rulings, Banks is not only off death row — unless Texas resentences him to
death at some point in the future — he also has a fresh chance to be acquitted of the crime entirely*"
(The Boston Globe, *February 25, 2004*).

"*It took Delma Banks and his lawyers 19 years to discover the truth. State prosecutors at his 1980
murder trial allowed two key witnesses to lie to the jury that sentenced Mr. Banks to death. But even
after the deception was uncovered, a federal appeals court said it did not matter. . . . At the center
of Banks' appeal is the failure of prosecutors to disclose fully contacts and cooperation between
prosecutors and two key trial witnesses, Charles Cook and Robert Farr. . . . Mr. Farr provided key
testimony against Banks during the penalty phase of the trial, suggesting to jurors that Banks was
potentially dangerous and thus should be executed.What neither Banks nor the jurors knew was
that Farr was a paid informant hired to help gather evidence against Banks. Nonetheless, in closing
arguments the prosecutor told jurors that Farr had been "open and honest with you in every way.*"

(continued p.76)

I am happy to hear that many people are finding inspiration in the letters that I write. I only write what is in my heart, and try to tell you as accurately as I can all the things that I see. I do not write them for recognition of any kind. But it is still very good to hear that they are helping others. Thank you for all your wonderful words of encouragement.

I am very tired all of a sudden. I hope I will be able to go to sleep. My arms are tired from exercising all night. I have been pretty tired lately, so forgive me if I do not answer all of your questions. I hope I helped you out concerning what you wished to know about my living conditions.

I am going to close this letter now, and maybe get some rest. Please give Elly once again my love and greetings and also to you as well. I will keep you in my prayers as I know I am in yours. *(April 25, 2000)*

My dear brother Pierre, how are you, you and your beautiful wife Elly? I hope and pray that God has and always will provide you with everything you will ever need. Just before I received your letter, I was telling my neighbor how God blesses us in ways we can never understand and that He blesses us when we do not even know it.

I was explaining to him[13] that God's hands never stop moving, they are always working, and just because we cannot see them does not mean they are not shielding us and protecting us from harm. And then I received your letter and when I opened it, I did not know what to do – I had no idea that you were working on something like that [this book of Roger's letters]. All I can say is: thank you from the bottom of my heart. May God bless you. It makes me feel so very good to know that something I do can help someone in some kind of way. I am still quite speechless.

We have been placed under another lockdown, for reasons that have not been made clear to us. It seems that since we have been brought here to this prison, the authorities use any excuse they can to lock death row down. So once again we are locked down in our cells 24 hours a day. We are not given showers nor are we given hot meals. We are being fed cold sandwiches and whatever else they can find in the kitchen to feed us.

---

13   Inmates talk to each other by shouting through the slit in the door. These exchanges frequently occupy quite a few hours each day.

The Delma Banks Case (continued)

Mr. Cook's testimony was even more crucial to the State's case. He told jurors that Banks had confessed to having killed someone, that Banks asked Cook to get rid of a gun that turned out to be the murder weapon and that Banks asked Cook to dispose of the victim's car.When asked on cross-examination by Banks' lawyer whether he had previously discussed his testimony with authorities, Cook said no. Prosecutors knew the statement was false.They had in their files a transcript of Cook's pretrial preparation with authorities.

Cook's denial of involvement with authorities prevented the defense, and ultimately the jury, from learning that the prosecutors intervened in a pending arson case involving Cook.According to court documents, one month prior to Cook's testimony in the Banks trial, the prosecutors filed habitual-offender charges against Cook in the arson case, a move that substantially increased his potential prison time if convicted. But after Cooks testimony against Banks, the arson case was dismissed" (The Christian Science Monitor/Monitorworld, Week of December 13-19, 2003).

Murder victim's mother speaks out against the death penalty

"When Aba Gayle's 19-year-old daughter was murdered in 1980, she found herself seeking revenge and consumed by bitterness. Although the District Attorney assured her that she would feel better when the murderer was convicted, and in turn executed, Gayle was not convinced that the death penalty would quell her anger and lead to the healing she desired. Today, Gayle shares her story with the public and speaks out against the death penalty. 'I know that I didn't need the State of California to murder another human being so that I could be healed,' she notes. 'It's time to stop teaching people to hate and to start teaching people to love. The whole execution idea as closure is not realistic.' A member of Murder Victims' Families for Reconciliation, Gayle states, 'Anger is just a horrible thing to do to your body. Not to mention what it does to your soul and spirit. Forgiveness is not saying what he did was right. It's taking back your power.'" (Silverton Appeal Tribune, March 12, 2003)

But once again I have to remind myself of all the men that were put to death this year - last month as a matter of fact, men that were good friends of mine – and be thankful to God for the little things that He does bless us with. We may never get what we want, but we have to be ever mindful of those who have even less. If we forget that even for a second, we are throwing the little that we do possess in God's face and making a mockery out of the blessings that He gives us.

Pierre, I wonder every day why I have not lost my mind. So many brothers have died at the hands of this state, and every day brothers are getting death dates, and you can see the fear in their eyes. Many of them do not want to show it, but you can see it, and you can feel it exuding from their bodies. They know that relief is almost non-existent. It cuts me to the depths of my soul to know that these young people will probably not see another year, and it hurts so bad. The only comfort I get is knowing that there are those like yourself who have taken up the fight with us, to see that justice prevails, not man's justice, but God's. Thank you on behalf of all of us.

The next paragraph refers to a letter I wrote telling Roger that I had met his then law-yer, G. T., along with three other Americans – Rick Halperin, a leader of the anti-death penalty movement in the US, Sonia "Sunny" Jacobs (a former death row inmate and wife of J. Tafero mentioned under "Botched executions,") and Sue Zann Bosler (who witnessed the murder of her minister father and was nearly stabbed to death herself). I met this remarkable trio while they were in Europe campaigning against the death penalty. Sue not only traveled the long road to total forgiveness, but pleaded at her assailant's trial that he be given a prison sentence rather than the death penalty. She is one of many in a growing movement of murder victim families who oppose the death penalty.

I am so happy that you finally met G.T. He has so much passion, so much commit-ment. Sonia "Sunny" Jacobs suffered greatly, and very little in the way of apology was given, if any. Of course, everyone knows Rick Halperin. Concerning Sue Zann Bosler, it is so wonderful to hear when someone who has been victimized comes to the realization that to hate the person responsible [for the misdeed] will only make your hurt go deeper, and that the only way to find peace is to let go and forgive. It takes a very strong person with much love for God to acknowledge that to forgive is divine.

I know in my heart that God directed you my way and me your way. I do believe that certain things happen for a reason. Sometimes God will make us go through some ter-rible experiences to gain just one lesson.

The ultimate healing

"Is not this the fast that I have chosen:
to loose the bonds of wickedness,
to undo the bands of the yoke,
to let the oppressed go free,
and that you break every [enslaving] yoke?

Is it not to divide your bread with the hungry,
and bring the homeless poor into your house?
When you see the naked, that you cover him,
and that you hide not yourself
from [the needs of] your own flesh and blood?

Then shall your light break forth as the morning,
and your healing [your restoration and the power of a new life]
shall spring forth speedily."

(Isaiah 58, in *The Amplified Bible*, p. 826. The [brackets] are in the text)

I sent Roger that biblical description of true fasting given in Isaiah, chapter 58. For me, it is one of the most powerful statements of non-dualism (or the philosophy of the Oneness of all things). Roger's earlier quoted statement that what we do to others, we do to ourselves, mirrors this famous passage, which stresses that our individual healing (our wholeness – both words stem from the same root) depends on the healing of the world.

This is a very beautiful prayer, Pierre. That prayer is for all of us who are fighting against the death penalty. The Spirit of the Lord is a powerful force and He will proclaim liberty to the captives and open all the prisons to them that are bound. I truly believe that the Spirit of the Lord is at work here.

I try every day to live up to the divine love that is in us all, and when I find myself slipping, I remember that Jesus died to show us that we possess all that he possessed, and it is our reward to claim these possessions. I remember that I am a divine being, and I will start my day with divine love, because these walls cannot enclose my spiritual senses, which tell me that I dwell in divine love. I have learned through and by the grace of God to be patient and content because the little we have today may be gone tomorrow.

I love you, my Brother, my Friend. I will always think of you, always. *(June 10, 2000)*

Hello my beautiful brother in Christ. How are you and Elly? I hope that you are continuing to walk with God and allowing Him to lead the way regardless of how narrow the path may seem to be at times.

I love you and Elly very much. When I think of you, I think of you in the form of strength and energy, something that I can always count on to lift me up and fuse me with power when I am down. That is how God uses us. He uses us to empower one another, so that the cycle of love is never broken. God comes in the form of a brother to lend a hand when you need one, or a shoulder to lean upon when your strength has failed. He comes in the form of a finger that wipes the tears away from the eyes of a crying friend. God comes to us in all forms, but we are so busy looking for what we think the image of God is, that we miss Him each time. I see and feel Him each time I receive a letter from you. It is a feeling that one cannot describe, but I know it when I feel it.

2008: 60th Anniversary of the Universal Declaration of Human Rights

This declaration is the most important document on human rights ever accepted by the nations of the world. Drafted by a committee working under US chairwoman Eleanor Roosevelt, it was adopted and proclaimed by the General Assembly of the United Nations on December 10, 1948. It has of course been ratified by the United States.

The full text of the declaration can be downloaded at:

http://www.un.org/en/documents/udhr/index.shtml

The conditions prevailing on many death rows around the world, including the United States in many cases, explicitly violate the following articles:

Art.1 All human beings are born free and equal in dignity and rights. They are endowed with reason and conscience and should act towards one another in a spirit of brotherhood.

Art.2 Everyone is entitled to all the rights and freedoms set forth in this Declaration, without distinction of any kind, such as race, color, sex, language, religion, political or other opinion, national or social origin, property, birth or other status. . . .

Art.5 No one shall be subjected to torture or to cruel, inhuman or degrading treatment or punishment.

Art.7 All are equal before the law and are entitled without any discrimination to equal protection of the law. All are entitled to equal protection against any discrimination in violation of this Declaration and against any incitement to such discrimination.

Art.10 Everyone is entitled in full equality to a fair and public hearing by an independent and impartial tribunal, in the determination of his rights and obligations and of any criminal charge against him.

———

Thank you very much for the [quotations from the] Scriptures. There is hope in every one of these words. God will deliver, He has never failed me.

"No weapon that is formed against thee shall prosper" God says!! Man, what hope and power these words bring to my ears, because I know that what God says is true. We not only have to read His words, but we have to believe in them and act as if the promises made in them had already been granted. These are very beautiful scriptures. How can anyone read them and not be touched? Or not feel the presence of God? Thank you very much for sending them to me. They really help at a time like this.

You asked me how things are getting along. They are getting along. First, I am not taking two shots anymore for diabetes. I am only taking one shot now, and my insulin has been reduced drastically. My blood sugar has been really good. I pray and thank God constantly for being so good to me. He is good to me when I do not know it. When I think He is not moving, that is when He is moving for me.

The food has not improved at all. Actually, if you can believe it, it has gotten worse. It seems as if they do not even take the time to cook it at all, and all they serve us is pork. But I guess it could always be worse. I thank God that I have friends such as yourself and M. and L. who make it possible for me to take care of myself enough to keep my body sugar under control without really having to depend on the food that is served here. Because I can go to the prison store and purchase food to cook and share with those around me who are also diabetic but do not have any means. That way we can all try to stay relatively healthy.

The lockdown was over on the 23rd of June. This was the worse one yet, but it was somewhat understandable. One of the guys here who is mentally handicapped cut up one of the volunteer ministers really badly. It was one of those senseless acts of violence that no one can understand. Thank God the minister is going to be alright and his arm will regain its full use. But yes, the lockdown is over. However, there is no telling when they will come with another one. One can never really prepare. We just have to stay as ready as we can. *(July 10, 2000)*

Thank you very much for your lovely letter. God provides me with the strength and compassion that is needed to sustain my soul and keep me rooted in His words and divine love, and He gives me friends such as yourself to keep me inspired to keep seeking and moving on.

On occasion I have relapses like every one else and allow the actions of others to enter my world and affect me. But most of the time I am able to throw them off and move on. However, I wonder if that is a good or bad thing?

Media concentration and the
poor information of the US public

It is remarkable that the US public has not reacted to the startling injustices taking place in the country's prisons, the serious dysfunction of the judicial process (the scope of which is only hinted at in these pages), and an estimated seven to nine percent innocent men and women on death row.

As a non-American who lived and studied in the United States for some time (I spent two of the best years of my life at the University of Michigan, and have visited the country yearly since the late 1960s), I know from experience that Americans are basically honest and decent people with a deep hunger for justice. So, how is this acquiescence or blindness to injustice possible?

The basic explanation seems very simple: few Western countries have such a concentration of media ownership in so few hands as the United States. Thirty percent of Americans say their primary news source is talk radio, 90 percent of which has a strong conservative bias. Another 32 percent claim their primary news source is Fox News, MSNBC, CNBC or the Sinclair Network, all of which are fundamentally conservative. This is nearly two-thirds of the US population.

Today, six giant multinational corporations control practically all 14,000 radio stations, an overwhelming majority of the 6,000 TV stations, 80 percent of the newspapers, and practically all the billboards – plus a great part of the internet information. This means that six media owners are controlling advertising and what Americans perceive as unbiased, objective news.

The content of programs is influenced not only by the highly conservative political views of the owners, but to a great extent by advertisers. Advertisers want programs that encourage what they call "audience flow," i.e. continued viewing of programs to maximize advertising rates and revenues. This necessarily implies avoiding any programs with disturbing or challenging information, as well as unsettling controversies that dampen what advertisers call "the buying mood."

Giving too much air time to human suffering interferes with the buying euphoria. Advertisers want people *"tranquillized, pacified, and entertained."* As media historian Robert W. McChesney puts it, the fundamental mantra of the dominant media to viewers is: *"Shut up and shop."*

This is hardly an encouraging environment for debates on the conditions prevailing on death row!

(Source of all figures: Robert F. Kennedy, Jr., Speech to Sierra Club Summit, San Francisco, 17 September, 2005)

On one hand, if I do not say or do something about the wrong that I see, am I not condoning it by keeping silent? On the other hand, by me saying something and becoming involved, I am opening myself up and allowing it to affect me. And when I do, then I am pulled down with it. The choices are never easy when one's emotions are involved, but I have to do the right thing. And doing the right thing can sometimes hurt like an open wound.

Now they have labeled me a member of a gang!! I have no idea how they came to this conclusion. I have never been involved in any kind of gang activity, ever!![14] So now they have a reason to tear my cell apart any and every time they feel the need to. They can keep me locked up for as long as they wish without giving any reason and they can confiscate all my mail. I have talked with everyone and they tell me to write to the Unit Gang Intelligence Sergeant. But I have written three times and he has not answered me. So I am trying to get a lot of people to write and/or call the prison and speak with the warden to inquire on my behalf as to how they can move me here to this new unit, and, without provocation, place me in a gang!!

Just last week, they came to everyone's cell and took our fingernail clippers. Now we are not even allowed to clean and clip our nails.

The more I pray and ask God to give me the strength to overlook the things that are done to us in the so-called name of justice, and, regardless of what happens, to never allow me to lose the love and compassion in my heart even for the officers here in this prison, [the more] it seems they come up with some new form of harassment. This leaves me still more bewildered, and it is getting to the point that I wonder how far they are trying to push us.

When I write to explain what is going on here, it is because I want you and others to know exactly what we are daily faced with and how fragile our peace is here. My anguish only lasts for a few seconds, and I never allow it to totally consume me. But at times, I do feel like a tree whose roots are being uprooted little by little. But believe me, I will not lose faith. The things that are done to me here only make me pray harder.

I am very happy to hear that you used one of my letters in your workshop. It honors me to know that at least something that I have gone through is helping others realize how valuable their lives are.

---

14   The accusation is all the more ridiculous, given the fact that inmates have no physical contact with each other whatsoever, and whatever they share by shouting from one cell to another is heard by all the officers.

The true stuff of space

*"Concerning the space that I occupy, in itself it no longer
bothers me, because it is filled with love."*

(Roger McGowen, August 24, 2000)

*"The depth, breadth, height, might, majesty and glory of
infinite Love fill all space. That is enough."*

(Mary Baker Eddy)

"If I make my bed in hell, behold, Thou art there."

(Psalm 139:8)

*"Can any hide himself in secret places
that I shall not see him? saith the Lord .
Do I not fill heaven and earth? saith the Lord."*

(Jeremiah 23:24)

The lockdown is over for the moment, but there is never any telling when they will just decide to lock the prison down, leaving us once more with cold pancakes and peanut butter sandwiches. And, yes, being locked up 23 [or 24] hours a day does take its toll on the mind.

Texas is so terrible when it comes to compassion and forgiveness for their own citizens, but one day we must all reap what we sow. The universe is so balanced that it all must be straightened out before the end.

The Christ mind is indestructible and no imprisonment or bad treatment can mutilate it. I know that. I strive to always understand and hold on to that. But we are human, and I do allow certain things to manifest that should be given over to Christ. But I will try harder, because it is the duty of all Christians to strive for that Christ-like perfection. And there is no harm in not reaching it, as long as we never stop trying.

Thank you for all your concern, love and understanding. Concerning the space that I occupy, in itself it no longer bothers me, because it is filled with love. *(August 24, 2000)*

*T*hank you for your letter and for writing to me while on your vacation. Please, that is unnecessary – enjoy yourself as a vacation is meant to be enjoyed.

I am sorry that it has taken me a while to respond to your last letter. But when I received your letter, which was in August, the officials here had turned off the air conditioning and the weather was about 120 degrees outside in some places. It was so hot here I almost felt that I was suffocating. At Ellis, we were at least able to get a little air from outside because of the windows. But here, we can get no air because our rooms are almost like closets. There is nothing stirring. The walls that are facing the sun got so hot one could barely touch them. Man, was it hot here! We could barely breathe, let alone write. When they finally turned the air conditioning back on, they turned it so low that it felt like winter in the cells.

Once we finally had the situation under control, I allowed the doctor to place me on some new diabetes medication – even though there was nothing wrong with me. It made me sick – it dehydrated me pretty badly, and gave me very severe stomach cramps. I am still recuperating from the medication. It has made me very weak.

All I have been able to do is sleep, which is not bad in itself, because before, I had insomnia. I was sometimes staying up two days straight, and then only getting two or three hours sleep. I really am very tired now, but I realize that I have put your letter off too long and that you would be worried about me. I just wanted to let you know what is going on and why I have taken so long in writing back

When innocents are put to death

"A legal regime relying on the death penalty will inevitably execute innocent people, not too often, one hopes, but undoubtedly sometimes. Mistakes will be made because it is simply not possible to do something that perfectly, all the time. Any honest proponent of capital punishment must face this fact" (US District Judge Michael Adrian Ponsor).

The book *Actual Innocence* by Barry Scheck (co-founder of the now famous Innocence Project), Peter Neufeld, and Jim Dwyer should probably be at the top of the reading list for people wishing to educate themselves on the complexities and *systematic* patterns of legal ineptitude, bungling, outright deception, and error that plague the administration of the death penalty in the US (and probably most other countries where it is still practiced). According to the well-known conservative columnist George Will, *"You will not soon read a more frightening book. It is a catalog of appalling miscarriages of justice, some of them nearly lethal. Their cumulative weight compels the conclusion that many innocent people are in prison, and some innocent people have been executed"* (Washington Post, April 6, 2000).

In recent years, the increasing number of death row inmates exonerated and freed, growing public awareness of fatal distortions that plague the system, and acknowledgment *that a good many innocents* may *have been put to death,* have made innocence emerge as the central issue in the long-standing debate on the death penalty. This awareness, say Scheck et al., *"has been accelerated in recent years by the development of DNA technology, the new gold standard of forensic investigation. This science, along with a vigorous re-investigation of many cases, has led to the discovery of a growing number of tragic mistakes and freed inmates."*

Clearly, those numerous cases establish that *"the risks associated with capital punishment exceed acceptable bounds."* As of early 2009, at least 130 people have been freed from death row after being declared innocent. If one adds up all the years they spent in jail, the combined time amounts to *well over 1000 years.* Imagine how high the figure would be if it included innocents who were not and will not be exonerated in time to stay their executions! As Scheck et al. point out:

"The pace of exonerations has risen sharply, raising doubt about the reliability of the whole system [...]. The public perception of the death penalty in the United States has radically changed in recent years.When thinking about crime and punishment, people no longer see only the threatening image of a dangerous criminal convicted of a terrible crime; they also recall the face of the innocent defendant walking into the sunshine of freedom from the confines of death row.

(continued p.88)

Thank you for all the information you sent me concerning Professor Protess and his students.[15] Many of the guys here get news clippings from internet web sites from their friends. I too get a chance to read a lot of that information. We are very much aware of what is going on in the courts and of the latest rulings. Texas does need a David Protess. But Texas is too arrogant. There have been many cases where death row inmates have proven that their prosecutors fabricated evidence.

Sometimes I feel really discouraged. But it is not very often, and when I do feel that way and I happen to be writing to you at the time, I will tell you what I am feeling. But I also try my very best to look for the sun that I know is shining behind the clouds.

This is a very bad place. What makes it even worse is that we know we are not supposed to be locked down like this. We are supposed to be treated like the regular [prison] population [those who are not on death row]. That is the law. But the people running this place lied, and made all kinds of promises just to get us over here [the Allan Polunsky Unit in Livingston]. We know we are supposed to be able to work, to watch television, and have contact with each other. But the officials decided that they are going to disregard the law and do what they wish instead.

I get very frustrated at times, especially with the noise, the constant screaming and shouting and wall banging. It drives me up . . . the wall. But I can't allow it to get to me all the time. I have to block it out. H. asks me about the situation, and I tell him. But I do not want to bother all of you with these problems.

Pierre, you are my way out of here. I ride on your words to a place far away - your mountain [chalet] - and I am there with you. I do not like discussing this place all the time, and most people don't understand that. I want you to be able to pull me out of here with you. I do not wish you to come and sit in here with me.

There is no regular routine in this prison. Chow is never served at a regular time and recreation is any time they see fit. They may allow you to shower early in the morning, or in the middle of the afternoon, so it is hard to adjust. They do not even pass the mail out at a given time. Nothing is done regularly here, so it is hard for anyone to set a schedule or routine. Just two weeks ago, they came and made everyone pack up and move to different pods [wings]. So now the little view that I had is gone.

---

15   A professor of journalism from Northwestern University, Illinois, who made national headlines when his students managed to prove the innocence of a series of death row inmates who would otherwise have been executed.

When innocents are put to death (continued)

The issue of innocence, and the powerful examples that have thrust this issue into the public's eye, has done more to change the death penalty debate in this country than any other issue. It has slowed the death penalty down at a time when the political climate and the fear of terrorism might have led to a substantial increase in the use of capital punishment. . . . Virtually everyone is aware of the mistakes that have been made in capital cases. In polls, the public believes that the most tragic of errors has already happened – that innocent people have been executed in recent years. The evidence of near misses, exonerations based on fortuitous circumstances, and the obvious fallibility of the justice system inexorably leads to that conclusion."

Inadequate representation is a key issue in the US legal system, according to a comprehensive study of the death penalty led by Columbia University law professor James S. Liebman, and published in 2000 (see Liebman et al., *Capital Attrition: Error Rates in Capital Cases, 1973-1995,* 78 Texas Law Review [1839,1854], 2000). Having reviewed every death penalty appeal from 1973 through 1995, Liebman et al. came to the following conclusions:

- Of all the thousands of cases that had completed the appeals process, an astonishing 68 percent contained errors so serious that guilt or sentencing trials had to be done again.

- Eighty-two percent of the cases in the sample ultimately resulted in a sentence of less than death when they were done over, correcting for the error of the first trial. And 7 percent of those defendants turned out to be innocent.

- Of the 151 Tennessee death sentences reviewed on appeal since 1977, half were overturned, primarily because of inadequate representation. Thirty-nine of the lawyers representing defendants in capital cases had been disciplined by the state, including a lawyer convicted of bank fraud, one of perjury, and one whose failure to request a blood test caused his innocent client to linger four years in jail.

- In Washington State, it was discovered that a fifth of the 84 people who faced execution in the past 20 years were represented by grossly inadequate or incompetent lawyers, i.e. individuals who were later disbarred, suspended or even arrested.

In 2001, calling for a death penalty moratorium, former US Supreme Court Justice Ruth Bader Ginsburg told *Associated Press:* "*People who are well represented at trial do not get the death penalty [. . .]. If you are white and wealthy, you do not go to death row. If you are black and poor, you often do*" (In *Innocence and the Crises in the American Death Penalty* by Richard Dieter. See www.deathpenaltyinfo.org).

(continued p.90)

I can't even exercise in the morning like I used to, because it's always very cold in the cells. And if you exercise in the morning and they take you to recreation in the afternoon, then you have to sit in your cell sweating and tired all day long, with a risk of catching cold. I said it once and I will say it again: they do what they want to do here. I believe they do that to keep us off balance.

There is no personal relationship with the officers. They barely talk to us, and we barely talk to them. They do not go out of their way to bother us, but everyone keeps their distance. They are very scared of us – you can see it in their eyes and the way they react to us. They are told outrageous lies about us and they believe them.

They read all the incoming and outgoing mail. To tell you the truth, I doubt they feel uplifted by any mail going to, or coming from, a prisoner. Please tell Elly thank you for the flowers [a few tiny dry- pressed mountain flowers on a post card], but I never got to see them. They were torn off before they were delivered to me. Sorry, but I really do appreciate the thought.

I am so tired, Pierre. I truly believe the doctor experimented with several of us who are diabetics, because we all became sick. Once we complained, he rapidly took us off the medication. But [earlier] he did everything in his power to get us to take it. My stomach and eating habits have not been right since taking that stuff. It is called Metformin. He lied when he said it had no side effects. He lied.[16]

Take care, Pierre. Please give Elly a hug and a kiss from me. I am sorry if I do not sound enthusiastic. I thank God every day for you being in my life. Stay in God's grace. *(September 27, 2000)*

Hello, how are you and Elly? I hope that you are fine and well grounded in God's truth and love. I really do love and appreciate everything you do for me, especially for never questioning or misunderstanding what I am going through here. I try with all my heart to walk with my shoulders straight and my head held high, because I know that greater is He that is in me than he that is in the world. That is my favorite [Bible] quotation, and I really believe it. But at times it is hard to remember all that we have been taught and all that we know when we are subjected to such blatant hatred and oppression.

---

16   A check of www.drugs.com mentions that "some people have developed a life-threatening condition called lactic acidosis while taking metformin." It also stresses the very careful medical supervision needed while taking this drug, which is clearly not available on death row.

When innocents are put to death (continued)

In 1997, official, professional, and public concern over the sometimes unbelievable errors, systematic distortions, and serious official misconduct performed almost daily in the administration of justice, prompted the American Bar Association to issue "*a historic resolution calling for a national moratorium on all executions to 'minimize the risk that innocent persons may be executed.' Over two thousand organizations, governmental bodies, including numerous bar associations and county councils, have responded by similarly calling for a moratorium*" (In Dieter, op cit). And in *US v. Quinones* (2002), the court found that "*The best available evidence indicates that, on the one hand, innocent people are sentenced to death with materially greater frequency than was previously supposed and that, on the other hand, convincing proof of their innocence often does not emerge until long after their convictions*" (In Dieter, op cit.).

The gentle art of blessing

*"On awaking, bless this day, for it is already full of the unseen good which your blessings will call forth;
for to bless is to acknowledge the unlimited good that is embedded in the very texture of the universe and
awaiting each and all.*

*On passing people in the street, on the bus, in places of work and play, bless them. The peace of your
blessing will accompany them on their way, and the aura of its gentle fragrance will be a light on
their path.*

*On meeting and talking to people, bless them in their health, their work, their joy, their relation-
ships to God, themselves, and others. Bless them in their abundance, their finances . . . bless them in
every conceivable way, for such blessings not only sow seeds of healing, but one day they will spring
forth as flowers of joy in the waste places of your own life.*

*As you walk, bless the city in which you live, its government and teachers, its nurses and street sweepers,
its children and bankers, its priests and prostitutes. The minute anyone expresses the least aggression or
unkindness to you, respond with a blessing: bless them totally, sincerely, joyfully, for such blessings are a
shield that protects them from the ignorance of their misdeeds and deflects the arrow aimed at you.*

*To bless means to wish, unconditionally, total unrestricted good for others and events from the
deepest wellspring in the innermost chamber of your heart: it means to hallow, to hold in reverence,
to behold with utter awe that which is always a gift from the Creator. He who is hallowed by your
blessing is set aside, consecrated, holy, whole. To bless is yet to invoke divine care upon, to think or
speak gratefully for, to confer happiness upon – although we ourselves are never the bestowers, but
simply the joyful witnesses of Life's abundance.*

*To bless all without discrimination of any sort is the ultimate form of giving, because those you bless
will never know from whence came the sudden ray that burst through the clouds of their skies, and
you will rarely be a witness to the sunlight in their lives.*

*When something goes completely askew in your day, some unexpected event knocks down your plans
and you too, also burst into blessing: for life is teaching you a lesson, and the very event you believe
to be unwanted, you yourself called forth, so as to learn the lesson you might balk against were you
not to bless it. Trials are blessings in disguise, and hosts of angels follow in their path.*

*To bless is to acknowledge the omnipresent, universal beauty hidden to material eyes; it is to activate
that law of attraction which, from the furthest reaches of the universe, will bring into your life
exactly what you need to experience and enjoy.*

(continued p.94)

I was very low and feeling bad because I have been going through some pretty rough times with these people. They have been shaking down the cell I am in. They have been doing everything they know to continually punish us for acts that only they hold us accountable for. When it was really hot, they turned off the air conditioning and made us suffer in terrible heat for weeks. And then when the weather changed due to the change in seasons, and it began to get cool, they turned off the hot water in the showers, and those of us who wished to shower had to shower in ice cold water for at least a week. Then as soon as everyone started complaining and had their relatives and friends call the prison, they turned the hot water back on.

Now they have the air [conditioning] turned up so high that it is freezing in the cells. They are telling us they have no heating system, so all the winter we are going to have to wear anything we can find to stay warm inside the cells. I could go on and on about the things that they are doing to us here, in America, supposedly the most civilized society in the world.

I was really feeling the effects of it all. I was at the bottom of the barrel, asking God for the strength to hold on. I was ready to explode. I prayed, but for some reason, I could not find comfort in my prayers, and I would get up feeling empty.

Then you sent me your letter. I looked at it, and, to be honest, Pierre, the first thing I thought was: "More to read!" I have so much stuff to read, so much spiritual literature. I am tired of receiving it.

Finally, one night, before I went to bed, I read the first sections of the book you sent me, The Gentle Art of Blessing. I can tell you that, that it changed my thought process. After reading it, I just started asking God to bless all of these people, to bless them and their families, to bless them in their finances, their spiritual life, every aspect of their lives. Very gently, very slowly, the weight began to lift from my shoulders, not all at once, but gradually.

And now, every morning when I wake up, the first thing I do is bless them, and in the middle of the day, and again before I go to sleep at night. There is no structure to this place, there is no routine to live by; hour after hour, nothing happens, so I just do the first thing that comes to my mind. And lately, that has been to pray.

The gentle art of blessing (continued)

When you pass a prison, mentally bless its inmates in their innocence and freedom, their gentleness, pure essence and unconditional forgiveness; for one can only be a prisoner of one's self-image, and a free man can walk unshackled in the courtyard of a jail, just as citizens of countries where freedom reigns can be prisoners when fear lurks in their thoughts.

When you pass a hospital, bless its patients in their present wholeness, for even in their suffering, this wholeness awaits in them to be discovered. When your eyes behold a man in tears, or seemingly broken by life, bless him in his vitality and joy: for the material senses present but the inverted image of the ultimate splendor and perfection only the inner eye beholds.

It is impossible to bless and to judge at the same time. So hold constantly as a deep, hallowed, intoned thought that desire to bless, for truly then shall you become a peacemaker, and one day you shall, everywhere, behold the very face of God.

*P.S. And of course, above all, don't forget to bless the utterly beautiful person **you** are."*

(Pierre Pradervand, **The Gentle Art of Blessing**, pp.6-8).

Racial bias in justice

"The [justice] system has proved itself to be widely inaccurate, unjust, unable to separate the inno-cent men from the guilty, and at times, a very racist system" (Governor George Ryan of Illinois, January 10, 2000, when commuting all death sentences in Illinois into life sentences).

African-Americans constitute about twelve percent of the US population, but 41 percent of the prison population. Almost one in three black men can expect to spend some time in prison, compared to one in 25 for whites. In 1995, the USA ratified the UN Convention on the Elimination of All Forms of Racial Discrimination, yet American courts and legislatures have failed to act decisively in the face of evidence that race has an impact on capital sentencing, perhaps out of a collective blind faith that *"America will always stand firm in the non-negotiable demands of human dignity, including 'equal justice,' as President Bush has asserted"* (Amnesty International USA, www.amnesty.org/library/index/engamr510462003 Spring, 2007).

Racial bias in the administration of justice is all-pervasive, unrelenting, and at times extreme, as statistics have shown over and over again. As far back as 1990, a US General Accounting Office study of surveys on this subject found that *"in 82 percent of the studies, the race of the victim was found to influence the likelihood of being charged with capital murder or receiving the death sentence, i.e. those who murdered whites were found to be more likely to be sentenced to death than those who murdered blacks. This finding was remarkably consistent across data sets, data collection methods and analytic techniques"* (AI, op cit.).

The New Jersey Supreme Court candidly admitted the existence of disturbing statistical evidence that murderers of white victims were far more likely to be condemned than those whose victims were black. A detailed study of over 500 murders committed between 1993 and 1997 in North Carolina showed that an accused whose victim was white was 3.5 times more likely to be sentenced to death than if the victim was non-white.

The behavior of District Attorney Jack McMahon from Philadelphia in the case of African-American William Basemore illustrates a common practice in death penalty trials. Both the prosecution and the defense have the right to eliminate potential jury members if they suspect them of bias, or for any other reason. McMahon eliminated 19 people, all of them black. There was even a video of a course given by the same District Attorney in which he was instructing future D.A.s on how to exclude certain types of African-Americans from the jury.

The Texas Defender Service, in a study covering the years 1995 to 1999, discovered that 0.8 percent of murder victims were white women, whereas close to 20 percent of prisoners arriving on death row during that period were convicted of killing white women. Of 55 murders in the 85 percent white population of Montgomery County (Texas) during the same period, 31 percent involved non-white victims, none of which resulted in a death sentence. The rate at which cases went to trial varies according to the race of victims.

(continued p.98)

[Recently] I talked to an intern from my lawyer's firm. At the present moment, nothing is going on concerning my case. The judge that has my case has not yet released it. But I realize that God is the only true judge that counts. I have been asking God to bless her, as well as the district attorney and the federal judges that will eventually rule on my case. So there is really nothing [my lawyer] can do at the moment but wait.

The US Justice Department did its own study on the death penalty and found that it was racially biased. Prosecutors had lied and paid informants to lie, and promised jailhouse snitches leniency in sentencing for testimonies against defendants facing capital punishment. But the Justice Department also said that the information available was not enough to call for a moratorium on the death penalty. Here in Texas Governor George Bush has already shown that he will not even consider a moratorium on capital punishment. So even though there are significant changes in the air and many studies have found the death penalty biased, racist, and unjustly administered, no one wants to be the first to say that it needs fixing. And until that happens, many more innocent people will die at the hand of over-zealous politicians.

I know that nothing is impossible to God. But I have to remember that not just once in a while, but every second of every day. I know it more than others, Pierre. I have felt God's presence. He has been working in my life for years. I just have to find out what it is He wants me to do. God has been so wonderful to me. I say this with tears in my eyes and the truth in my heart. I would rather be in prison with Him than free without Him. When you wrote [in The Gentle Art of Blessing], "For one can only be a prisoner of one's self-image, and a free man can walk unshackled in jail, just as citizens of a free country can be prisoners of the fear lurking within their thoughts," that touched me deeply, because there is no place with walls that can shackle a man who wishes to be free in God.

Pierre, I know my life is not Livingston jail. I fight with all my heart to understand and believe that my life is in Christ. But I believe that God makes us go through things that we believe are the worst to test our faith and believe in Him. It will just take time. I am trying very hard to understand it all. I am really trying. God will in time give me all that I need to understand His glory, as long as I keep seeking. I know that we are all the true body of God with Jesus as the head. We are the light of the world as Christ was the light of the world. We are all the children of God as Jesus was. We just have to remember that when we need it most.

Please give Elly my love and greetings and tell her I will be alright. We all stumble sometimes, and sometimes we even fall. But our strength in God shows when, in spite of all else, we rise again because what is inside us is too strong to stay down. I love you both very much and you keep lifting me up just when I think I can't stand it any more. *(October 19, 2000)*

Racial bias in justice (continued)

Ninety percent of cases involving white victims went to trial, whereas only two cases involving non-whites (16 percent) were tried. Countless blacks have been put to death for killing whites in Texas, but only two whites have been put to death for killing a black. That happened in a case so horrendous that even the most racist District Attorney could not have avoided requesting the death penalty. It is all the more remarkable that in that particular case, the son of victim James Byrd put in a plea for mercy, arguing that *"all [the death penalty] does is bring more hate into the world"* (Roger speaks of this case, see letter of July 3, 2002).

Stanford University professor Jennifer Eberhardt's article, *"Looking Deathworthy: Perceived Stereotypicality of Black Defendants Predicts Capital-Sentencing Outcomes"* (*Journal of Psychological Science*, May, 2006), showed that the more stereotypically "black-looking" defendants were twice as likely to receive the death sentence than lighter skinned blacks, when the victims were white. This relationship disappeared when the victims were black!

In a 2005 landmark case highlighting systematic racial bias in the administration of justice in Texas, the Supreme Court overturned the conviction of black death row inmate Thomas Miller-El, recognizing that Texas prosecutors had *"unfairly stacked his jury with whites [and] issuing a harsh rebuke to the state that executes more people than any other."* As reported in a *New York Times* editorial:

"At the start of the third week of jury selection [...]. the first four prospective jurors up for questioning were black. The prosecutors requested a 'jury shuffle,' a procedure allowed under Texas law that rearranges the order of the prospective jurors who are waiting to be questioned. After the shuffle, the four blacks were sent to the back of the room, a position that made it more likely that they would never be questioned or allowed to serve. [...] There were 108 prospective jurors in Mr. Miller-El's case, 20 of whom were black. But when the jury was finally selected, there was only 1 black member. The attorneys for Miller-El contended that Dallas County prosecutors (where the accused was judged) had a long history of excluding blacks from juries, and pointed to training manuals that were distributed to prosecutors from the 1960s to the early 1980s. The manuals advised prosecutors to remove blacks or Jews from death penalty juries on the theory that those groups would be more favorable to criminal defendants" (New York Times, June 13, 2005).

Perhaps the last opinion on this issue should be that of black mothers, rather than abstract statistics, however compelling they may be. In a brief, already quoted autobiographical document, Roger says that a black mother: *"knows that the color of her child's skin alone is a strike against him, and it triples if that child is a male.*

(continued p.100)

Thank Elly for the magazine [of her foundation]. It was great reading it. It is so difficult to believe these courageous women had to fight so hard just to seek justice in educating their fellow villagers on so many fronts. Some were even jailed! It is so good to have an organization that recognizes them and their achievements. It is a good and well written magazine.[17] I congratulate her. Elly certainly is a Godsend. She seems tireless. Is there anything I can do for her from here?

Thank you for sending me the Bible lessons.[18] I read them every day, and I have been sharing [the manuscript of] *The Gentle Art of Blessing* with a few guys here interested in reading it.

Yes, I am constantly growing, Pierre, but all things take time as you know. As long as I do not give in to the fear and doubt that has been plaguing me the last month or so and remember to take my problems to God, they are not as hard as we believe. The hard part is remembering that God has control over all things, and that if we just ask, He will help. I have always had a beautiful relationship with God, and I let it go to try other methods of how to attain salvation. But no method works better than your own. I can read all the material I want that others send me, but in the end, my salvation rests in my hands. I thought that if I did not read what others sent to me and did not try their methods, I was somehow being untrue to my friendship with them. But I was wrong. I have since grown a little each day, remembering to keep God first in all things.

In a previous letter to Roger, I told him about the publication of my latest book, Happiness can be learned. *Referring to this topic, he wrote:*

I have not been very happy lately, not in the gleeful sense, but I still try to remember to laugh in spite of all that is happening here. Last week, two good friends of mine were put to death by the state. Last night, another was killed, and tonight one is being killed while I sit here and write to you. Tomorrow, another will die. And I ask myself: Will it never end? And now the person who signed each of the death warrants is fighting to become the next president of the United States.

They finally turned the heat on, albeit barely. But it is more than we had at first, and it is more than many in the free world have now. We complain about many things here, but we never stop to wonder if these things we complain about are not worse in the outside world. Despite all the treatments we are subjected to, I still thank God for all that I have.

---

17   The newsletter of the World Women's Summit Foundation which is now published solely on the Internet at www.woman.ch . The newsletter describes the amazing courage of rural women from the South and East who have to perform daily miracles of endurance, creativity, and courage just to stay alive, and for whom the foundation has created a unique prize recognizing their achievements.

18   These lessons are based on the Bible and *Science and Health*. See www.spirituality.com

Racial bias in justice (continued)

She knows that every force aligning the universe will set a judgment against him. She knows that no matter how much love she provides, understanding she instills, wisdom she imparts, or tears she sheds, it will not be enough to carry him to adulthood. But for her, the journey is one that she cannot abandon for fear of what might be. In the ghetto, a mother lives in constant fear that her child, once he leaves his home, may never return, because once she turns her child loose, sets him free in a world where the color of his skin, the texture of his hair, and his very culture, are already strikes against him, the chances for his survival diminish for every hour he lives."

"Even under the most sophisticated death penalty statutes, race continues to play a major role in determining who shall live and who shall die" (Former Supreme Court Justice H. Blackmun).

Prison expert: Texas solitary cells inhumane

"An expert on maximum security prisons said that Texas solitary confinement cells are among the most inhumane he's ever seen. 'The level of despair [...] was unparalleled in my experience,' said Professor Craig Haney, chairman of the University of California in Santa Cruz, Psychology Department, who has studied high-security prisons for 25 years.

In a December visit to three Texas units, Haney said he saw inmates smeared with feces; urine puddles in cells and hallways; and apparently mentally ill inmates screaming and banging their heads against the wall.

'These are not subtle diagnostic issues,' he said. The isolated inmates were 'in profound distress and pain,' he said. 'It was shattering,' he said of his visits, adding, 'I was told this was an everyday occurrence. . . .'

'Many complained the deterioration of hygiene was part of their overall (psychological) decline,' Haney said. 'They felt they had their dignity taken away,' because the inmates don't have access to commissary items such as deodorant and are given one roll of toilet paper a week. . . . . Haney described the level of deprivation he observed as 'rock bottom.'

'Prisons routinely — and constitutionally — inflict psychological damage on inmates,' Haney conceded to prison attorneys. 'But those in Texas' 8000 solitary confinement or "administrative segregation" cells are subjected to far harsher conditions than in some of the nations toughest lockups, including the. . . . California "super-seg" prison at Pelican Bay,' Haney said. Conditions in the three cited Texas units - Estelle, Beto, and Eastham — 'were as bad or worse than any I've seen,' Haney said."

(John W. Gonzales. *Prison Expert: State's Solitary Cells Inhumane* in *Houston Chronicle, Austin Bureau*, February 5, 1999)

It is not so much the mean way the officers treat us, or the harsh conditions we face that get to me, but the loneliness, the lack of human contact, a warm hug from a friend, a kind word or the warmth in the eyes of a stranger when you shake their hands. If I could, I would give every person I ever met a hug and a kind word of encouragement, from this day on until the day God called me back to Him.

People take so much for granted. My God, they do not realize what it feels like to have not been hugged in fifteen years. It is like a wedge that is driven between you and all that you hold sacred. But I had better stop talking like that. It tears me apart inside.

Thank you for being my friend. I mean that from my heart. If I ever say something hurtful, remember it is my hurt that is saying it, and not the one who loves you. Thank you for remembering me in all you write.

I agree that love is always addressing us. That is something I know and try to remember. I do not only look for it, I try to send it as well. So I will go into the silence with you. God knows that I need it badly. I will meet you there. You have taught me a lot. I love you and Elly very much. I have to keep going no matter what is in front of me, and I am so happy to have you with me, keeping me on my feet. *(December 6, 2000)*

[Roger's birthday is two days before Christmas]

Thank you for the beautiful birthday card and the Christmas wishes along with the pictures. You shouldn't have bought a birthday card for a death row inmate, but for a friend instead. We are all on some death row or another. Our rebirth in Christ is the only real birth that matters, because that is where our true life exists. All else is an illusion created by our own fears and doubts. I am grounded in Christ and will remain that way.

I still prefer being in prison with God than being free without Him. God has held my hand and carried me through storms that I did not realize I was in until it was over. He has proven Himself to me time and time again. Now I must begin to prove myself to Him.

Take care of yourselves, you and Elly, and remember God's love conquers all. I will always remember your love – just remember mine. *(December 28, 2000)*

*"Place love before anger
and God before all"*

(Roger McGowen, January 4, 2001)

2001

To Monica, Sweden

I have been able to learn so much through my struggles here, and yet I am still learning so much. At one time I thought I was at the end of my tolerance, but God showed me I could go much farther. And I have realized that nothing can enter our lives and hurt us unless we open our lives to it and let it in.

I have at times argued with God, become disenchanted with the Bible, and cried out to God for allowing this to happen to me. But He always led me back and restored my faith and not once did I ever lose hope.

I have been so angry at times, Monica, that all I could do was love. When people get angry their first thoughts are of hate and revenge. But our first thoughts should be of love, because God is love, and we are one with God. God does not have to decide to love, it is automatic, it is a pouring forth from a universal source that never runs empty. And that same source is in us. Love is so easy. Hate is what is hard.

We are under a lockdown. Actually, we have been since January 2, and once again we start the year with peanut butter sandwiches and pancakes. But I will not complain. I have had worse to eat, and there are those who do not even have that to start the new year. God is and has been more than wonderful to me.

Place love before anger, and God before all. *(January 4, 2001)*

Thank you, Pierre, for the Bible lessons, they really do help me keep a steady pace each day. I must tell you, The Gentle Art of Blessing has really helped me. I keep it where I can reach it easily. You see, since we have been moved to this prison, the officials have been trying to associate me with one of the prison gangs. I have no idea why. They have no reason to even suspect me of anything like this. I have always carried myself with respect, I have never fought or threatened any of the officers.

I was on death row at Ellis One Unit for 14 years before coming here, and there never was any sign of gang activity on my record, because I simply do not belong to any gang, unless Christ is the gang leader. But upon coming to this prison, Terrell Unit [later renamed Allan Polunsky] they have taken upon themselves to make me a gang member in four months, and they have been making my life a living nightmare.

> ## *"Everything ... happens to teach us"*
>
> (Roger McGowen, February 27, 2001)

In 1987, I undertook a 14,000 km trip through more than 100 African villages to describe the amazing things that African farmers at the grass roots were doing to help themselves.

It was a remarkable learning experience to talk with truly courageous people who had decided to learn from life's challenges rather than wait for handouts.

I will never forget my discussion with Dondo Peliaba, chief of the tiny village of Minti, in the Dogon country of Mali in West Africa.

The drought had been so terrible that people had been eating grass, bark, insects. Yet this gentle man told me: *"Before the drought, everyone worked for themselves. But the drought has taught us to build small anti-erosion walls across our fields. Before, we never planted beans, now they have become one of our staple foods.* **Hunger has become a teacher prodding us to innovate and invent***."*

Much of my personal property has been destroyed, and they tore my cell apart twice a day. They tore it apart on December 23, my birthday. They came back and did it again later on that same night. They tore it apart again on New Year's Eve – they really destroyed things that day. Then they locked the prison down on January 2, and for the next 11 days we were fed cold pancakes and peanut butter sandwiches. Between the 2nd of January and the 14th of January, I have had what was left of my property destroyed, or I should say torn apart, at least six to seven times. They have been making us recreate outdoors in 20-degree weather, sometimes in the rain.

I was upset, very upset for being treated this way. I was so upset in fact that I stopped talking to anyone. I wouldn't even answer the officers. I would just come out of the cell, wait till they tore it apart, go back inside and just sit in the middle of the things thrown everywhere.

Then I received The Gentle Art of Blessing and began to read, and my burden began to lift. I closed my eyes and I told God that I did not know what lesson I was supposed to learn from this. I knew He would not allow me to suffer like this without cause. So I started blessing the officers, all of them, especially those who had just torn apart my belongings. And I realized that God was showing me the calm in the middle of the storm, and that love is so easy. Like the Polish lawyer in your book who decided not to hate the Nazis after witnessing the death of his family at their hands, I will not bow to hatred. They cannot make me hate them. I will continue to bless them, regardless of what they destroy, because they cannot destroy the love I have for them as children of God. I have to forgive them a thousand times for the wrong they do. I will not be a victim. Blessings for others are blessings for us. God never forgets. When we bless others, we also bless ourselves, mind, body, and self.

Pierre, I was thinking, the $150.00 you send to me [each quarter] why don't you donate it to the World Day for the Prevention of Child Abuse and I will get it the next time? God has blessed me so much, and despite everything I am going through, I still have no reason to complain.[19] *(January 12, 2001)*

I must admit that living in a place like this prison at times tests one's love and commitment to continue to bless, but as you said, "everything that happens in our lives, happens to teach us." It [learning] is something that I love doing and feel good while doing.

---

19   This day was launched on November 19, 2000, by the Women's World Summit Foundation (www.woman.ch). The "pocket money" a few friends send Roger enables him to supplement the very poor diet at Allan Polunsky, to purchase stationary, stamps, and hygiene products – and to help other less fortunate inmates.

Divine Love's perfect plan

August L. Reader, a clinical associate professor at the University of Southern California School of Medicine in Los Angeles, recalls a near death experience (NDE):

"In that moment of understanding, there was a panorama. . . . of everything that occurred in my life, from the most trivial detail to the most important events, and displayed equally and with no favor, connected by golden threads, showing me that everything that had occurred to me in my life was important, was part of who I was, and was essential to who I had been. And in that knowledge was the understanding that my life had been worthwhile and I had nothing to regret in dying" (Quoted in Larry Dossey, *Reinventing Medicine*, HarperOne, 2000).

"Tis God that girdeth me with strength
and maketh my way perfect."

(Psalms 18:32)

"I have made the earth
and created man upon it;
I have raised him up in righteousness,
and I will direct all his ways."

(Isaiah 45:13)

Actually things have gone smoothly over the last month, and I recognize it is because of my blessing everyone all day and night, no matter who they were or what they have done to me. I love The Gentle Art of Blessing. Everyone who has read it says they have incorporated the teachings into their lives. Many recognize the benefits and the love they gain as it returns to them.

Yes, things are a lot easier here, not because the officers have changed, but because my outlook has changed. I look at things with a renewed sense of love and understanding. I now try to look for the goodness and perfection in all of God's children, even those that hate me, because God made us all perfect. However, at times we do imperfect things.

I no longer look at myself as a victim of these people's assaults. I now look at myself as a divine being able to accept any and everything, and to love everyone, because I am "a product of love," and I search for the lesson in all things now, instead of calling them curses when I perceive them wrong.

I know that God has really blessed me. I know in my heart that God has something wonderful planned for me. Yes, God's plan for us all is perfect – but knowing and understanding that is another matter altogether. We have allowed the illusion of separation from God to cloud our judgment and make us trust our own understanding. So we have forgotten our relationship with God, and thus His perfect plan for us. It feels really good to know that one is perfect, and that the plans for our perfect life are already laid out.

Please thank your friend Jill for me, and for her prayers. I know they are being answered. Also for her statement: "The will of God can never lead you where the grace of God cannot help you." I feel very light and at peace inside. I can feel the love of the friends who are praying for me surrounding me. It does my heart good to know that you are sharing my letters with others, just as I am sharing your book with the men here.

It is good to feel contented in life. I cannot say that I am contented – I will never be until I regain my freedom. But I do feel blessed and at peace. Not a day goes by that I do not thank God for all He has given me, especially all my beautiful friends.

It is the small things that I miss the most. I can't even now look up at the sky, or touch the grass. I have not felt the wind on my skin for a very long time. But I still remember that there are people who are in prisons of their own making, those who have their liberty, yet are not free. I am blessed to be able to pray to God and I thank Him for everything, including what He hasn't given me. *(February 27, 2001)*

What corresponding with Roger has meant to me

Roger speaks so glowingly of our correspondence and what it means to him that I must attempt, however imperfectly, to convey the amazing changes corresponding with him has brought into my life.

As mentioned in the introduction, after my first visit to Roger in Huntsville in 1999, I remember making the vow never to complain again about anything in my life. This vow was strongly reinforced during our 2003 visit. I was sitting opposite Roger, and at one moment during the discussion, he stated. *"You know Pierre, I have a roof over my head, I have three meals a day, I have a bed* [a narrow, hard bunk] *and,"* he added, holding his grayish-white inmate shirt between thumb and forefinger, *"I have clothes - they are not exactly the ones I would choose, but I have clothes."* Then, with his immensely beautiful, warm smile, he concluded, *"I am a happy man."* I will never forget his words in my whole life. Here was a man held in hell for 16 years (at that point) for a crime he never committed, speaking about happiness. How could I ever again complain about anything?

For me, Roger is an example of indomitable courage, of unrelenting perseverance, of never, never giving up or giving in. He is a living example of Winston Churchill's state-ment, *"When you're going through hell, keep going."* I have heard many – including priests of every creed, condition, and consciousness – speak of forgiveness. I have often listened politely, thinking. "That's nice theory, man, but do you always practice it?" But when Roger writes about unconditional love or forgiveness, I listen intently, with my whole being, because I know his words were forged and hammered out on the anvil of the most intense suffering, and that he walks his talk, as intensely, honestly and sincerely as he possibly can.

Roger has come to inhabit my thoughts almost perpetually and taken up residence in the innermost chamber of my heart. Sometimes I just walk through our apartment thinking, wow, I can move freely from one room to another, while Roger is cramped in a small cage that affronts human dignity. And yet, in his letters he repeatedly writes: SMILE. Yes, Roger is God's smile in my life. And what a smile!

He has brought additional meaning to my life in a way he might never understand. His fight is the fight of all humankind for dignity, respect, simple decency, uncondition-al love and win-win solutions in every single area of life – including victims' families and murderers – and he has given me the rare gift of joining in this fight with him. And finally – well, no, not finally, because there is no "finally" in our ever-unfolding

(continued p.110)

In these very difficult circumstances, I do feel God's touch and unchanging love, and it is in the most difficult times that I feel His presence and love the strongest. And one day soon God will keep His promise and allow me to embrace my brothers and sisters with open arms.

Never in my wildest dreams did I imagine that what I was sharing with you could inspire others. God does not care what method He uses to open the eyes of the blind, as long as they eventually see. Anne Frank never imagined that her diary would have the effect it did.[20] We all have work to do in this life, and we each have our own part to play. Together, we are creating a web of love, respect, and compassion that is spanning the globe. It was written that we would do so even before we took up our pens. Nothing can contain or imprison God's love and divine plan for us. I am angry at times, and confused at others, Pierre, but we are all placed where we are supposed to be so that God's love and divine plan can manifest itself through us. *(April 4, 2001)*

It is almost impossible to explain to anyone what my correspondence and friendship with you and my other friends has meant to me. It has enriched and filled my life beyond measure. Where I once felt alone, I have a beautiful family of people whom I love with all my heart. I have a reason to get out of bed in the morning with a song on my lips, a prayer in my heart, and compassion and love at all times on my mind. You have helped me to realize that divine Love rules all, and forgiveness is the cornerstone and foundation of that divine Love.

Corresponding with you has helped me realize that we all need one another, that to make mistakes is only human, and that we must try to find the divine lesson in everything. Corresponding with you and my other friends has given me a beautiful family. Through your love, patience, understanding, and devotion, you have given me hope and a new outlook on life, one that I will never take for granted.

It has been many years since I smelled the perfume of a flower, ran my hands over the soft, velvety grass, or smelled the fresh newness of a newborn baby. There are so many small things that I cannot do anymore. But your love and friendship has never left me wanting, and I am sure never will. Put simply, you, Elly and my other friends give me an unspeakable joy: I could never return all the love I receive. And each day I live, I will never stop trying to pass it on to everyone I meet. *(April 8, 2001)*

---

20   Anne Frank was a German-born Jewish girl who hid in Amsterdam from the Nazis until she was captured and died in the Bergen-Belsen concentration camp. Her diary has been translated into many languages and has become a classic.

What corresponding (continued)

relationship – he has made me understand as never before that the true essence of religion and spirituality can never be in a fixed form, a theology, a guru's teaching, a liturgy or fixed holy practice of any kind, but only in love lived moment by moment. For me, one of the most powerful statements he ever made was in a letter to our dear common friend Monica where he wrote: *"Love is only one thought away. It can never be depleted. Remember to use it often."*

"God uses us to empower one another," he once wrote to me.

Tank you, Roger, for empowering me!

Always in your right place

We can never be *out* of our right place, because our only right place is our oneness with divine Love.

The right place is not a geographical location, the perfect occupation, a certain school, partner, family, church or club. Our right place is the awareness that all we are is simply God, being. As a drop of water is one with the ocean we cannot be in a wrong place when we are one with God. We are a note in the song of Life sung by the great Singer.

As we develop a deep feeling and awareness or consciousness of our present oneness with God's infinite Love, our human material situation adjusts naturally whether it be another job, partner, apartment, getting out of jail, or the fading of tensions with our neighbor, boss, church, whoever, whatever, wherever.

Psalm 18 makes the amazing statement: "*It is God that girdeth me with strength and maketh my way perfect.*" This means that wherever you are is the perfect place, way, or moment to learn what you need to learn – or to just relax and bask in the sunlight of the Soul, and simply be an emanation of infinite Love expressing Its unlimited creativity and joy.

The belief that our right place is a physical location comes from the belief that we are merely material beings in a physical world. Our perfect oneness with God is *now*, at this very instant – and always. Could we ever be *out* of our right place *in* God? And why would we ever want to be anywhere else?

Mary Baker Eddy once wrote: "*Whatever diverges from the one divine Mind, or God – or divides Being into beings – is a misstatement of the unerring Principle of [divine] Science.*" Only we as human beings believe that we are not in our right place. The divine Being, God, is omnipresent, and as we grow in our awareness of our pure divine essence, we will be in our right place.

Remember: we don't have to make an effort to *become* one with God. We simply need to be aware that this is already the only truth about ourselves. We are already perfectly one with God. The two can never become one because **the One never became two**. We can never be out of our right place, because our right place is consciousness, not geography.

Many of us are unaware of the freedom we have to simply walk from room to room, and to go and fetch a glass of water – so many things we take for granted in this life. But I thank God for the air I breathe, the water I drink and use to wash in. I even thank Him for dirt on my shoes or the fly that annoys me, because all comes from God. I am constantly reminded of all the men I knew who have gone back to their source, who can no longer swat at a fly or walk on the same dirt from which they came. We are each other's teachers, Pierre.

Loving is so easy and simple that people simply forget it. We only have to remember who we are, and where we come from, and who sent us, and remember that we do nothing on our own, that it is the divine Mind and Creator who directs our very path. *(May 1, 2001)*

Sometimes I do not wish to get out of bed in the mornings, because I know the day that lies ahead is much, if not exactly the same, as the one that has just gone by. But then I remember the family and friends I have out there fighting for me, and expecting me to do the same, and get ashamed of feeling that way.

But at times, Pierre, I get tired of everything and just want to lie down and fade into nothingness. And then I get a letter from you or M. or L. that inspires me to keep fighting for only one more day. Because with each new day come new hopes, new prayers, and a stronger desire to seek God. Never take my silence as a sign that I do not wish to write to you. But I get tired after a while and must turn my face completely to God.

I loved your article [Always in your right place]. It is very beautiful. After reading it, I sat back and looked around at the drab prison cell that confined my physical body and I knew at that moment that I was in the right place because I was in God's divine love and was in fact one with His divine allness. Actually the very first sentence of your article said all that needed to be said: "We can never be out of our right place, because our only right place is our oneness with divine Love!" *(June 26, 2001)*

I'm happy to hear that your workshops went well. We were under lockdown most of July, and I always use the time as a kind of "self-workshop," reflecting on how bad things could be, opposed to how they are. This makes me realize that happiness cannot come from anything outside of us. Happiness is knowing that. That is all there is to it. There is no tomorrow, and yesterday can never be replaced. All there is, is now. Happiness is not as people believe it to be, i.e. a state of mind. Happiness is a state of being: being, or coming into oneness with all there is, because nothing exists outside of oneness.

To be really content, to enter the state of being called happiness, we must break the yoke that binds us, whatever it may be. It is very hard for people to leave what they have been taught for years. I see it every day right here: minds closed to new ideas, to new teachings, afraid to break the yoke.

"Loving is so easy and simple
that people simply forget it.
We only have to remember
who we are,
and where we come from,
and who sent us,
and remember
that we do nothing on our own,
that it is the divine Mind and Creator
who directs our path."

(Roger McGowen, May 1, 2001)

"You ARE love,
so do not waste precious energy
deciding that you are love,
because love decided that
long before you did.
You just have to realize it."

(Roger McGowen, November 13, 2001)

People bog themselves down in all kinds of spiritual and religious rhetoric. Why do people complicate simple things? Love, truth, and happiness are not complicated, nor were they ever meant to be. They are free, light, and beautiful.

Hate is a strong illusion. It makes people feel they are holding on to something. It is also a very self-destroying emotion, binding you to all that is false and negative. It is not hard to let go of hate. I learned that in your book, The Gentle Art of Blessing: just let it go, and bless it as it flies away. But one minute of hatred is long enough to destroy a lifetime.

I would love one day to visit one of your workshops. I truly believe that God has already granted this request. **I only have to realize it**.

I did receive the magazine of Elly's foundation. I like to read it. It is something to see how these women struggle daily to make a living and raise the awareness concerning aids, poverty, and pollution in their countries. These are the women movies should be made about. It breaks my heart to see how they struggle – and here we complain about being too fat. But we won't stop eating! *(September 5, 2001)*

I have written to you twice since I received your last letter. I have been waiting to hear from you, but we have been having some really bad problems here with our mail. I have had many letters come to me from people to whom I had written, asking me why they had not heard from me, when I know that I wrote to these people weeks ago. I wrote you on September 1 (I keep the dates of all the mail I send). They are throwing our mail away. I have written to my attorney asking him to call the warden, and I have asked the mail room to send me the information I need to place tracers on the mail that I sent out. It is very frustrating Pierre, because I feel I am being cut off, isolated from all my family and friends.

I am not even sure this letter is going to reach you. I am so tired of writing and sending out letters, only to have the people to whom I write ask why I have not written to them. Even now as I write to you about the mail situation, I am thinking of how bad it is, because I feel isolated from my friends when I do not hear from them. But God has already decided the outcome. He knows what is best for everyone involved. Even though the mail room is doing what they are doing, I do not hate them, because I realize that everything happens for a reason, and all that is hidden must one day be uncovered. *(September 29, 2001)*

"We are one with all things"

(Roger McGowen, January 24, 2002)

"I know nothing of two worlds – all I know is One.
I seek only One, I know only One,
I find only One, and I sing of only One"

(Jalaluddin Rumi, Sufi poet and mystic, 13th century)

"See one in all things.
It is the second that leadeth astray"

(Kabir, Indian mystic, philosopher, and poet, 1438-1518)

To Monica

Yes, the attack on the World Trade Center towers was indeed planned by a very diabolical mind. So many people were caught and trapped in those airplanes and buildings. The world will be changed forever, not just because of the attacks, but because of the lack of effort in attempting to understand what kind of pain creates an illusion [of separation] so powerful that it leads the mind to strike out at itself. We cannot harm anyone without harming ourselves.

I am not a teacher, only a student searching for himself. I am glad to hear that you are beginning to feel much better, and that your inner peace is becoming more apparent. You deserve the peace that is yours. Claim it as yours. You cannot decide what has already been decided. You ARE love, so do not waste precious energy deciding that you are love, because love decided that long before you did. You just have to realize it. *(November 13)*

2002

I had written to Roger that I thought the New Year season must be a difficult period of the year for him, as it marked one more year in prison. Here is his reply:

All praise to God in the highest that we are able to share in His glory for still another year, and with so much to be thankful for in this world of tragedy and sorrow. For love still abounds in the hearts of those who have lost much.

New Year is in fact the most blessed time for me here on death row, because God has allowed me to step over the hole that I tripped into yesterday. He has allowed me to be able to praise His name at least one more year. I do not look at it as being another year on death row. I look at it as another year during which God's blessings can flow through me. My only focus is on what is inside, what I can do to make the stay of the new guy next door a little easier. I am happiest when my service to others creates a smile.

Actually, we are one with all things, and being one with all things, we have experienced all things, because we live in God and He lives in us.

You have experienced what I have, and I have experienced what you have. You told me how you left your job [in 1986] with so much bitterness and anger. You were your own prison and your own torturer.

Compassion in action – the story of Martin Avdeitch
How a poor cobbler recognized the Christ in his neighbor

This is a summary of Leo Tolstoy's story about a pious widower named Martin Avdeitch – a cobbler who ekes out his living in a small Russian town.

One evening, while reading the Bible story of the Pharisee and Mary Magdalene, it occurs to Martin that he is more like the self-oriented Pharisee than like the woman. After a moment of deep repentance, he falls asleep. Then, suddenly, he is awakened by a voice calling, "Martin! Look out into the street, for tomorrow I shall come."

Martin doesn't know if he has heard these words while he was dreaming or awake. But the next day, he gets up early, prepares his cabbage soup and buckwheat porridge, and, still pondering what happened the evening before, settles down in front of his window to work. Since his lodging is below the street level, the first thing he sees of passers-by is their shoes. He knows most of the shoes in town because at one time or another he has repaired them all! One of the first he recognizes are those of the poor old soldier, Stepanich, who lives on charity. Seeing Stepanich shoveling snow on the street, Martin has an image of him so surprising that he laughs out loud: "I must be growing crazy with age," he says to himself. "Stepanich comes to clear away the snow and I must needs imagine it's Christ coming to visit me!"

Nonetheless, feeling deep compassion for this man who barely has the strength to clear the snow, Martin invites the pauper into his home and offers him some tea. "May God bless you," says Stepanich. "My bones do ache to be sure." As they sit together, Martin tells him about the strange voice he heard the previous evening and speaks to him of the Scriptures. After three glasses of brew, the ex-soldier departs, thanking his host for nourishing not only his poor body but also his soul.

The second person Martin notices from his shop window is a woman dressed in summer clothes despite the biting cold. She is holding a baby, drawing her own used clothing over the little one as best as she can, desperately trying to protect the child against the wind's icy blasts. Hearing the baby cry, Martin calls the woman in, puts a clean napkin on the table and offers her soup and porridge. The woman has no more milk, so Martin gently tends to the baby while she eats. He even manages to make the child laugh.

The woman tells Martin her long story of woe, and he gives her an old but warm cloak to protect her and the child from the cold. As she leaves, Martin gives her sixpence to retrieve a shawl from the pawnshop. Looking into his kind face, she says: "The Lord bless you, friend. Surely Christ must have sent me to your window, else the child would have frozen."

(continued p.120)

I have stopped trying to learn to love, now I just love. I try to look at people as reflections of me, only having a bad day. Sometimes I still get angry, but you know what? The best part comes when I have gotten angry about something, then catch myself in the act of being angry, and smile. Then I say to myself that for a moment I was being less than who I AM! Then I start over again.

You live where God has placed you for the reason He did. Just think, if you had not been where you are now [in Switzerland] you may not have known L., who introduced me to you, or vice-versa. You would have nothing that you have if God did not wish you to have it. So all that you have, and where you live, is a blessing from God. I guess I can say that I was placed where I can be most effective for the time being, and I will do what I can do to make sure that my stay here is not in vain.

Actually Christmas was great, because there are 14 guys to a pod, seven on row one and seven on row two. We have been locked down most of November and the prison administration wanted to lock us down for Christmas, but came under tremendous pressure [from inmate's families and friends], so they backed off. For as long as Texas prisons have been standing, I guess you could say there has always existed a certain dignity. One could go to the unit store and buy canned goods like roast beef, chili, and other foods. Well, Texas prison officials have just decided that they would not allow us to purchase any more canned goods, so they have terminated their sale, and many people were caught off guard.

But I always buy more than enough, because I know that there are always people who need something. So, as you know, my birthday was on the 23rd, two days before Christmas. I cooked all the canned goods I had [in my coffee heater], and made enough tacos to feed the entire wing! An officer wanted to know what the occasion was. I told him that it was my birthday and that I just wanted to share. He looked at me and said: "That is unique, McGowen. It is your birthday and you are feeding everyone instead of them feeding you?" I just kind of shrugged my shoulders. And everyone was happy about being able to eat roast beef for the last time.

So when Christmas came, everyone took small items that they had bought for themselves, and made little packages for everyone else. Some packages only had typing paper, a candy bar and an aspirin, others had small store bought brownies, little tea packs and whatever else they could put together. It made my heart sing with joy to feel so much love in a place where hatred is bred and taught

The story of Martin Avdeitch (continued)

Later that morning, Martin intervenes to prevent a woman from calling the police to arrest a poor street child she has caught stealing an apple. Then he has the joy of seeing them continue on their way as friends. Later that evening, after eating and sweeping the floor, Martin settles down with his Bible. The vision of the evening before suddenly comes to his mind, and he hears footsteps. Turning toward the sound, he hears a voice whisper in his ear: "Martin, Martin, don't you know me?" "Who is it?" mutters Martin. "It is I," says the voice, and out of the dark corner steps Stepanich, who smiles and then vanishes. "It is I" says another voice, and out of the darkness steps the woman with the baby. The woman laughs, the child smiles, and then both disappear. Then, again, "It is I," and this time the old woman and the boy appear, smiling with their whole faces and then vanishing like the others. Martin feels his soul growing glad as he crosses himself and reads in the Gospel: "I was hungered and ye gave me meat; I was thirsty and ye have me a drink; I was a stranger and ye took me in." Continuing, he reads, "Inasmuch as ye did it unto one of these my brethren, even these least, ye did it to me." And Martin rejoices, realizing the Christ had truly visited him and he had taken him in.

(Adapted from Leo Tolstoy, *Twenty-Three Tales*, London, Numerous editions)

"Christ has no body on earth but yours,
No hands but yours,
No feet but yours.
Yours are the eyes through which
Christ's compassion looks out into the world.
Yours are the feet through which
he is to go about doing good.
Yours are the hands with which
he is to bless men now."
(St. Theresa of Ávila)

"The hands that help are holier
Than the lips that pray"
(Sathya Sai Baba)

The time to be happy is now.
The place to be happy is here.
The way to be happy is to make others so.
(Anonymous)

So, our Christmas was wonderful, Pierre, one of the best I ever had. One guy wrote home, telling his mother how I was always helping and looking out for him and the others. He had his wife send me a late Christmas card. She thanked me, saying she did not have the money to take care of him and that she really appreciated all I did for him.

I cried, because I know that the world is filled with love. And if people don't believe you, tell them to come to Death Row, 12 building, R-R pod, and they will find much love.

I would like to know what, if anything, I can do to help Elly in her work. I would very much like to be of service to her and the cause that she is fighting for [the rights of women and children]. Please let me know. I reread [the Foundation document] on circles of compassion. I believe that a great many people have lost touch with their compassion. Many feel that to show compassion in a world filled with so much suffering, death, and misery is to show weakness. Yet deep down inside they would like to be able to show compassion. However they are afraid of what their neighbors and family members might think, so they keep their mouths shut.

But to show compassion is not a sign of weakness. On the contrary, it is a sign of strength, a sign of the divine, because by showing compassion, we show that we are Christ-like, that we are not above forgiving. And sometime, in our lives, we will all need compassion. I hope that it sprouts a million buds of compassionate interest. *(January 24, 2002)*

By all means, publish my letters if they can help someone, anyone, through whatever hardship may be befalling them. I know that anything you do is for the good of all.

I no longer think about what I do not have, what I am missing or think I am missing. Now I only thank God for all He has given me, and also for a lot of bad things that He has allowed me to miss as well.

Pierre, I have rather bad news to report to you. I received a case from a sergeant the other day – a very bogus case.[21] I went to our day room [22] Saturday morning. An inmate who is a friend of mine had asked the officers to call a certain sergeant.

---

21   A "case" is a complaint that an officer files against an inmate for breaking a prison regulation. It becomes part of the inmate's permanent prison record.

22   A room where inmates can exercise physically outside of their cells. Since the day room is on the opposite side of the corridor from the cells, it is possible to talk to other inmates when in the day room.

Responding to insults: A story about the Buddha

The Buddha taught wherever he went. One day, he was speaking in a village and a man came to listen to him, mingling in the crowd. The listener was soon overwhelmed by feelings of envy and rage. The holiness of the Buddha exasperated him. He could no longer stand it, and hurled insults at the holy man. Buddha remained unmoved. Boiling with anger, the man left the place.

As he was walking along a rice field, his anger calmed down. Already he could see the village temple silhouetted behind the rice fields. Slowly, he became aware that his anger was the expression of his jealousy, and that he had insulted a wise man. He felt so ill at ease that he turned back on his steps, fully decided to present his excuses to the Buddha.

When he arrived at the village square where the teaching was still going on, the crowd parted to let him, the man who had insulted the Master, through. Hardly believing what they saw, the people observed him. They nodded at each other and a murmur followed his steps. When he was close enough to the Master, he knelt, begging the Buddha to forgive the violence of his words and the indecency of his thoughts.

Full of compassion, the Buddha made him stand up, and said:

"I have nothing to forgive you, I was not the object of any violence or indecency on your part."
"But I insulted you in the grossest manner!"
"What do you do if someone offers you an object you don't need or don't care to accept?"
"Well, of course I don't extend my hand, I just do not accept it."
"What does the giver do?"
"Well, what can he do? He must keep his offering."
"That is why you seem to suffer from your own insults and rudeness. As for me, you can be assured that I was in no way upset. There was simply no one to receive the violence you were offering."

(Translated from *Au Bord du Gange*, Martine Quentric-Séguy, Seuil, Paris, 1998, p.118-119.

> *"Arrows of hate have been shot at me too; but they never hit me,*
> *because somehow they belonged to another world, with which I*
> *have no connection whatsoever."*
> (Albert Einstein)

Apparently he had had some problem with the sergeant earlier that morning, before I came out. The sergeant finally came on the wing, and in the process of talking to inmate W. who is a friend of mine, he started screaming and yelling at him, saying that he knew how to do his job. And I mean really screaming and yelling, like a crazy person. As for me, I was just walking around the day room minding my own business.. Finally, after he and W. had finished talking, he left the wing. Another inmate in the day room across from the one I was in asked to speak to him also.

The next thing I heard the same sergeant screaming and yelling at this man, telling him not to ask questions about an officer or sergeant. The gist of the matter is that he was really unprofessional, way out of order. So, my friend W. asked me to ask the sergeant for his name. So, I walk to the bars, and in a very light and friendly manner, say: "Sergeant, cell 17 wants to know your name." He then turns around and starts yelling and screaming at me, and that if I say another word to him, he is going to write a case against me. As for me, I am totally blown away. I point out that I never said anything to him to begin with, apart from asking him for his name.

He runs over to the day room where I am standing, and puts his hands inside the bars, with his finger pointed to my face, yelling and screaming at me about talking to him. I could not interject a word. He was spitting and cursing at me and threatening to fetch other officers to beat me up. All this time I am just looking at him, wondering in God's name where all this madness came from so early in the morning! To make a long story short, he filed a complaint saying that I created a disturbance by yelling and screaming at him.

Everyone who is on the pod has written statements and grievances saying that I never said one word to him, apart from asking his name, and that he was the one that created the disturbance.

But if they find me guilty, then they may put me on another level, and withdraw certain visiting rights, which might mean we could not see each other. They will take away all of my property, and move me to the worst wing of the prison called F-wing. There they feed you very little, you cannot have any glass to drink from, you are not allowed radios, fans, typewriters, coffee pots - not even your clothes. They only shower you every three days, and you are only allowed five very small soap bars every two weeks. You cannot shop. They have guys on F-wing for years at a time.

It is really the most horrible place you can imagine. A report aired last week on the radio mentioned that Texas had the worst death row in the entire nation! It is horrible here. I cannot find words to describe to you the things being done here in the name of the people and justice. People are being gassed and beaten, their property is destroyed and they are talked to and treated as animals - all of this just before they are executed.

The cost of the death penalty: equivalent to *three times* that of prison for life without parole

By and large, the cost of putting someone to death is about three times that of life imprisonment without parole – and that despite the very poor quality of, and limited funds for, representation of the accused. In a country that is so cost-conscious when it comes to government expenditures for social programs, there seems to be a strange blindness concerning the extravagantly high cost of the death penalty.

There are very few recent studies on this issue, but the rare figures that are available should be a cause of deep concern for citizens who wish a careful use of their tax dollars. In Texas, in 1993, already (the actual figures are certainly much higher today), the extra costs of the death penalty were estimated at $2.3 million per inmate per year. Florida spent an average of $3.2 million per execution from 1973 to 1988. It could save $51 million each year by punishing all first degree murderers with prison for life without parole. Based on 44 executions carried out between 1976 and 2000 (nationwide only twelve percent of those condemned to death are actually put to death), that amounts to an approximate cost of $24 million *per execution*! Death penalty costs in North Carolina are very close to those of Texas - $2.16 million. Nationwide, the costs of capital trials between 1982 and 1997 amounted to an additional $1.6 billion. What if that sum had been used to fund prevention measures, such as high quality, low profile community police patrols? Prevention has always been the best cure, in all areas…

A revealing Kansas Performance Audit Report of the Kansas Department of Corrections concluded that:
*   investigation costs for death sentence cases were 3 times that of non-capital cases
*   trial costs for capital cases were about 16 times greater than for non-capital cases
*   appeals costs for death-penalty cases were 21 times higher
*   trials for capital sentences averaged 34 days versus 9 days for non-capital trials

Since only twelve percent of those condemned to death are actually put to death, *"the death penalty without executions is just another name for life without parole; and this is the most expensive form of life without parole because the sentences that are obtained occur after the high costs of death penalty trials"* (Richard C. Dieter, executive Director of the Death Penalty Information Center, DPIC website, spring, 2007).

But I want you to know that through all the cursing and yelling and humiliation, I never once lost my focus. I stayed grounded in truth. I looked the sergeant in the eyes and took everything he had to offer, without once returning his hatred with the same hatred, or his curses with the same curses. I could not do to him what he what he was doing to me, because that is not who I am. I did not believe that the person who was screaming and hollering and cursing at me was the person he wanted to be that morning.

I believe it was done to see how strong I was. God's ways are God's ways. All of us must learn to stand the strongest during the greatest storms and howling winds. God did not make me weak and cowardly, he made me strong and courageous. When I stand up for something, I stand up for God. I stand up with grace in Christ and love for all humankind, not only the ones I love and that profess their love for me, but more so for those who think they hate me and for those who think love has abandoned them. The love I have is Christ love, and it is for everyone.

The sergeant was wrong in what he did, which could cause me the hardest time since being in prison. If that is the case, then I will do what I have to do in Christ, in order to overcome whatever I find facing me. But never will I bring myself to hate the man hating me. I prayed for him that night, and I will pray for him every night from now on, because by loving him and praying for him, I know that someone, somewhere is loving me and praying for me for the wrongs I committed toward them, whoever they may be. I will be very sad if we are not able to visit, but I am trying to get some people from the outside to help me contact the warden and the major for death row, because even though I am not angry, or hate any one, a serious wrong was committed that can go into my record and cause me trouble if ever I get a re-trial. I wrote M. and asked her to contact friends requesting they call the warden and have them check into those allegations.

I love the teachings of the Hindu Master Ramana Maharshi. I have a friend named J.W. who owned quite a lot of property in Switzerland. She sold everything she had and moved to India, where she lives in an ashram and is studying to become a guru.

Give Elly a hug from me. I know all will be right because I walk in God's love and His light. *(March 3, 2002)*

"Never stop reaching out.
When you pass the moon, reach for the stars,
and once you pass the stars,
reach for yourself,
because you stand higher than both of them."

(Roger McGowen, March 17, 2002)

To Monica

What a great pleasure it was to hear from you. Yes, I do have others who write to me, and each holds a special place in my heart that no one else can fill. If I had a hundred friends writing to me, I would still miss hearing from the one who did not write.

I hope that you are well and allowing the spirit of oneness to carry you on the wings of understanding and love, so that your soul may fly higher and further than it has ever before. You are a special person, Monica. Please believe that God does not make mistakes. His every creation is a perfect one, and so are you. Never stop reaching out. When you pass the moon, reach for the stars, and once you pass the stars, reach for yourself, because you stand higher than both of them.

We have been locked down all of November and for Christmas. In December, there was a lot of moving around, and another lockdown. The new person in charge here is a very unfocused man. He does what he thinks is his own doing. But none of us do what we want to do. Sometimes God hardens a heart so that His glory can be shown through that person. Did He not harden the heart of the Pharaoh, so that he would not allow the children of Israel to leave, even after he had lost his first born, suffered famine and many other calamities?

This person is very hard. He will not allow even the Christian workers to bring cookies to the death row inmates. He will use every opportunity to deepen the misery that is already present here. But each time, God gives us the strength to overcome, and each time it fuels this person's hatred for us still more. So his battle with himself continues. The things he does to us only hurt him more. So each night I pray for him and ask God to bless him and his family. So sometimes I do not even have the time to write when I wish to. But I will never abandon you.

A very good friend of mine [at Ellis One Unit], named A. W., was hated by most of the inmates because of his gambling habits. He would steal and cheat to gamble – he was the most underhanded person I ever met. But I loved him when everyone else hated him. I saw the good in him when everyone else only focused on the bad. He was my cellmate for a long time. We were cellmates the day they came to get him and move him to a single cell to prepare him for execution. On more than one occasion, he got into debt and couldn't pay, so I would have to pay his way out to keep people from hurting him.

Now, he was not a small person, and we used to call him "Black" because he was very dark. He stood every bit of 6' tall and weighed around 250 pounds. He could barely read or write, and I paid him five dollars a week out of my pocket to let me teach him how to read and write every night before bed. He was progressing quite well by the time he was executed.

Autobiography in five short chapters

[how being a victim or being responsible is a choice] by Portia Nelson

1

I walk down the street.
There is a deep hole in the sidewalk.
I fall in.
I am lost ... I am helpless,
It isn't my fault.
It takes me forever to find a way out.

2

I walk down the same street.
There is a deep hole in the sidewalk.
I pretend I don't see it.
I fall in again.
I can't believe I am in the same place.
But, it isn't my fault.
It still takes a long time to get out.

3

I walk down the same street.
There is a deep hole in the sidewalk.
I see it is there.
I still fall in ... it's a habit.
My eyes are open.
I know where I am.
It is my fault.
I get out immediately.

4

I walk down the same street.
There is a deep hole in the sidewalk.
I walk around it.

5

I walk down another street.

(Portia Nelson: www.strawberrycheesecake.wordpress.com/autobiography-in-five-short-chapters)

At the Ellis Unit in Huntsville (before we came here to Livingston), when someone had an execution date, they would be taken to what is called "Death House." They could request to have a last visit with five or six people, and I was the last one Black wanted to see.

I will never forget looking into his eyes and holding his hand, listening to him tell me that he loved me, because I was always there for him even when his family wasn't. But I told him that it was not me, it was only my body. It was God who had looked after him all these years, [simply] using me. Then he said the strangest thing to me. "I wish I had one more chance, Rock. I would make you proud of me this time, I would be strong, like you are. But I guess I don't have another chance – or do I?"

I looked at him as the tears rolled down my face and his face, and I grabbed his hand and held it tighter. I told him we are all what God has wanted us to be, He loves me no more than He loves you – and if I thought He did, I would give all His love back.

The last thing he told me was, "I know you are worried about me, but I will be fine. I just realized why I have been strong all these years. It's because I have been using your strength." I asked him if he could really read and write, and we both laughed. When I left him, he was still laughing. They killed him that night at 6 p.m., March 17, 2002.

There are very few of us that will ever get a second chance to do it all over again. So we must do it the best we can the first time, and live the life that God has given us so that there will be no regrets when we pass from this life into the next. So stretch your arms out to heaven and let the sand fly, it is what we are all made from. And as that sand flies with the wind, so let your troubles and fears fly with it. You are a special person. Embrace what you have and do not worry about what you don't have. *(April 6, 2002)*

To a Canadian correspondent who read one of Roger's letters in my (French) book, "Plus Jamais Victime" (Never Again a Victim), *Roger wrote:*

X is a very beautiful soul. He came into my life when I needed him. The creator often sends us the right tools for the right job at just the right time, does He not? Your letter was an inspiration to me. Regardless of our attempts to do things alone, we cannot. We were made for one another, and we are all a perfect fit for each other. What I lack, you possess, and what you lack, someone else possesses.

It is only when we start to consider ourselves as victims that we do injustice to ourselves. We forget the strength we possess, and start looking for excuses as to why we should or should not do something. In the end, it is all the same, we fail to use the strength.

Grace [on death row]

By Paul Ferrini

"When we know that we are worthy of love, we no longer need to engage in a profusion of activities designed to prove our worthiness to ourselves or others. Our inner sense of worth enables us to give love without demands or expectations, thereby creating the pathway through which love spontaneously returns to us.

Our relationship to the world, and therefore to each other, is no longer one of manipulation, struggle or greed, but one of trust in the natural unfolding of all organic processes. What needs to occur happens through us, because we are willing and able, not because our egos need it to happen to validate self.

Grace unfolds in our lives and we are naturally drawn towards events and circumstances to which we can contribute our energy and attention. Because we are flexible and cooperative, we meet our goals seemingly without effort."

(Paul Ferrini's *Weekly Wisdom Messages*, www.paulferrini.com, May 29, 2006. info@ heartwayspress.com)

I hope the message in the [forthcoming French] book will lift you to the height you aspire to, so that you can become the greatest version of the grandest vision of whom you wish to be.

My sufferings are no greater than anyone else's. I only learned that to hate with the same hate as the one who inflicts hatred on us is not worth the effort. I found it was easier to love them than to hate them. To love is so very easy, it takes no effort whatsoever. Hate, on the other hand, is an unnatural emotion. It does the mind and body more harm than good, and makes you no different than the person who hates you.

We were created from love and with love, and love leads our way. So why waste our time hating? *(April 7, 2002)*

Yes Pierre, I remember the sentence I wrote to you, "I do not try to love, I just love." I believe that if I had to try, I might not be able to love everyone. I would pick and choose, so I do not try. I just love, and in doing that, I cannot be biased. Does that make any sense to you?

I never know what to say to you, when you mention that you are putting a book of my letters together. I am always grateful that I am able to help others by what I have experienced. At the same time, I do not take any credit for anything that I have said or done, because everything I say comes directly from my heart, from the experiences that the Creator allowed me to experience. I guess they happened so that I could share them, so I never really think that I am responsible. I just hope these letters will help someone in need.

[In reply to your question], yes, we [the inmates] see each other daily. The day rooms are set directly opposite the cells, so actually you can walk up to the bars and talk to another inmate. And we see each other when we are escorted to the showers.

When [in March 2000] we first came to Livingston, there was no regular schedule for anything. Meals, showers, mail, everything was done when the officers had time to do it – or felt like doing it. Exercise was anytime in the morning, and they would even put us out in the pouring rain without any coats. The outside recreation yard is just a room with walls 20' high, no bigger than the day room, with no shelter [roof] whatsoever from the elements. So, when it rains, it rains right on top of you.

I guess some things have changed [since we arrived]. For instance, there are two rows [of cells]. One day row 2 will be out for recreation first, the next day it will be row 1. So we do have some idea of when we shall get out. But food is still served whenever it gets here. Sometimes, it is very cold, and a couple of times we received food that had not even been cooked! When we complained, they replied that it was a cold meal, and it was meant to be that way! Mail is distributed whenever the officers have time.

> *"God is one and all, and*
> *governing Himself,*
> *He governs the universe."*
>
> (Mary Baker Eddy)

We thought it was bad when we first came here, but then we got a new officer in charge. He has let it known that he hates death row inmates, and that if it was up to him, he would take us out and shoot us all without a trial! He has suspended all phone calls, he has taken away almost all of our property, he has changed all the rules regulating the visiting area, mostly to harass our visitors. His hatred has trickled down to the regular officers, so they realize they can do just about anything they want to do and get away with it, because this person will back them. So that is the kind of environment we find ourselves in now.

I often wonder, can anyone get a good feeling treating human beings inhumanly? And of course I know the answer is no. However, sometimes people do things without actually knowing why, and sometimes their actions make others stronger for trials that lie ahead. So I do not hate them for what they do. It is all a learning experience for me.

God is indeed great. I believe that most inmates in Texas know who the true ruler is, and that is why there has not been a great deal of protesting like everyone expects. "God does indeed govern all." Those are some very powerful quotes you sent me. "The real jurisdiction of the world is in Mind, controlling every effect and recognizing all causation as vested in Mind." That is so powerful and so very real! The entire world is in Mind, isn't it? There is nothing that we need outside of Mind. I agree with the statement: "God is one and all, and governing Himself, he governs the universe."[23]

You know, I have always felt that way, that God is everything and all things, and that whatever I do to you, I am doing to myself, because all is one. The sergeant who yelled at me so offensively was yelling at himself, and simply not recognizing it. That last quotation is powerful. I will never forget that, it sums up so much for me. That is Oneness. Completely.

I will keep standing on the love and truth I know to be the only sure and solid foundation there is. *(April 7, 2002)*

---

23   These three quotes are from Mary Baker Eddy, whose writings Roger has been studying for years.

> *"Love is only one thought away.*
> *It can never be depleted.*
> *Remember to use it often."*
>
> (Roger McGowen, May 21, 2002)

To Monica

An officer entered my cell and destroyed some of my personal affairs. When I came back and saw what had happened, I immediately became angry. I wanted to say something nasty to him, and he knew it. He was waiting for me to say it. In fact, he acted in that way without really being aware of what he was doing. Because a few hours earlier, I was on my knees, asking God to give me the strength to face any kind of evil that I could encounter during the day. So when the officer did what he did, he was playing a role in which he had been placed unwittingly. I realized that the minute I looked at him. And so, instead of saying something mean and becoming a victim, I stole the victory and smiled at him, saying: "Thank you, I needed to do something. And you know, officer, we all have our roles to play." That evening, before going home, he stopped by to present his excuses to me.

Love is only one thought away. It can never be depleted. Remember to use it often. *(May 21, 2002)*

To Monica

Yes, I do see and experience many things in my mind and heart, and that is where all things originate, whether good or bad. In my case, it is the only place where I am allowed to go. I go there because that is where all our truths lie, inside us, and where, eventually, sooner or later, we will all turn.

I grew up in Houston, Texas, in what most people would call the inner city ghetto. Life was very dangerous, and hard at times, but there was love. I could say many bad things about growing up there, and indeed there were many. I saw many of my young friends killed or commit suicide out of despair. I lost so many friends and family members at very young ages.

But when I remember them now, it is not as victims of senseless crimes, but as souls who had completed their task here on this plane and were called back to the source from which they all came. I had to grow up and become a man before I knew what the meaning of the Word was. However, I truly believe that God has planned something for me, something I must learn or do before my time on this plane expires.

Remember that love is alive, Monica, and it can never die. Nothing that God has breathed life into can ever die. *(June 10, 2002)*

Harassment

It is very difficult for someone who is not part of the death row system to imagine what it means to live in a setting where harassment is a constant feature, sometimes in extremely mean, cruel, or even violent forms, such as gassing inmates when it is totally uncalled for, and often inflicted in random, arbitrary fashion. Too often, the guards themselves have to apply rules they perceive as totally meaningless, such as closing the aeration slot in the shower door, which can make taking a shower (one of the very rare "pleasures" of death row) painful. Guards vary in degrees of zealousness. Rules are applied one day, often arbitrarily, but not the next, and the types of punishment for not observing rules change all the time, without warning.

Any normal being (be it of the human race or of any other species) needs a certain consistency in his/her environment in order to function with a basic sense of sanity and security – with the understanding that if I perform action A (cause), result B (effect) will follow.

However, it must be added that the personnel hired as guards often have very little formal education and receive only minimal training. To their credit, quite a few guards do attempt to apply regulations as humanely as possible. That being said, here are a few examples of harassment experienced by inmates, garnered from their letters:

- Destroying an inmate's personal affairs without any reason other than to provoke him.
- Ignoring low temperatures that leave inmates shivering in their cells for weeks on end in early winter.
- Allowing shower temperatures to be so hot the inmates scald themselves.
- Searching an inmate's cell without reason 2-3 times a day.
- Disciplining inmates for negligible reasons such as: keeping a spoon from the dinner tray in the cell, not shaving due to medical reasons, having something other than hygiene items on a cell shelf, placing a family photo on the wall, eating breakfast delivered at 3 a.m. at 6.50 a.m., and hanging one's washing on a string instead on letting it dry on the floor.
- Shining flashlights on a sleeping inmate's face in the middle of the night (thus waking him up) during the few hours rest they have (10 p.m. to 3 a.m).
- Confiscating a book from an inmate because he did not mark it with his name (as if another inmate could steal it!) or because he left the book on the bunk when leaving the cell. (A spiritual book Roger cherished and studied daily was seized when he left it on this bunk while taking a shower).
- Accusing an inmate of masturbating because he was urinating when a female guard passed his cell - and then imposing discipline as severe as sending him to level 3 (extreme deprivation).

(continued p.138)

Hello my beautiful Pierre and Elly, how are you doing this lovely summer day? I hope that all the colors of the rainbow are at your fingertips, and that just the thought of being is enough to bring you bliss.

I am so sorry that Elly did not get the chance to come [with you on your recent visit] – I was so looking forward to meeting her. But it does not matter. I already know her, and she is an occupant of my heart and mind forever.

I have been doing a lot of thinking lately, trying really to understand how man can be so cruel to man, even when one is down. The foot of the state and all its supporters is already pressed tightly and securely on our necks, and they push ever harder. I was telling you during our visit of all the changes that were being adopted, but little did any of us realize how radical these changes would be. The bottom line is that if one looks close enough, all the changes that are being forced on us are for financial reasons.

Starting July 1, they are only allowing the prisoners to buy 15 stamps a week from the commissary. Now, keep in mind that many people here, especially on death row, depend mostly on the help, generosity, and love they receive from overseas. Some inmates have their entire support network overseas, and sometimes write to 20, 30 or even 40 people. To mail even one letter overseas costs three stamps. 15 stamps will only allow prisoners to write 5 letters a week overseas, and this does not include their correspondence with their friends and family here in the States. We all know what is coming. They have for a long time been trying to stop us from writing overseas, especially the victim's rights groups here in Texas, because they realize that much, if not all, of death row's help comes from other countries. So, by stopping the correspondence from and to these countries, they will most likely cut out all assistance.

When a prisoner is shipped to another prison, all the property that he owns is destroyed or sent home. He cannot take his property with him, apart from one bag. Guys [sometimes] have hundreds of dollars worth of property they have accumulated over many years in prison. And whenever you are shipped elsewhere, you have to start all over again, and buy everything from the prison store. That is racketeering! They sell us products, then six months later tell us we are not allowed to have them, but that they will replace them with other products we can choose to purchase. That is exploitation! It's ridiculous.

For instance, take the typewriter ribbons. They usually cost $6.95. Now we are being charged $10.20! They told us the company had gone out of business and had raised the price on the ribbons! That is a lie – the prison hiked the price. Everything has gone up. I have to laugh, but then I also feel like crying.

Harassment (continued)

- Strip searching inmates in front of female guards (this involves bending down stark naked so that the rectum can be searched). Throughout the world, prisoners experience these searches as extremely humiliating.
- Keeping inmates waiting 30-40 minutes for medical assistance, even in emergency situations.
- Disciplining inmates for tying their sheet corners in knots (which prisoners do to prevent the sheets from slipping off their small, thin mattresses).
- Disciplining inmates for having an extra piece of soap.
- Confiscating an inmate's radio because he extended a small wire from the antennae to the window to improve the very poor quality of reception. (This happened to Roger. Hearing about it, I phoned the chief warden to express my surprise and was told the small wire constituted "contraband.")
- Constantly changing regulations and thereby making prison life still more unsettling for inmates.
- Repeatedly decreasing the number of possessions an inmate can have. In recent years Roger lost many precious books in this manner.
- Frequently moving inmates from one cell to another – one element in a long list of factors that increase instability.
- Prohibiting inmates, as of May, 2003, from writing to each other unless they are related. This is especially hard for inmates who do not receive any mail from outside the prison system – and all the more so for those who do not have visitors. (I know of an inmate who did not receive a single visitor for 14 years, and his first visitor was a volunteer prison chaplain. To be severed from human communication is like being buried alive).

Putting up with all of this is difficult enough if you are guilty – and let us not forget that the majority on death row are guilty of murder, sometimes horrendous murders (see any of the pro-death penalty sites for a sample). But when you know you are innocent – and sometimes strongly suspect that even the District Attorney who prosecuted you knows it too! - it verges on sainthood to put up with such a system. More often, it simply drives you insane.

(Source: *Lifespark* newsletters and various letters from inmates; Allan Polunsky prison regulations)

It is a shame that these people are profiting from our misery, but that is capitalism. Many of the guys do not know what to do, and to tell the truth, neither do I. I can't hate the persons in charge, I can't curse them, but at this very moment I can't really feel pity or love for them, because they know what they are doing is wrong, and yet they do it gladly, with smiling faces. We are locked up 23 hours a day, we never really get to see the sun, the food they serve us is terrible and it is always cold and just looks uneatable. The showers are usually cold, and when they are hot, the heat is such that they are almost scalding. They give death row disciplinary cases much faster than [in the prison's] general population. We get the worst medical treatment and the worst verbal abuse, and yet we sit here and take it, hoping that maybe it will change if we only just accept the abuse for a few more days.

And the more they see that we are accepting it, the harsher they get. They will succeed in cutting off all of our air supply. It is a sad state of affairs that we are living in, but I continue to pray for them, asking the Creator what lesson lies hidden in this that I might have overlooked. As of yet, I am still searching. But regardless of what they do to us, I will not allow them to make me hate them.

I am going to close this letter, Pierre. Remember that I love you very much. Please kiss Elly for me. Take care and give my love to all the people who sent me their love. Thanks again for the visit. *(June 23, 2002)*

I wrote to Roger that Elly went to a meeting in New York despite having broken a bone in her foot. His response:

She had a broken bone, and it never even affected her. She went to New York and did the work God ordained her to do, and through it all she felt no pain. It was only after she completed the journey that she felt pain! I truly with all my heart believe that when you are working for God, no evil or calamity shall stand against you. The work Elly is doing is too important to allow a broken bone to get in the way.

God is amazing in all His wonders. How can we even begin to grasp the magnificence that is in us, that is Him, that is **God being us!**

I will also be praying for Elly's healing, despite of all the horrors that I see right here every day. Elly gives me hope and confidence, she gives me strength to hold my head high and, regardless of what I have gone through, still believe in the goodness of the human heart, soul and existence. May God bless her for all times!

How easy it is for people to believe in, and allow, the mortal human mind to suggest to them that they are hurt, that they are sad, that they are sick. That causes them to fear, doubt and place limitations on themselves that God never intended. In the book The Power of Now by Eckhart Tolle, he says that we are not our minds, we are more than our minds, and until, we realize that, we will forever be led by our minds. We are not mortal mind. We are the divine in its entirety.

The Ravensbrück Prayer

At the end of World War II, this prayer was found scrawled on a piece of paper next to the dead body of a child in the Ravensbrück camp, the only Nazi concentration camp for women. Ninety-two thousand women and children died there.

"Lord,
Remember not only the men and women of good will
but all those of ill will.
Do not only remember all the sufferings they have subjected us to.
Remember the fruits we brought forth thanks to this suffering -
our comradeship,
our loyalty,
our humility,
our courage and our generosity,
the greatness of heart that all of this inspired.
And when they come to judgment, let all those fruits we have borne
be their reward
and their forgiveness.
Amen."

(Source: www.healingenvironments.org/archives/pdf/2001Prayer.pdf)

Nothing can, nor should, prevail against the absolute, divine truth, and that truth is that *we are God manifested in this experience*, to make our experience that much more magnified. Nothing can harm us unless we adhere to it, recognize it, and/or accept it. And that I refuse to do.

Forgiveness is something so many people struggle with, mainly because most people do not want to forgive. It is not that they are evil, it is that we have been brought up in a society where we have been taught that everyone must be punished, where the highest courts in the land show no mercy, and leaders of our country, while claiming to be the embodiment of freedom, justice, liberty and equality for all, will at the same time kill their own citizens, drop bombs on countries halfway across the world in their misguided ideology and belief that it is God's will. Forgiveness is something that most people practice only in theory, but it is not something that is taken seriously. I discovered today the most selfless and sincere act of forgiveness that I have witnessed in my 38 years of life.

In 1999, in a backwater Texas country town, three white men picked up an intoxicated black man walking home alone from a family function down a back road. They knew the man, James Byrd, Jr. They beat him severely, cut his throat, tied him to the back of their pickup truck, and dragged him until his head came lose from his body. They actually dragged his body to pieces.

Two of the men received death sentences, and one received a life sentence. The ringleader of the group, whose name is William King, has exhausted all his appeals in the courts and has received an execution date. Today, the news stated that the father and family members of James Byrd, Jr., begged the state of Texas not to kill the man who dragged him to death! They said they would do whatever it took to keep the state from killing him, because it was wrong. They did not want him free, but they did not believe he should be killed either. The father made a powerful statement, saying, "I can't take a gun and go out and avenge his murder by killing them – so why should the state be able to do it?"

What forgiveness! The world should stand up and be glad that God has placed such angels in our midst, to teach and guide us. Love and forgiveness take no effort. They ask no payment, only that you take them and apply them – as in the beautiful prayer that was found next to the dead child [in the Nazi death camp].

Since being here, I have witnessed so many acts of kindness, not only between the prisoners, but also between guards and prisoners, and I have witnessed also the worst acts of violence and deprivation imaginable. I have cried and I have laughed, I have cursed and I have blessed, and I have at times been so angry that I could not think. But through it all, I will never allow hate to be my companion behind these walls. And when I feel I am at the end of my rope and hatred for the acts done against me is all my vision will allow me to see, I would rather be blind in both eyes and without a tongue before I allow hate to be the blanket my weary bones are laid to rest in.

Love is what brought us here, and I hope with all that is good in me, that it will be love that takes me home. *(July 3, 2002)*

Foreign nationals on death row

"Under article 36 of the 1962 Vienna Convention on Consular Relations (VCCR), local authorities must inform all detained foreigners 'without delay' of their right to have their consulate notified of their detention and to communicate with their consular representatives. At the request of the national, the authorities must then notify the consulate without delay, [...] facilitate consular communication and grant consular access to the detainee. Consuls are empowered to arrange for their nationals' legal representation . . . . The United States ratified the VCCR without reservations in 1969; so fundamental is the right to consular notification and access, that the US Department of State considers it to be required under customary international law in all cases, even if the detainee's home country has not signed the VCCR. As of February 9, 2009, 172 countries were parties to the VCCR."

"While not all of the reported foreign nationals currently on death row were deprived of their consular rights by the arresting authorities, there is overwhelming evidence that prompt notification of these rights remains highly sporadic across the US. No comparative study has been done yet, but available data indicate that timely consular assistance significantly reduces the likelihood that death sentences will be sought or imposed on foreign nationals facing capital charges."

"Even applying the less stringent definition of prompt notification used by the US State Department, only seven cases of complete compliance with Article 36 requirements have been identified so far, out of more than 160 total reported death sentences (including those executed, reversed on appeal or exonerated and released). In most of the remaining cases, detained nationals learned of their consular rights weeks, months or even years after their arrest, typically from attorneys or other prisoners, and not from the local authorities. As a consequence, consular officials were not able to provide crucial assistance to their nationals when it would have been most beneficial: at the arrest and pre-trial stages of capital cases. For example, Arizona authorities did not inform German nationals Karl and Walter LaGrand of their Article 36 rights **until 17 years after their arrest and just weeks before their execution.**"

"In *Sorensen v. City of NewYork*, a Danish national sought punitive and compensatory damages for the failures of the New York Police Department (NYPD) to inform her upon arrest in 1997 of her right to consular notification. Official records produced by the plaintiff revealed that over 53,000 foreign nationals were arrested in New York City during 1997, but that the NYPD Alien Notification Log registered only four cases in which consulates were notified of those arrests – a failure rate well in excess of 99 percent."

(Source: www.deathpenaltyinfo.org/article.php?did=198&scid=31 February, 2009)

One of the most enriching aspects of corresponding with a death row inmate is that it is a mutual learning experience. I feel I have learned some of the most important lessons in my life from Roger, above all gratitude for the good that is present, and especially refusing to feel a victim (a choice one can make; see p.55). In this letter, he echoes his vision of this mutual learning.

You have taught me so much. You are my light in the darkness of night. You have shown me how to look at life from inside these walls with new eyes. You have taught me how to find life on death row. Thank you for being you and for allowing me to be me. I truly love you and Elly.

I am sitting here in a very quiet wing. The wing is deathly quiet. One of our brothers is being prepared for execution. He is a Mexican national to whom the police lied when he was arrested. He was not informed that as a Mexican national he had the right to contact his consulate, and was denied the right to counsel. Everyone, from Colin Powell to the Pope to the UN High Commissioner on Human Rights have pleaded the governor of Texas for his life. As of now, there has been no response. I have just looked at the clock. He has less than 30 minutes left to live if the governor [of Texas] does not step in…

Please forgive the mistakes in this letter. My mind is in "Death House" with Xavier Madina, my friend who is being executed at this very minute. I'm sorry this letter is so bland. It is now 6:37 p.m., and executions start at 6.00 p.m., so chances are, they have already killed our friend. I will let you know what happens.

Please give my love and thanks to the participants of your workshop for their nice and comforting words. The cards were beautiful. I love the landscape that surrounds your chalet. These cards are a constant reminder to me of the love that still exists in this sometimes cold world. I felt so much love and compassion in those signatures, Pierre. *(August 14, 2002)*

Arbitrariness in sentencing

"These death sentences are cruel and unusual in the same way that being struck by lightening is cruel and unusual. The petitioners are among a capriciously selected random handful upon whom the sentence of death has in fact been imposed" (Supreme Court Justice Stewart in *Furman v. Georgia*).

One of the most amazing facts about the way the death sentence is meted out in the USA is, as Justice Stewart has stressed, its completely arbitrary nature: depending on where you are born, the color of your skin, your financial resources, your sex, the integrity of the prosecution and the defense, the quality of representation and whether or not the jury understands the instructions, you might walk out of the tribunal a free man or be condemned to death. Here are just a few of the main factors involved:

Geography One would not expect justice to depend on the place where you live. If I live in the center of Washington, DC, or a suburb, for an identical crime, I should get the same sentence. Well, this is not the reality of things. For instance:

- Baltimore City had only one person on Maryland's death row, but suburban Baltimore County, with only 10 percent of the murders committed, had nine times the number.

- In New York, upstate counties account for 61 percent of capital prosecutions, although only 19 percent of the homicides occur there, and three counties out of 62 account for a full third of death sentences. This list could cover pages. One could expect that sentencing at the federal level, where local biases presumably don't exist, would be less chaotic, but that is hardly the case. Thus it could happen that between 1995 and 2000, 42 percent of the federal cases submitted to the Attorney General came from just five of the 94 federal districts.

- Texas is by far the state with most executions, and Harris County in Texas has sent more people to death row than any other county in the United States. *"Harris County is the capital of capital punishment (if Harris County were a state, it would rank third in executions after Texas and Virginia)."*

(www.allacademic.com/meta/p_mla_apa_research_citation/0/1/7/5/4/p17540_index.html)

Race We have already mentioned the extreme bias of a system where black people are very heavily overrepresented among death row inmates. So, we will simply quote Supreme Court Justice Harry Blackmun, who stated, *"Even under the most sophisticated death penalty statutes, race continues to play a major role in determining who shall live and who shall die"* (in *Collins v. Collins*).

Representation The *National Law Journal*, in a June, 1990 study of death penalty representation in the South, concluded that capital trials are *"more like a random flip of the coin than a delicate balancing of scales"* because the defense attorney is *"too often . . . ill-trained, unprepared and grossly underpaid."* Nothing has significantly changed since then. States still vary enormously in the quality of representation provided to indigent defendants.

In Washington State, over a twenty-year period, one-fifth of the 84 individuals sentenced to death were represented by attorneys who had been, or were later, disbarred, suspended or arrested. (The statewide disbarment rate is less than one percent). In Texas, about one in four death row inmates have been defended by lawyers who have been reprimanded, placed on probation, suspended or banned from practicing law by the State Bar.

(continued p. 146)

Living on death row, one gray day after another, month after month, year after year, KNOWING THAT YOU ARE INNOCENT, is bad enough. When compounded with constant harassment, it is not close to, but constitutes an extreme case of "cruel and unusual punishment," forbidden by the Constitution of the United States of America. At my request, Roger described some additional examples of this harassment in the following letter:

We are forced to eat food that is always cold, and when served, has been spilled all over the trays and onto other foods. The bread is soaked with water of different juices. Punch or supposedly iced tea is always bitter, without sugar or sweetener, and the juice containers it is brought in are always filthy.

They have taken our finger nail clippers so that we cannot clip our nails. We must wait until the officers in charge decide when we can clip them. It is sometimes months between clippings. The clippers are never sanitary, so many inmates prefer to just bite their nails off.

We have one set of fluorescent lights in the cells, because our only window is only three inches high by two feet wide.. We barely get adequate light from either source. When the only light in the cell goes out, which is often, people can sometimes be left in their cells for a long period without light.

Same thing with the toilets. You can stay for weeks in a cell with a broken toilet that will not flush, and when you complain, the reply is: "We have written it up, so maintenance knows about it."[24]

We are sold clothes and detergents in the prison commissary, but we are not allowed a clothes line! When we ask where to dry our clothes, we are told to lay them on the floor!

Once you are found guilty and convicted of a major case, which you always are, you will be "leveled" on level 3. There, prisoners cannot have any property, not even a radio. Only as recently as last month, they were only allowed toothpaste and soap! They cannot have deodorants, [extra] clothes, food, anything. They are only allowed to recreate three times a week, and many prisoners are kept in these conditions for months, sometimes years. When they behave themselves, they are moved to Level 2, which means they can keep deodorant and go to the commissary once a month.

---

24   This means that each time an inmate needs to go to the toilet, he has to call the guards, be handcuffed, led to the WC and back.

Arbitrariness in sentencing (continued)

Roger's own lawyer was called "one of the worst of Texas lawyers." *The Austin-American Statesman* of September 14, 2005, wrote of his *"shoddy work in capital murder trials"* in relation to his extremely poor defense of Frances Newton, the first woman put to death in Texas in many years. The newspaper added *"No less than sixteen people whom* (name deleted) *represented were sent to death row [...].When asked by a trial judge, he could not mention a single witness he had interviewed on Newton's behalf"* - a repeat of what happened during Roger's trial when this lawyer did not attempt to contact a single witness.

Juror misperceptions A study of 1200 jurors in fourteen states concluded that the *"constitutionally mandated requirements established to guide juror discretion and to eliminate arbitrary sentencing **are not working**."*This is an extremely serious situation: the mechanism supposed to guarantee the democratic and impartial functioning of justice has such major flaws that it is sending people to the gurney by the dozens instead of adequately protecting their constitutional rights. Among the major flaws:

Premature decision making About fifty percent of jurors had already *"decided what the penalty should be before the sentencing phase of the trial.This is **before** they have heard penalty phase evidence or received instructions on how to make the punishment decision."*

Bias in jury selection *"Researchers found that jury selection methods resulted in disproportionately guilt-prone and death-prone juries."*Jurors that are opposed to the death penalty are removed for cause (not being able to follow the law and give a legally available sentence), and jurors that are able and willing to give the death penalty as a sentence have been shown to have a lower threshold on the question of guilt, and are therefore more likely to convict in close cases than a truly representative jury would.

Failure to understand judge's instructions to the jury Many jurors simply do not understand the extremely obtuse legal language of jury instructions, which led Supreme Court Judge Sandra Day Connor to admit that often juries passed judgments *without the foggiest notion of what was really happening.* Close to half the jurors in the above-mentioned study believed the death penalty was required if the defendant's conduct was heinous, vile or depraved. Harris County district attorney Chuck Rosenthal went as far as saying it was not his problem if the jury did not understand jury instructions. Most juries do not even understand the key concept of mitigating circumstances (i.e. facts or situations such as background and educational factors that reduce the degree of culpability of the accused and thus may reduce the severity of the sentence) – two-thirds of them in a South Carolina research. This is particularly true in Texas as well, where so many death sentences instead of life sentences are handed out, because of the lack of clear instructions given to the juries by the presiding judges.

(continued p.146)

If a prisoner gets sick and needs immediate medical attention, he may have to wait and suffer for 30-40 minutes before he can receive any help. In August, my neighbor cut his wrist in the middle of the night, and it took 30 minutes before they came to get him. First, they had to get the sergeant, who did not believe the officer on the wing, and had to come and see for himself. Then they called for a suit-up team, meaning they had to run in on him in the cell to make sure that he was not hiding any weapons. Once that was done, they placed him on the gurney. By that time, he had almost bled to death!

Pierre, they do not care, it is only a job for them. Everyone is looked at as an object, not a person. So whatever happens, they do not have to feel anything.

I must not forget to mention that we are made to strip search in the freezing cold if and when we are coming from the outside. We have to stand on the cold concrete and take off all our clothes and be inspected like an object before male and female officers alike. If inmates complain about this mistreatment, they are run in by the prison riot squad and gassed. Then they are pepper sprayed and beaten up badly and sometimes thrown back into the cells without medical attention.

We are placed in very small showers with no ventilation and often left there for 40 minutes to an hour. When we complain, we are told to "stop crying." The air [conditioning] in the cells is often turned down until it is so cold it is physical torture.

The whole process is harassment. Just living in these cells 23 hours a day when you know you should not be here is harassment. And every time we turn around, they are changing the rules. *(September 25)*

To L. (The following undated letter, written by Roger sometime in the fall of 2002, is included here, as it also deals with the theme of harassment)

As of July, they have changed a lot of rules, and one of them has to do with sending money to prisoners. For some time, they have been attempting to stop us corresponding with our overseas friends and families, as many victims' rights groups have been protesting about us receiving help from overseas. They do not like it. So, very quietly, they are creating rules to stop us from doing so. One of the rules states "No prisoner can solicit money from anyone but a family member."

They are taking the remainder of our property and making us send what is left home. Otherwise it is destroyed. If you remember, before I left Ellis One Unit in Huntsville, they allowed the inmates in the property room to steal all my piddling [handicraft] tools while I was in solitary confinement. Then, as soon as you had paid for me to buy some more, they decided that we could not have it anymore, so they took it again.

Arbitrariness in sentencing (continued)

In an effort to remedy this situation, the Texas legislature has added questions the juries need to answer, to help them come to a correct conclusion, but the changes were not made to apply retroactively.

Racial bias. We have already mentioned research stressing the very important role of racist attitudes in the functioning of justice. The famous Philadelphia district attorney Jack McMahon, commenting on the fact that the law required the jury to be competent, honest, and impartial, openly stated that he considered this ridiculous, and that the District Attorney's role was not to make sure that justice was done, but to win his case. He even recommended the elimination of specific categories of people from juries, such as social workers, MDs, most teachers, and especially young black women.

(Sources: www.americanradioworks.publicradio.org/features/deadlydecisions   and www.deathpenaltyinfo.org Spring, 2007, and also *The Celling of America*, Daniel Burton-Rose, ed., Common Courage Press, 1998)

North Pole: Livingston, Texas

In many of his letters, Roger mentions how cold it can become on death row (and, during the summer, how unbearably hot). Coming on top of all the other forms of stress described in these pages, uncomfortable temperatures can drive inmates up the wall – and also down to hell. In a country by far the world's biggest energy consumer (both in absolute and relative terms), the inadequate regulation of heating and cooling on death row would appear to be more an attempt to intentionally increase inmate stress rather than to relieve the state budget–the fact that the air-conditioning will often stay on throughout day and night at the coldest possible temperature in the fall and early winter months confirms that. Any reader who has been exposed to cold for long periods of time knows how rapidly it can become unbearable, and that preserving one's body heat becomes the almost sole focus of activity. It is unquestionably a cruel form of punishment.

What is termed in medical jargon as "thermal stress" has been the object of many scientific studies. When the body no longer manages to generate enough heat, a variety of cold-related illnesses and injuries, some of them serious, start manifesting themselves. One result is *permanent tissue damage*.

Among the more benign conditions manifested by inmates, one can mention mood swings, irritability, lassitude, lethargy, confusion, loss of motor coordination, slowed reflexes, etc.

Actually, they took property from us twice before I left Ellis. Then since we have been here, they have taken property from us. Now they have decided to go ahead and take most of it. So, I wrote and told M. that I was going to get rid of everything I had. I will never give them the opportunity to take anything else from me. So I will only buy food, writing material, and the few disposable reading things I need.

Speaking of food, yesterday afternoon they served us chicken and mashed potatoes. The guy about five doors down found a piece of rat in his food. After he yelled and everyone started inspecting their food, pieces of rat were found in almost everyone's food. I got sick to my stomach. I have not eaten since. *(Fall 2002)*

The two following letters are to the same correspondent, L. They express real discouragement at the continual, day-after-day harassment meted out to inmates. If someone with the inner maturity and spiritual strength of Roger can feel this way, it is not difficult to imagine what it must be for inmates with fewer psychological and spiritual resources.

We have been under lockdown since October 16. It has been 17 days so far, and we still have about two weeks to go. We have not had a hot meal in 17 days. It is freezing in here. It is cold and rainy outside, and we are sitting in the cells with the air conditioning blowing like a Northern wind. It is so cold that every few minutes I have to sit on my hands to warm them so I can keep writing.

They took all our property. I am sitting in a virtually empty cell. They lied to us. We have three small shelves welded under the steel bunks. When they took most of our property last November, they told us we had to keep everything off the floor and store things on those three shelves. So everyone threw out or sent home a lot of their property, so what remained could be stored properly. We were all pretty much in compliance. We figured they would come through and inspect, as they are supposed to. But they came with these very small boxes 1x1x2 feet and told us everything we wanted to keep had to go into the box – and what did not fit into the box was to be sent home or destroyed. So I lost most of everything!

It can become extremely difficult to even get a simple magazine someone orders for us. We have to struggle with the mail room just to get them. The officials lie to you, purposefully try to deceive you or simply ignore you. I have been waiting for some magazines I ordered months ago and that have already been approved. But the person who oversees book distribution keeps them until she feels like bringing them. We feel like nothing ever gets done.

List of Roger's belongings

Depending on the shifting prison regulations, the list of Roger's personal possessions has varied slightly over the years, but has always been austere. The day he finally walks through the prison gate and is a free man again, he will not need a truck to haul his belongings. During my April, 2003 visit, when visitors were still allowed to take a pencil and some paper into the visitors room (this is now forbidden), we made the following list together:

• Three books: an English dictionary, a book on the history of the United States (Roger is a history fan) and a book of poems.

• Two T-shirts, three underpants, one undershirt, one long underwear, two pairs of socks, one face flannel, a ten-year old pair of boots, and a pair of sneakers.

• A coffee pot, one cup, one bowl, and one spoon.

• One poorly functioning radio.

• A ballpoint pen and some writing paper.

• An old typewriter which no longer functions. (Due to the erratic performance quality of the low-grade prison-furnished typewriters – paid for by the inmates – Roger spends a great deal of time doing his correspondence by hand. This can be especially trying when he faces hand-numbing temperatures in his cell for weeks on end).

• A set of sheets and a thin blanket.

I'm really tired, in ways I never thought possible. I'm tired of being pushed. I'm tired of being robbed of all my property and constantly treated like trash. I do not understand why they don't just leave us alone. I'm so tired of being punished over and over again for nothing.

There is no such thing as justice in America, my friend. They should just do away with the word. It means nothing. Here, in this place, it means nothing. I agree with Earl Warren: "Permitting just enough justice to justify the injustice." But even that small amount that is permitted is only shown to those who can afford it.

I sit and look around this empty cell and wonder when – if ever – my heart will feel as empty. I pray to God that I die before that day comes, because if you bend anything enough, it will eventually break. I fight every day. One day I will win. *(November 3 and 12, 2002)*

Thank you very much for your letter. It was indeed a rare light in the middle of much darkness. Actually, we did not get out of lockdown until November 16, which makes 29 days. We were locked down, freezing, with cold meals. The only thing that has changed since is that we are getting our usual lukewarm meals. I myself make my own meal when I have food from commissary. But they deliberately made sure that we had very little food before we went under lockdown, and they took most of the little we did manage to keep.

I now honestly believe they have meetings to decide what is to be the next step to make our already hard and painful existence just that more painful. I have never experienced so much hatred concentrated in one place for a few men. Even now, they have the heat on everywhere except in Building 12, which is death row.

We are constantly being submitted to freezing air coming from the air-conditioner. But what is worse is that most of the guys have stopped complaining. They are beginning to believe that they are supposed to suffer, and accept their conditions. Most guys don't talk to one another anymore. It is as if they were zombies.

Yes, my friend, they cleaned us out this time, but after everything was gone, and I had looked around, a peace settled over me. I do not need any of those possessions. I just thought I did because they connected me to the outside world. I thought that to be human, to feel good about oneself, I had to have possessions, a sort of illusory wealth.

"I have to keep trying at all costs"
(Roger McGowen, November 24, 2002)

*"I fight to remain always filled with the spirit of Christ.
And yes, I do believe with all my heart
that one day I will win.
I will never, never give up on those beliefs."*
(Roger McGowen, November 30, 2002)

"Be ye steadfast, unmovable..."
(I Cor.15:58)

...for over 21 years on death row

Steadfastness

Firm, strong
Unwavering
Unrelenting
Unshakeable
Unyielding
Untiring
Persistent
Uncompromising
Determined
Immutable
Irreducible
Inalterable
Steady
Perpetual
Settled

Enduring, resolute
Adamant, persistent
Unfaltering, indefatigable
Unflagging, tenacious
Entrenched, unremitting
Unbending, unwavering
Undeviating, unflinching
Undefeated, insistent
Invariable, courageous
Irreversible, irrepressible
Unfailing, single-minded
Immovable, intractable
Constant, irremovable
Ineradicable, irrevocable
Rooted, deep-seated ...

*"Be sure you put your feet in the right place,
then stand firm."*
(Abraham Lincoln)

But I now realize that they were holding me down, because even with those few possessions I could never make this cell home – nor would I wish to. With an empty space, it looks just as it is supposed: a prison cell. And I never even want to forget that.

Thank you for all those beautiful things you said about me. However, at times I feel like a glass with a hole in the bottom, and slowly I'm being drained of what once made me, me. Like a person with a finger in a dike, I know its only a matter of time before it gives. But my finger is all I have, and I have to keep trying at all costs, because this cause is much, much bigger than I am.

Thank you for always being there for me and for never judging me, no matter how crazy I sound at times. I fight to remain always filled with the spirit of Christ, but at times I still feel very empty. And yes, I do believe with all my heart that one day I will win. I will never, never give up on those beliefs. Thank you for never forgetting me in your heart and prayers. I love you, my friend.

As I told you, they took my property – well, I gave it up, but they would have taken it anyway – books, legal books and tablets, history books, you name it. In September, they changed the policy concerning us, stating that we could only buy 30 stamps a week from the commissary, and that we were only allowed to have 60 stamps in our possession at a time. The new policy was that if we needed extra stamps for postage, we could apply for a special purchase from the warden. I was going to send my property to M. [in Switzerland]. The property room officer weighed my boxes and said it was going to cost me $ 80.00. So I applied to the warden for a special purchase, explaining that I only had 60 days to mail my property. He denied my request. Can you believe he said no? So I wrote the property room asking if I could send the things to C. and G. [in Texas]. And they said no, as they were not on my visiting list! I explained that they were my lawyers and did not have to be on my list. They still said no!

Almost everyone to whom I can send these things on my [visiting] list is from Switzerland. And I will not be able to purchase $80.00 of stamps from the store in time. So they are putting me in a lose-lose situation, which will ensure that they destroy my property. They are deliberately stopping me from being able to mail my property.

My Blackstone law dictionary alone cost $ 85.00. I am not going to let them get away with this. You see what I mean about being evil? They are sick, my friend.

I am going to close now. Just know that I love you with all my heart. You have constantly given me strength. Thank you. *(November 24 and 30, 2002)*

Executing the innocent

*"The best available evidence indicates that, on one hand, innocent people are sentenced to death with materially greater frequency than was previously supposed and that, on the other hand, convincing proof of their innocence often does not emerge until long after their convictions. It is therefore fully foreseeable that in enforcing the death penalty, **a meaningful number of innocent people will be executed** who otherwise would be able to prove their innocence"* (Emphasis added. U.S. District Court Judge Jed. S. Rakoff, quoted in Texas Defender Service, *Lethal Indifference*, op. cit).

*"The thought of executing an innocent person is repulsive. This is so even though the accused person may be a habitual criminal guilty of numerous crimes against persons and property. Yet few have the benefit of diligent services. . . . **The process is so fatally flawed that the only solution lies in abolishing capital punishment**. Most nations with which we share a common heritage have already taken this step. The relatives of the victim have the right to demand swift and sure punishment, but they do not have the right to demand death when the process is so severely flawed"* (Emphasis added. Former Missouri Supreme Court Chief Justice Charles B. Blackmar).

State capital punishment *"systems [are] so riddled with errors that for every eight persons executed in the modern death penalty era, one person on death row has been found innocent"* (Senators Russ Feingold and Jon Corzine, Editorial, *Baltimore Sun*, May 16, 2002).

"Perhaps the bleakest fact of all is that the death penalty is imposed not only in a freakish and discriminatory manner, but also in some cases upon defendants who are actually innocent" (United States Supreme Court Associate Justice William J. Brennan, Jr., 1994).

(Sources of quotes: Texas Defender Service and DPIC)

In this next letter, Roger mentions the strength he receives from our correspondence. What I wish to add here is the immense strength I have received over the years, when going through a deep valley, thinking of him and his incredible courage and resiliency. For some death row inmates, having a pen-pal is very literally a matter of life and death, of sanity and insanity. Organizations that put potential correspondents in contact with inmates in the US have long waiting lists of prisoners desperately waiting for a correspondent.

It is so cold here, Pierre, that guys are walking around with blankets and anything else they can find to keep them warm. They won't turn on the heat and they won't give us coats or extra blankets. We get one old, dirty, very thin blanket when fall first arrives. After that we keep warm as best we can. It's been very hard to write while freezing at the same time.

When we were placed under lockdown in October, we had no idea what we were in for. But we soon found out. We lost almost everything. I do not have anything in this cell but food. I'm tired of ordering books and other things only to have the prison administration take them. I'm reading and buying only what I can give away. It does not really bother me that I lost all my property. It was how it was taken [that troubles me]. They lied, schemed, connived in order to catch us off guard so they could take as much of our property as they could. Now that they have taken our property, they are doing everything that is humanly possible to thwart us from mailing our property home, thus ensuring that the prison will destroy it.

I never really gave evil much thought. I never believed anyone was inherently evil, but I am beginning to reassess my thinking in that area. Since coming to this prison, I have witnessed some of the cruelest acts imaginable. I now believe some people really appreciate causing evil to others. I have witnessed it and experienced it. These people do terrible things, and then they laugh about the destruction they cause.

When we first encounter a truth that has been kept from us, when a long-believed myth has been shattered with truth, it causes us all to stumble and sometimes even fall. But if we are strong in our belief in our Creator, then we know that He makes no mistakes and that all we learn today is to prepare us for tomorrow.

I thank you, my friends, you and beautiful Elly, for your strength. Please believe that not a day passes that I do not hear your voice, feel your love and prayers working in my life. Have a joyous Christmas and New Year. I will be with you in prayer and in Spirit. Your strength and love constantly pull me through.

PS. It's freezing in here. My fingers are freezing. *(December 8, 2002)*

*"You are as close to God
as you are to the person
from whom you feel the most alienated."*

(Statement of the former Moral Rearmament Movement)

*"Loving your neighbor as yourself
means your neighbor is yourself,
and that recognition of oneness is love."*

(Eckhart Tolle)

I wrote to Roger that I had cried thinking of him when I viewed the film about Hurricane Carter, the African-American boxer who was unjustly incarcerated on death row for many years. His reply:

Yes, I know who Hurricane Carter is. He was cheated out of so much of his life, and yet he felt no bitterness at his release.

Please, never, never cry for me, my friend. I have cried enough for both of us. The river of my tears has flowed for seventeen years, and I cannot and will not allow you to travel down that same river. We have both been sad, but Malcolm X said that no one can change their conditions by being sad. Pierre, at times I get very sad, so sad in fact that I wish I could go to sleep and never wake up. Sometimes I get so lonely my heart physically hurts. I would never want anyone to feel that kind of mind-crippling pain. However, I love you for putting yourself in my shoes. We all need to walk in one another's shoes once in a while. *(December 18, 2002)*

2003

Hello, how are you this beautiful day? I hope that God has continued to bless and enrich your lives this New Year as He has all the years before.

I truly love you guys. You are always on my mind and in my heart. You are a part of my life, you walk with me and talk to me every day.

The people who run this prison think that by taking away everything the prisoners possess and treating them like sub-humans, they can somehow make society feel safer. [They seem to believe that] people will not want to commit crimes because they will not want to go to prison, due to the cruel punishment and treatments prisoners receive. But they have been trying that since the first prison was built!

There were times when I was so angry I could not picture myself loving any of these people. But it came to me that maybe they hate so much because they do not love themselves, nor do they have love in their lives. So maybe someone had better love them. I realize that I could not continue to hate anyone, and still confess to love God. Hate and love cannot coexist in the same body. So I gave them all my property if that was what they wanted. *Could I do that.*

A historic decision

"I have always found that mercy bears richer fruits than strict justice."
(Abraham Lincoln)

In January 2003, three days before retiring, Illinois governor George Ryan (who voted to restore the state death penalty in 1977) commuted the sentences of all Illinois death row inmates to life in prison. Announcing this at Northwestern University Law School, Ryan said, *"Our capital system is haunted by the demon of error, error in determining guilt, and error in determining who among the guilty deserves to die.[...] To say it plainly one more time - the Illinois capital punishment system is broken."* This decision was the result of a thorough review of the state justice system by a high-level commission led by leading legal experts and former District Attorneys. The review was launched after it was discovered that thirteen death row inmates would have been put to death, had professors Larry Marshall and Dave Protess and their students not proved them innocent. In all, seventeen men *"wrongfully convicted and rotting in the condemned units of our prisons"* were freed. *"Seventeen exonerated death row inmates,"* said Ryan, *" is nothing short of a catastrophic failure."*

Among the more glaring factors mentioned in Ryan's speech:

- Over half of the convictions in Illinois were reversed for a new trial or re-sentencing. (Commenting on this figure, Ryan added in another speech *"When I was a pharmacist, I know I couldn't have stayed in business if I only got it right 50 percent of the time. There is virtually no other profession where that level of mistake would be tolerated. Yet that is the situation we have with the police, prosecutors, defense lawyers, and the courts in capital cases in Illinois."*)
- Forty-six inmates were convicted on the basis of jailhouse informants ("snitches,") one of the most unreliable forms of testimony.
- Since the reinstatement of the death penalty in Illinois, 93 people had been condemned to death and later released (or the sanction rescinded).
- In the famous "Ford Heights Four" case, the primary testimony came from a 17-year-old girl with an IQ under 60, who the police said was an accomplice to the murder. In this case, *the police were given the name of the actual rapists and killers days after the crime*, but failed to follow up because they had already made up their mind about the guilt of the four defendants. *"A system that is so fragile that a journalism student has to do the police work is badly flawed,"* said Ryan.

(continued p.162)

The reason I did not write to you is that I was saving stamps to mail out my property. But the property that I claimed was what was giving them power over me! So I told them to destroy the property if they wanted. Now their scale broke down and they can't weigh things. God never sleeps. He is always there, watching and waiting, waiting for us to realize He is only one problem away!

All that property was not really mine to begin with. If it had been, it would not have been taken away. What is truly ours can never be taken away. God allowed me to become weak, so that I could realize that true strength dwells in our oneness with our Creator.

We all must stop at times and make a pause, and that is what I have been doing, learning to humble myself more and stop fighting the lessons of this life.

But we must be ever on our guard. Starting the 2nd of February 2003, they will stop feeding us three square meals a day, and begin feeding us two hot meals and one cold sandwich for the last meal of the day. We never received fresh vegetables, only canned. Henceforth, we will only get one helping of canned vegetables a day. They have already cut down on the size of the portions. Their punishment never ends. *(January 25, 2003)*

I wrote to Roger that I had finished the French manuscript for the first edition of this book. I also mentioned that Governor George Ryan of Illinois had commuted all death sentences of the state into life sentences, a decision that made national and international headlines.

Thank you, my brother, for taking the time to put the book together. My only hope is that someone is truly helped by it. I never pictured myself as a teacher or as any kind of inspiration. But actually, we are all teachers, healers, counselors, and sources of inspiration to one another.

What Governor Ryan of Illinois did was a thing of Biblical proportions. Yet, for his love of right and moral conviction, he has become hated and scorned and talked about as being a criminal himself. What many people do not see is that Governor Ryan has to sign each death warrant that comes across his desk before an execution can be legally carried out. He almost signed three death warrants of men who turned out to be innocent. How do people believe this honorable man would have felt, after signing a death warrant, only to find out the man was innocent?

Rick Perry, Governor of Texas, let it be known immediately that he would never do such a thing. But prisoners here were very excited, because, regardless of what Perry said, there would be a great deal of focus on the issue, and indeed there was.

A historic decision (continued)

A key claim among those favoring the death penalty is that victim families find deep satisfaction and even appeasement from the death of the murderer of their beloved one(s). However, Ryan noted that in 2002, over a thousand murders were committed in Illinois, *"but less than two percent of those murder defendants will receive the death penalty."* And of those so sentenced, many will never be executed. Commission president Thomas Sullivan noted: *"The police who conducted the investigations in these cases remain on the force. The prosecutors who over-stepped the bounds of fairness, and the defense lawyers who gave incompetent defense remain in practice. The judges who permitted or caused errors, remain on the bench."*

(http://dir.salon.com/story/news/feature/2003/01/14/ryan/index.html)

"The spirit cannot be held down.
It was created to soar,
and I have witnessed the spirit triumph
over unbelievable odds."

(Roger McGowen, early 2003)

I can only hope my victory over our cruel and inhumane treatment can help others. I must say that even though the struggle gets harder, my level of love, compassion, and tolerance gets stronger. I no longer expect anything from anyone here. I only expect it from myself. Nothing outside of me can do anything to me. As long as I am talking and showing [the officials] how they are breaking their own rules, they are happy, because it is what they expect. But when I do not say anything, they get worried and want to know what is wrong. Sometimes, I go weeks without talking. I love silence because it soothes me. But I cannot hate, because hate is not in me. I can only give what is in me. I get angry at times, I get upset, but these are natural emotions. But I will never allow them to turn into anything else. So I give not only to you, but also to my torturers, only that which I know: love. *(February 16, 2003)*

In addition to the early letters to Conor and Mirjam included at the beginning of this book, the letters starting with the following one were not in the original French edition, published in 2003.

To Monica

Christmas was cold and the inmates had very little to be happy about, at least, that is what was being thought. The wardens have taken just about everything we owned and left us sitting in cold empty cells, so spirits were not as high as last year. But we manage, as we so often do, and after looking back, we realize it is always what is in the heart that matters most, not what is in the cell. *The spirit cannot be held down. It was created to soar and I have witnessed the spirit triumph over unbelievable odds.* These inmates here realize that today could very well be their last day on this planet, so they try to treat each of us as if it were their last day. There is much love and life on death row.

I'm sure your prayers have reached me. Prayers are hopes that truly never go unanswered. Your mercy and compassion fill me and surround me with love. Take care of yourself, and remember that love cannot be contained. If you try, it will find its own way of manifesting.

Thank you, Monica. I love you and see you and am with you as you are with me. *(Undated, early 2003)*

I would have written earlier, Pierre, but we are under another lockdown. It seems to be the regular operating procedure. Five days after your visit, we were placed under lockdown. It has been sixteen days now that we have not been to commissary. We have no food to eat in our cells, and we get very little from the kitchen.

The broken thread of life

Two members of Roger's international support group, Monica and Robin, took part in the Journey of Hope in Texas in October, 2007. The Journey of Hope is composed of people who lost a family member or close relative due to a violent crime and are opposed to the death penalty. The following passage is an extract from the report Robin wrote on her experience:

"One of the biggest windows into the failure of our legal system, especially in the area of capital murder cases, is the wrongful conviction and imprisonment of innocents on death row. Three of these men were with us in Houston. Somehow these situations hit me harder than all the tragic stories I heard. I just kept thinking: 'What could be worse than knowing you were going to be executed for a crime you did not commit?' They explained that inmates on death row have experienced their execution mentally thousands of times before they actually die. It is a mental torture that destroys you. Just think how much greater that torture might be for someone who was innocent. That is why, even in the unusual case where innocence is legally proved and they are released, these men are never the same.

It is similar to having been a POW (prisoner of war). You never get over it mentally and your physical health frequently deteriorates with the terrible food and bad health care in prison. It is still difficult to get a job even when you have been exonerated just because of the stigma of having been accused of murder and of having been in prison. Marriages dissolve, children grow up without you, the thread of life you were trying to live can never be picked again. Very few of these people have even gotten an apology from the state, let alone monetary compensation.

It is the rare person who can pick up their lives again without great bitterness and go on with the semblance of a normal life" (Robin).

It is now 4:39 a.m. and they just served breakfast. The chow cart was late this morning. We usually eat at 3 a.m. Anyway, I was very hungry and still am very hungry. They served us two very thin pancakes with syrup, one small milk and three cooked prunes! I could not go back to sleep, I was going to exercise but thought better of it, and decided I had better save what little strength I have. It looks as if we are going to be locked down for another two weeks.

There are many decent human beings working here. Most will not go out of their way to harass inmates. Many just want to do their jobs and go home to their children, and they are really good people. But they do not know, when they apply for this job, that the state of Texas requires them to be as mean and hateful as possible, and if they aren't, the state will try and make them feel that way. The officers cannot be as decent as they would like to be, because they have been putting hidden cameras all over the prison, and the officers are afraid of being fired for doing something for the prisoners.

So the kindness expressed by the officers that I focus on is e.g. in always saying "Hello, how are you today?" or not putting the handcuffs on too tight, or just being courteous. I have thought a great deal about this, and some acts of kindness cannot be put into words. All I can say is that there are some beautiful people with beautiful hearts working here.

You know Pierre, I sometimes find myself unable to fully express myself as I used to. It's like I am stuck in a virtual parallel world. [During lockdown] we are locked up 24 hours a day, cut off for the most part from the world, and wondering if indeed tomorrow will bring a day brighter than today. An [inmate] friend who works here in 12 building – which houses death row – and who lives in general population, stopped by yesterday to tell me he was going home in a few days after spending ten years here. He was very happy, but he was also afraid. I could see it in his eyes – this not knowing what to expect. And it dawned on me that he was afraid of being free. They had beaten him down to the point that he was afraid of being free! And I wondered if I would feel the same after being here for so long? I can only hope not. *(April 29, 2003)*

A "soul story" by Gary Zukav

Many of the guys here have found the strength to forgive. (Roger McGowen, June 22, 2003)

"Kill him!" said the brother. His face was set like stone. "Kill him," said the mother through her tears. "Kill him!" said the sister, her voice quivering. Around the council fire each member of the family spoke. In the balance lay the life of the young man sitting restlessly outside. Murder is a terrible thing. Murder of a friend is more terrible yet. Yet there he sat, the blood of his friend still on his hands, awaiting his fate.

"Let us think this through," spoke the grandfather softly. Sorrow deepened the lines on his wrinkled face. Generations spoke through him. "Will killing him return our boy to us?"

"No." "No." "No." The word moved slowly around the tortured circle, sometimes whispered, sometimes murmured, sometimes spoken spitefully.

"Will killing him help feed our people?" asked the old man, his eyes steady.

Again, "No," then "No," then "No," moved around the circle.

"My brother speaks the truth," said the great-uncle. All faces turned toward him. A tear ran slowly down his cheek. "Let us look at this matter carefully."

They did look at it carefully. They deliberated through the night. Then they called the young man to his fate.

"See that tepee?" they said, pointing to the tepee of the young man he had killed. He nodded. "It is yours now."

"See those horses?" they said, pointing to the dead man's horses. He nodded again.

"They are yours now. You are now our son. You will take the place of the one you have killed." He looked up slowly to the faces surrounding him. His new life had begun, and so had theirs.

Brown Bear looked across the table at me. "That happened in the late 1800s," he said. "They could have killed him. Tribal law gave them the right."

I sat amazed as Brown Bear's words sank into me. Could the family of a murdered boy adopt the murderer as their son?

(continued p.170)

I shared with Roger two quite amazing testimonies of spiritual healing told to me by a friend of mine from California.

Those were extraordinary testimonies, Pierre. God never gives up on us. We give up on others. We give up on God. And we give up on ourselves. But God never gives up. When we are in our darkest hour, God remembers. The power of prayer is amazing, isn't it? There is nothing done that God cannot undo. When God's words are given, they perform. Thank you for those stories. I know God is real, I feel His presence daily.

God's angels surround us all. Miracles happen everyday, they are simply not reported, because many people do not feel they will be believed.

I have been doing some meditating. You asked me if I thought some people were "fundamentally evil." I do not believe any one is born evil. But I believe that people without a strong foundation in morality and decency are like water, they become the color of whatever is added to them. I believe people are shaped by their encounters when they are at an impressionable age, thus shaped by their surroundings. I do not necessarily believe that some people are evil, but some people just take a certain pleasure in seeing other people suffer greatly. *(May 18, 2003)*

To Monica

Yes, "my" Easter was peaceful and quiet. Actually, most of my days are the same. Although at times chaos invades them, in those times I search for the peace that is in the chaos. I guess many of the guys here have for the first time had the time to look deep within themselves and see what they could not see when they were free: their inner beauty, their inner child. And more importantly, they have found the strength to forgive. Many of the guys in here entered with much hate in their minds, but they soon learned that hate is a force that takes no sides. The more you eat it, the more it eats you. But in the end, Monica, peace is what we will all find, whether we wish to or not.

The freedom that is in me can never be chained - because the freedom I claim is being free within the oneness of all things. As long as a single bird flies, or fish swim in the ocean, as long as clouds sail in the sky and grass is green as far as the eye can see, I will always be free. *(June 22, 2003)*

A "soul story" by Gary Zukav (continued)

"The young man became a devoted son." Brown Bear continued. "By the time he died, he was known in all the tribes as the model of a loving son."

This is forgiveness. Authentically empowered people forgive naturally. They forgive because they do not want to carry the burden of not forgiving like heavy suitcases through a crowded airport. The family of the murdered boy could have killed his killer. Instead they took him as their son. [...] They did not have to hate him. They did not have to live with his death in their hearts, as well as the death of their son.

(Source: Gary Zukav, *Soul Stories*, Simon and Shuster, N.Y, 2000, p.113. Reproduced with the authorization of the publisher)

How Roger handles depression

"I get depressed at times but I confront the emotions. Sometimes I wake up and I am very lonely. Sometimes I say to myself: 'Man, there is a chance that I may never again feel the simple warmth of another human being's embrace.' I feel sometimes when things seem to be going right and I'm in the middle of laughing and just enjoying the moment, that its not going to last and I get depressed but I don't identify with it. I see it for what it is, but I also see it for what it is not. It is not part of me. I love to sing, it makes me happy, so when I feel that way I start to sing to myself or I remember one of those occasions that made me laugh until my stomach hurt and I laugh all over again. Then I know, it will be all right for the moment, for just that moment. I don't know about the next one, but for the moment I am all right. I'm doing fine. I am at peace. We can only deal with one moment at a time, because that is all we are given: moments."

(Letter to Monica, June 5, 2007)

I too go into bouts of depression, Pierre. I am quite certain that we all do, at some point. I actually believe that it is a normal reaction to our sometimes stressful lives. In order to learn what we must, we need to suffer the bitter with the sweet. I look around at times, Pierre, and I must be honest. I ask myself: "Is this it? Is this all my life is going to be?" But I have learned that at times we must learn to look beyond what is sometimes apparent to find what we need. Some of our greatest painters, singers, and writers created their greatest works after coming out of a period of depression.

Yes, the parable of the Prodigal Son is an amazing one, but as many times as I had read it, it had never occurred to me to think of it in the terms you described. I listen to the Christians here arguing back and forth about their interpretation of a particular parable. Often they ask me, and I tell them it needs no interpretation, just accept it as it reads. The meaning is clear! But I believe the Christians feel that they are not true Christians until they have found an esoteric meaning within the parable.

If we are made and created in God's image and likeness, and we are His reflection and He lives His experience through us, to be angry and punish us would be to be angry at Himself and punish Himself, since we are His reflection.

How many of us have been prodigal sons? We have no real idea of God's love for us.

Yes, all that God is, is ours, if only we ask.

How simple!

What is it in man that makes him turn his back on God's unconditional Love and seek it in places where it can never be found? All that the Father has is ours for the asking. Maybe it is the simplicity of the claim that makes us wary. The Christian Church has taught that the only way to God is through sacrifice, hard work, and suffering. *(June 30, 2003)*

Who was Epictetus?

An eminent stoic philosopher, Epictetus lived between 55-123 A.D. Born a slave in Phrygia (in what is today Turkey), he was a servant of Epaphroditus, one of Emperor Nero's bodyguards. It is said his master was torturing him once with a machine that was twisting his leg. Epictetus smiled and said quietly, "You are going to break my leg." When that happened, he simply added, "I told you so." Later he gained his freedom and left Rome.

His life radiated virtue, contentment, and simplicity. He practiced the morality that he taught. He lived for a long while in a small hut with few possessions, apart from a bed and a lamp, and no servants. When a friend of his had to give up his child due to pressing poverty, the philosopher not only adopted the child but took a nurse to take care of him. Epictetus is one of the greatest stoic philosophers and his famous maxim "Bear and forbear" summarizes his practice, and also suggests why Christiane Singer compares Roger to him in her foreword to this book.

This school of thought emphasizes the difference between what we can influence and change and what we cannot change and must accept. Thus Epictetus could not prevent Epaphroditus from torturing him, anymore than Roger can stop being on death row. But he could decide upon his response to the event, just as Roger has chosen to grow rather than wane on death row. Contrary to most stoic thinkers, Epictetus condemned suicide. The following statement, taken from his *Golden Sayings*, also unites him to Roger:

"Friends, wait for God. When He gives the signal and releases you from this service [i.e. life on earth], then depart to Him. But for the present, endure to dwell in the place wherever He hath assigned you to your post. Short indeed is the time of your habitation therein, and easy to those that are thus minded. What tyrant, what robber, what tribunals have any terror for those who thus esteem the body and all that belongs to it of no account? Stay, depart not rashly hence."

I sent Roger the foreword to this book, by well-known French writer Christiane Singer. She likens Roger to the famous Phrygian slave and philosopher Epictetus (born 50 B.C). who wrote some very profound texts on freedom. She writes (see p.5 "Holiness is that invisible force that keeps the world together since its creation. It is the deliberate choice a man makes to be whole (heilig, holy), to welcome good and bad, injustice and justice, cruelty as well as kindness, illness and health alike – to welcome and embrace the entirety of what is – without condition, without restriction, to hold against his heart this scandalous and sublime world as one would rock a sleeping monster.

In a cell of six by nine feet, where light trickles through a six-inch opening, Roger, Black American incarcerated for murder, sentenced to death and innocent, teaches us freedom."

Yes, I believe that if we can help only one single person with this book, we will have done a tremendous work. All of your efforts will be rewarded.

Pierre, I had to read the preface to the book twice before I realized who Christiane Singer was speaking of. It is more than I can grasp at the moment. I don't know what to say about it.

While I was reading it, I was drawn back to the days when I first set foot on the steps of Ellis One Unit, the first death row in Texas. I was a young man who was lost, but who never stopped searching, a young man who was green all over and whose life and awakening began soon after. I saw faces and lives and [heard] the last words of so many men now gone, flash by. Gone but for their memories. All caught up in a web of confusion and looking for compassion and mercy, yet finding only brutality, hatred, deceit and, ultimately, death. I made up my mind to set my eyes on a candle in the distance and to never stop putting one foot in front of the other. I sometimes stumbled and did not want to get up, but I had all of these beautiful people reaching down to pick me up, dust me off, and whisper words of encouragement.

You know, people love to thank God for everything good that happens in their lives. Yet God IS the people, the friends we meet on our journey. God manifests Himself through us. We are all God.

We only give back to ourselves when we give to others. By praising and thanking me, Christiane Singer is only thanking and praising herself, as well as everyone. Was there anything I did you would not have done, put in the same situation? I think not. Please give Ms. Singer my thanks for all of her beautiful words. I may not be worthy of them now, but it gives me something to strive for, and I will never stop reaching. *(August 17, 2003)*

An Arab legend

"Everyone is us."
(Roger McGowen, October 14, 2003)

THE FRIEND WHO SAID "I"

A certain man knocked at his friend's door: His friend asked, "Who is there"?

He answered, "I." "Begone," said his friend, "'tis too soon: at my table there is no place for the raw."

How shall the raw on be cooked but in the fire of absence? What else will deliver him from hypocrisy?

He turned sadly away, and for a whole year the flames of separation consumed him;

Then he came back and again paced to and fro beside the house of his friend.

He knocked at the door with a hundred fears and reverences, lest any disrespectful word might escape from his lips.

"Who is there?" cried his friend. He answered, "Thou, O charmer of all hearts!"

"Now," said the friend, "since thou art I, come in: there is no room for two I's in this house."

(Rumi, Persian Poet and Mystic)

To Monica

I am so sorry to hear of the passing of your young woman friend. I guess the universe gives and takes. It gives us the joy and beauty of having people such as your young friend with us for only a short time. They teach us love, compassion, and humility. We laugh, cry, hurt, and experience life together, and like a match in the wind, their flame is gone.

Some things are just not to be made sense of, Monica. I have watched so many young lives come to an end, and each time, even now, I still wonder why. But I have come to believe that each life, no matter how short lived, performed the task for which it was put here.

I do not know if I ever told you, but Paula's death was like my mothers'. My mother was only 42 when she passed on. Whenever someone I know and love passes, I celebrate it with silence. How else can one share the feeling of never having that person's physical presence in their lives? *(September 10, 2003)*

People in lectures often ask how one can be as strong as Roger. Well, Roger goes through his valleys, like all of us, as this letter makes very clear. But, in contrast to many, he stubbornly refuses the role of victim.

As of the spring of 2009, he has held on 21.5 years...

I am very happy to hear that the book project is nearing completion and that you are very satisfied with the results. You have worked hard to bring it to completion, and I am sure it will surpass both our expectations. Thank you for all the labor of love you have put into it.

I see *The Gentle Art of Blessing* has finally appeared in English. I am sure many people will find healing in its pages. I know I certainly did. It changed my entire outlook on how I viewed people. It made me realize that everyone is us, and that all our experiences are the same, so what we give we eventually get back.

No matter how hard we try, the illusion known as the past rears its ugly head and catches us unawares. Sometimes, Pierre, no amount of words, spiritual or other, can help. Sometimes we just get tired of it all. I can't really explain to you how I feel. I know you say we are helping people with the book, but still I feel so empty at times. I sit in this cell 23 hours a day, trying to believe in something better, but at times, Pierre, I find myself doubting everything. I have never been around people as cruel and filled with hate. I don't know what to believe anymore. Sometimes I find myself angry at the powers that be, wondering how one can allow so much pain, suffering, and injustice into this world. The bottom line: I get tired of it all.

"What is truly ours can never be taken away.
God allowed me to become weak
so that I could realize
that true strength
dwells in our oneness with God"

(Roger McGowen, January 25, 2003)

All I know is that at this moment I'm hurting inside because I only see despair and suffering. Everyone writes and tells me how good things are, that eventually things will change, and to just hold on. But from where I am looking, it does not appear that way. At the moment, I just can't handle all of these spiritual letters about God! I guess I am going through one of these phases where nothing seems to comfort me. Maybe it's depression, but at this moment I don't want to read, write or even talk for that matter. But my love for you and Elly has not nor will it ever lessen. I just need time to work these things out. Trust me, I have not gone crazy, just the opposite.

Remember the small box into which the prison administration made us fit our property? Well, they are talking of [a new box] about only half the size. And they don't want any pictures, posters, calendars or anything on the walls. Not even family pictures. It's crazy, and it's getting worse. I try not to let anything outside of me bother me. But what is happening is madness.

They have cut back on all the food they serve. The servings are like half an ounce of everything, when they are supposed to be two ounces. On top of that they have cut the size of everything in commissary by about half, while still charging the same price. So we are forced to buy almost everything from the commissary.

But I will be all right. I believe that at times we all have to do a bit of soul-searching. We all have doubts sometimes. Even Jesus did. *(October 14, 2003)*

One of Roger's new correspondents, Eve, is a young photographer from Switzerland who sent Roger some of the beautiful nature pictures she takes. One comment he makes about them says more on the drabness of prison life than pages of prose.

Thank you for offering to replace the books they took from me, but I have no room for any more books. We only have limited space for storage. Anything not stored properly is taken. Although my books were stored properly, they took them because they said I had not written my name in them.

When we bless others, God blesses us. When we bless others, it is also for our own peace of mind. Love can be understood by all. It is a universal feeling that transcends all boundaries. Thank you for spreading that love, Eve, it is our only salvation.

What's in the brown paper bag?
by Luis Ramirez, # 999309, executed October, 2005

The Swiss *Lifespark* network occasionally circulates particularly moving letters from inmates. The following letter about a "random act of kindness" on death row was sent to members on September 11, 2003. It challenges many stereotypical views about death row inmates. As Roger has said several times, they can express great love and caring toward each other. The letter is now posted on the Internet at: www.axisoflogic.com/ artman/publish/printer_23631.shtml

"I came here in May, 1999. I was placed in a cell on H-20 wing over at the Ellis Unit in Huntsville. A tsunami of emotions and thoughts were going through my mind at the time. I remember the only things in the cell were a mattress, a pillow case, a couple of sheets, a roll of toilet paper, and a blanket. I remember sitting there absolutely lost.

The first person I met there was Napoleon Beazley. Back then, death row prisoners still worked. His job at the time was to clean up the wing and help serve during meal times. He was walking around sweeping the pod in these ridiculous looking rubber boots. He came up to the bars of my cell and asked if I was new. I told him that I had just arrived on death row. He asked me my name. I told him, not seeing any harm in it. He then stepped back where he could see all three tiers. He hollered at everyone: 'There's a new man here. He just drove up. His name is Luis Ramirez.'

When he did that, I did not know what to make of it at first. I thought I had made some kind of mistake. You see, like most of you, I was under the impression that everyone on death row was evil. And now, they all knew my name. I thought, "Oh well, that's strike one." I was sure they would soon begin harassing me. This is what happens in the movies after all.

Well, that's not what happened. After supper was served, Napoleon was once again sweeping the floors. As he passed my cell, he swept a brown paper bag into it. I asked him: 'What's this?' He told me to look inside and continued on his way. Man, I didn't know what to expect. I was certain it was something bad. Curiosity did get the best of me, though. I carefully opened the bag. What I found was the last thing I ever expected to find ond, and everything I needed. The bag contained some stamps, envelope, notepad, pen, soap, shampoo, toothpaste, tooth brush, a pastry, soda, and a couple of Ramen noodles. I remember asking Napoleon where this came from.

He told me that everyone had pitched in. They knew that I didn't have anything and that it may be a while before I could get them. I asked him to find out who had contributed. I wanted to pay them back. He said: 'It's not like that. Just remember the next time you see someone come here like you. You pitch in something.'"

(continued p.182)

Yes, I can receive as many photos as you send. My only problem is that I can't keep them all, because of our limited storage. But please send them. I would be delighted to travel with you through your photographs. There are days, even weeks, when I do not see outside of these walls. All the colors are the same, white and gray. Through your pictures, I enter a world of colors. Thank you, Eve. I'm glad you purchased your finest camera yet and decided to continue to take pictures. Now you are sharing your talent with me, someone who is only able to see the world's beauty in pictures. I keep looking at the picture of the small church and the sky above. It is a very beautiful photograph. It has been a long time since I saw a sky like that.

I'm glad you went to the website *[www.rogermcgowen.org]*. Ginger did a wonderful job. I have been very blessed to be surrounded by so much love coming from so many beautiful people. Everyday I thank God and everyday I try to do something to spread the love and joy I feel to someone. We are all the same. We all come from one source, and will return to the same One. So when we reach out to help others, we help ourselves. *(October 23, 2003)*

In a letter to Roger written after his book was published in French, I told him that readers were sending in funds for his defense. The following letter came in response to this news and to the examples I gave him of the amazing inner healing the book was generating in many readers.

There are times when our sunny days are not as sunny as we would wish them to be. There have been times when I have really felt great about everything. All of creation seemed to be in harmony with my center. I stop and look around and know in my heart of hearts that there is much, much more than we believe there is. It is as if I had tapped into a source of truth and realization that is blinding, and I have been literally high from this source. And then I witness man's cruelty to man and I come crashing down back into the illusion. And I wonder: why can't everyone feel the love? Where has their humanity gone?

I sometimes feel so sad, Pierre, that I wonder how long I can stand it.

Then someone will send me a "kite" - a small note under the door, telling me they are hungry, or asking if I can help them to write a letter, or to just talk to them because they are lonely. And then I understand I have no other option open before me but to wipe my tears and keep smiling, because my strength does not lie in me: it lies in my ability and desire to assist others.

So at times I get discouraged, my step falters, and my voice trembles, but I will never give up hope, although at times I do ask myself: why do I hold on so tight? Then I see the faces and smiles of my friends. I love you and Elly very much, you are a part of my family now, and in families we sometimes lean on one another. Thank you for your shoulder. I feel your embrace. Thank you for holding me while I weep...

Ramirez letter (continued)

"I sat there on my bunk with my brown paper bag of goodies, and thought about what had just happened to me. The last thing I expected to find on death row was kindness and generosity. I thought of how many times I had seen "good people" of the world pass [by] some man, woman or child holding up a sign that read: "Hungry," or "Will work for food." I'm guilty of the same. I just passed them by. By the end of the block, or upon reaching my destination, that poor, hungry, tattered and perhaps dirty soul had been forgotten, lost among my daily challenges and struggles for life. Yet, here on death row, amongst the worst of the worst, I didn't have to hold up a sign.

They knew what I needed and they took upon themselves to meet those needs.

They did this without any expectation of reimbursement or compensation.

They did this for a stranger, not a known friend. I don't know what they felt when they committed this act of incredible kindness. I only know that like them, twelve "good people" had deemed me beyond redemption. The only remedy that these "good people" could offer us was death. Somehow what these "good people" saw and what I was seeing didn't add up. How could these men, who just showed me so much humanity, be considered the 'worst of the worst'? …

What's in the brown paper bag? I found caring, kindness, love, humanity."

About Luis Ramirez

Luis Ramirez was convicted of a capital murder (for hire) in San Angelo, Texas, in 1998. In this case, the state offered no tangible evidence to support the conviction. They had no DNA evidence, no physical evidence, no scientific evidence, no eyewitnesses, no murder weapon, and they could not place him at the crime scene. They relied primarily on the hearsay testimony of a *paid* informant. The informant was a self-described daily drug user. He was not someone Mr. Ramirez knew, nor did he know Mr. Ramirez.

In the courtroom, the informant was not able to identify Mr. Ramirez when he was sitting in front of him. Basically, the informant's testimony was about something he had heard. He offered no firsthand knowledge of the offense and even less regarding the alleged remuneration. The informant never said that he heard Mr. Ramirez offer anything, or saw him pay anything. And the state had absolutely no evidence to support this claim. The victim was a complete stranger to him. Luis adamantly maintained his innocence from the onset.

(Source: above-mentioned internet link)

Note: Napoleon Beazley, the death row inmate who first reached out to Ramirez, was executed May 28, 2002.

This is great news, Pierre. Finally, all the work put into the book can begin to help and heal those who read it. This IS great news! I am very excited about it. I knew it would be coming out, but I did not believe it would hit me like this. We all go through what we go through for a reason, don't we? We reach people in different ways, at different times.

I shared my feelings about death and dying with Monica – such a beautiful person, I love her gentleness – and how I had been able to look beyond the veil **and see not really death but a returning.**

Warden[X] left, and we received a warden named [Y]. He seems to be a pretty reasonable man, so we figured we finally had a decent warden. Then they sent us another person, who really runs the building. He hadn't been here two weeks before he had the officers writing major disciplinary cases [against the inmates] for anything, like having a [forbidden] rubber band and paper clips, for throwing any kind of trash on the cell floor, for placing small curtains over the opening in the door while we are using our toilets to show respect for the female officers. No pictures or calendars are allowed on the walls. I could go on and on about how we are being harassed with no reason.

We are trying to get all our family and friends to bombard the head warden with phone calls asking him why he is allowing this person to constantly harass for no reason. The sergeant has already told us that any case a death row inmate gets is to be upgraded to a major case, thereby ensuring that the concerned inmate will be put in solitary.

It has been hell, here, Pierre. So we are trying to get something done. We are hoping if enough people contact the warden, he will rein this major in before things get any worse. *(November 2, 2003)*

In the weeks that followed the previous letter, reader response to Roger's book grew, and he started receiving mail from innumerable readers in many countries as far away as Lebanon and sub-Saharan Africa. Monasteries began saying masses for him. School children took up writing letters and making drawings to send him. Magazines and newspapers carried reviews about the book, and I was invited to speak about Roger on talk shows. A Swiss distributor selected the book among thousands to be sold in post offices along with a few dozen other titles. As I write (early 2008) the stream of letters continues.

Do you know what a bird *really* is?

A Swiss journalist who accompanied me on my 2004 visit to Roger commented: "Roger explained to me how he had spent ten minutes looking at a bird from the slit in his wall that serves as a window: *'An officer made fun of me,' explained Roger, 'but he does not realize what a real marvel a simple bird is. And yet he sees them every day.'*

"Before returning to his cell, his eyes shining with amused curiosity, Roger looks at my digital camera and my Palm [Pilot]. He asks me, 'What are those things?' A question which reminds me that for 17 years he has been completely cut off from the world (Didier Bonvin, in *Le Matin Dimanche*, April 4, 2004).

One woman phoned from Brussels and told me she was going to take a crash course in English so as to be able to visit Roger. A French inmate incarcerated for a serious offense read the book three times, started corresponding with Roger, and then organized a collection among fellow inmates of his prison for the Women's World Summit Foundation mentioned in Roger's book. People everywhere pray for him daily. When I visited him in October, 2007, he was writing innumerable letters, and often did not have the stamps or time to respond to all the mail he was receiving.

Especially touching is the way Roger's example inspires people to improve their own daily behavior, like the gentleman who wrote that he stopped killing insects (something Roger mentions in one of his letters), or the teacher who said she's learning to be more patient and less irritable.

The rare combination of gentleness and towering strength, childlike trust and unshakable faith, humor and profound wisdom, and above all forgiveness and unconditional love expressed in Roger's letters continues to touch thousands – if one measures by book sales. It seems fitting to include at least a very small sampling of excerpts from the countless letters and emails I have received – and to place them on the same side of the book as Roger's letters. They give a modest idea of the kind of inspiration Roger brings to people in very different circumstances, and how, through his example, all are inspired to live better, more courageous, and loving lives:

Tell Roger how he fills my heart. It was so thirsty, and he soothes it by the purity of his love. He gives me the most unexpected gift. I feel blessed. Roger's letters have reawakened my faith. I have started again to pray, and I again meet God in my prayers. I now feel I can move mountains and be an instrument in God's hands. Tell Roger I have never felt so motivated to learn English!! *(R.A., France, nurse)*

Today I made a modest payment for Roger's defense. I am an old lady with a tiny pension, my modest means do not enable me to give more, but I am happy to participate. *(M.O. Switzerland)*

I believe in the miracle of having Roger come here one day to speak about the power of Love, which alone is capable of saving the world. In two weeks, our school will undertake a trip to Chechnya and Belgium, where we will visit prisons and bring Roger's message. *(M-C.B., private French school)*

It has been a long time since I have read a book with such fascination and emotion. You and Roger can add me to a long list of people who have been profoundly touched by what Roger writes. It so happens that I am in the middle of quite a complicated situation at work with a very difficult boss.

The last 24 hours

In the last 24 hours of his life, the inmate awaiting execution can receive the visits of his close family, a spiritual advisor, attorneys and, finally, friends. These visits take place in the death watch area or a special room. The following describes what happens in many states in preparation for the execution, although the order and exact events may vary from state to state:

- Last meal is provided - if possible, to suit the last requests of the prisoner. In Texas, it is served mid-afternoon.
- The warden and state-appointed chaplain visit and stay with inmate until the end of the execution.
- Witnesses arrive and are usually confined to a witness room, which has a glass viewing window facing the execution room. Witnesses often include relatives of the victim, friends/relatives of the inmate, and an official group of "reputable citizens," media representatives, prison guards, etc. Relatives of the victim are sometimes (but not always) placed in a different room than those of the prisoner. In Texas, the inmate may have a maximum of five pre-approved witnesses, and the victims the same number. Once the witnesses are in place, the warden allows the condemned person to make a last statement.
- The inmate makes final preparations, which vary from state to state (shower, clean clothes, etc).
- The inmate waits in the death watch cell with a spiritual advisor until the warden orders him to be brought to the death chamber minutes before execution (hence the expression "dead man walking.") Once attached to the gurney, the inmate is connected to an electrocardiogram (ECG) machine, which will be monitored by the medical personnel until a flat line indicates that death has occurred.
- Some execution chambers have a one-way mirror (witnesses see the inmate but not vice-versa), others a clear window. Once the IV's are inserted into the veins, the curtain covering the window is usually drawn.
- After the execution, witnesses are escorted out of the prison, and the state witnesses sign a document stating that the execution effectively took place.
- After the inmate is pronounced dead, the body is removed from the execution chamber and delivered to a local funeral home for burial by the family or the state. The inmate may request that his body be donated to the state anatomical board for medical research purposes.

(Source: www.usatoday.com/news/science/stuffworks/2001-05-10-lethal-injection. htm and TDCJ execution procedures)

Last week, I was ready to quit, but Roger's letters, and talks with my wife and a friend made me think again. If someone facing so much more adversity can forgive, not hate, and bless his adversaries, than surely it is possible for me in much easier circumstances to follow his example. *(M.C., UK)*

I am a photographer and am going to take part in an Art Forum. I would so like to be able to help raise funds for Roger's defense, so I have decided I will turn over the totality of the profits of my photo sales during this forum. *(E.F., Switzerland)*

I am unable to work due to cancer. Specialists give me few chances of surviving, but Roger's example impels me forwards. I do not complain. Like him, I thank God daily for all the good with which He blesses me. I would consider it indecent to complain. My life is under menace – his too. But I at least can move around freely. Roger is in the purest divine light. He has become Christ-like, and I assure you he never leaves my thoughts. *(A.L., Belgium)*

Your book is very moving. What struck me most is the courage with which you face the very hard conditions which life has imposed on you. No one can rob you of your moral courage. *(K.S., Burkina Faso, West Africa, letter to Roger)*

I am presently devouring Roger's book. I so admire his manner of thinking and his common sense despite being in such a sordid place. With a friend we are going to prepare a talk for school. In your next letter, please greet him on my behalf and tell him that many people uphold him. *(Emma, 13 years, Switzerland)*

You have given Roger to us as an elder brother, a light in our lives… or rather, he makes us enter into his light. *(M-C, a nun in a Catholic convent)*

I am a simple grandmother. I have read most of your books, and Messages de vie du couloir de la mort [the title of Roger's book in French] moved me to the depths of my being. Concerning Roger, I believe the only way to help him is to pray for those who condemned him, that their compassion may be awakened. I have his picture in my room, and, sometimes, when something futile enters my life, I ask him how he manages. I just look at his face with its wonder-filled smile. . . . What greatness. *(M.F. Switzerland)*

Please tell Roger that in my daily life I feel that I am a prisoner of certain reactions, be they simple irritation to outright anger, and that his example inspires me to free myself from these limits on loving. As for the affection he so cruelly lacks, I commit myself to expressing as much of this affection as possible in lieu of the affection he never received. *(C.V., France)*

A book that heals

An acquaintance of mine in Geneva, Switzerland, a businessman, facing problems with the tax authorities and a lawsuit born of tax evasion and other questionable financial deals, was wrestling with aggressive attacks of depression. He decided to visit a local doctor, expecting the MD to prescribe some antidepressants. As he poured out his tale of woe, the doctor listened attentively.

When my friend finished his story, the doctor said, "I'm not going to prescribe you any antidepressants. Instead, I'm prescribing this." Then, taking out his prescription pad, he wrote down the title of Roger's book and said, "Read this. It will help you."

My friend was both completely perplexed and angry. He had not come to the doctor for literature, but for powerful pills! Nonetheless, he finally purchased the book and read it – and pulled out of his depression. He told me few books had had such an impact on him in his life.

I was so impressed I visited the MD to check the story with him. He confirmed it.

I was strolling through the bookstore when my eyes lit on the beautiful photo [of Roger on the book cover]. I purchased the book, which I read as a prayer. It is both a revelation and a teaching. How could we ever complain. Roger McGowen is a luminous being who moves me deeply. I do not pray that he may be free, for he is already – that freedom of which no one can rob him. But I pray that American law recognizes his dignity and his innocence, and that it may one day become more human and more just. *(F.S, e-mail, no country of origin indicated)*

A week ago, I purchased Roger's book at the post office. After reading the book, I took my rosary and, for the first time in my life, prayed with real heart and in deep communion with God. I later returned to the post office and bought all the remaining copies to give to others. I would like the whole world to know Roger. Since reading his letters, I think of him every day. *(M.T., Switzerland)*

This is an extraordinary story you have shared with us. It gave me the greatest kick in the pants I ever received in my life! Both a lesson and an example to follow. I no longer see life in the same manner. The book has put many things into question. *(Unsigned letter with a donation)*

I was deeply touched by Roger's book. I never realized that there were people who suffered as much on this earth. I cried, so deeply did I feel for Roger and the other inmates. I would like you to tell him that he is the most humble, gentle, tolerant, and magnanimous of persons. Tell him that when one has faith, one has everything, and that I am sure God is preparing something wondrous for him in the coming years. I am a Muslim, and since reading his letters, I have started praying for him five times a day. *(S.L., student from Senegal, W. Africa)*

This book of your correspondence with Roger McGowen is so powerful I simply lack words to express what I feel. Please tell Roger that since reading his book I leave spiders alone at home, and that it has become very difficult for me, even impossible, to complain. *(O.C., Switzerland)*

Thank you, Pierre, for enabling me *[via the book]* to feel useful, to feel that I am contributing something back to humanity.

I have been getting letters and cards from so many people, all of them thanking me, saying beautiful things about you, me, and the book. People are placing the book on their web sites, telling friends, co-workers, and family about it. One young girl from Lebanon said she was going to give the book to her brother who is very bitter and filled with hate and revenge. I do not know what to say, except that many letters brought tears to my eyes.

> *"Some day,*
> *after we have mastered the winds,*
> *the waves, the tides and gravity,*
> *we shall harness…*
> *the energies of Love.*
> *Then, for the second time*
> *in the history of the world,*
> *man will have discovered fire."*
>
> (Teilhard de Chardin)

I try not to complain, because I realize how bad others have it, but the situation has become worse here. The officers have been given quotas concerning the number of cases[25] they must write up per day. They are turning many cases death row inmates receive into major cases, meaning you can be sent to level two or three for anything. Regardless of how hard we try to get along, they will not leave us [in peace]. But I will do my best to follow their rules and regulations.

Yes, I too have been praying for, and blessing, President Bush. We can only overcome hate with love. Not only do we all need it, we all deserve it. Bin Laden, Saddam Hussein, and George [W.] Bush are human and God's creatures and deserve love as we all do. *(November 23, 2003)*

Merry Christmas and Happy New Year! May your light never dim in God's eyes, and may the peace that you work so hard to bring to the world never leave you. God sent you to me because I needed you. God knows what we need, and when we need it.

I have been receiving so many cards and letters that I have not had time to read them all. Just tonight I received 10 letters from people who had read the book.

It seems the administration has given the officers quotas for the number of cases they should write up weekly, maybe even daily. But many of them despise the ranking officers in general. When the last warden, and the last major, left, there were not many people on level three. (That is where you are placed in a cell, 24 hours a day, with nothing but your mattress, sheets, and jumper. No radio, coffee pot, fan or anything else). Level 3 is supposed to be reserved for violent offenders, i.e. offenders who continue to break rules, and this is how it is applied to general population. But here on death row, ranking officers have been told that any case given on death row is to be automatically upgraded to a major case, ensuring a finding of guilty and transferral to Level 3.

You can't have a family picture or calendar on the walls. If caught, major case. The water faucets in the day rooms are broken and have been so since we arrived here. So, we used to take bottled water with us to the day rooms so we could have water to drink while exercising. Not any more. New orders: no water in day room, or outside. If caught: major case. If it's freezing and raining outside, and we get caught with something on our head, major case.

---

25   A "case" is an infraction of the prison rules by an inmate, which can be as minor as leaving a book they are reading on their bed when they go to the shower (instead of putting it back on the shelf), hanging a towel to dry in an unauthorized manner (e.g. spreading it on the cell floor), etc. Levels two and three are sections of death row where the rules are much harsher.

"I have seen the truth.
It is not as though I had invented it with my mind.
*I have seen it, **seen it**,*
And the living image of it has filled my soul
Forever …
In one day,
In one hour,
Everything could be arranged
At once!
The chief thing is to love."

(Fyodor Dostoevsky)

It was raining and freezing outside, but I just needed some fresh air. We have small rain-resistant coats with small, thin caps on the back against the rain, but it does nothing to protect from the cold. When the officer came to put me out for recreation at 7.30 a.m., it was cold and drizzling outside. I had a small bottle of hot coffee in my hand as usual. The officer, who is a good and decent man as many of them here, said: "McGowen, you can't carry any more liquids outside. Prison regulations."

I put the coffee down, and after being strip-searched and dressing again, he noticed the small knit cap I wore on my head. He said, "Sorry, Mac, you can't take your hat anymore." I replied, "You know it's cold and raining, and that I am diabetic." He said: "Yeah, I know, but they are writing cases on us and docking us off pay if we do not write you guys up."

Many of the employees who work here are decent men and women. We can't deny that. But it is the rules they are made to enforce, even when they know they are wrong, that make many of the prisoners dislike them. Many of the officers are angry with the inmates for not getting involved themselves. Some officers tell the prisoners to write up the ranking officers and get their families involved, but only a handful of us ever try to.

Well, Pierre, I have to get back to some of these letters and cards. *(December 30, 2003)*

2004

Thank you very much for the money you collected and sent me. This enabled me as usual to buy enough food from commissary to fix sandwiches and feed everyone in our section. In spite of all the harassment, we were able to have a pretty good Christmas. We laughed, joked and made fun of one another, and celebrated the true meaning of Christmas by being love and giving love, because we knew that love was all we really needed.

I don't know what to say concerning all the beautiful words and beautiful letters I have been receiving. I'm just happy that the book has been well received. I feel so much love from so many people all around the world. Love: it is a wonderful thing. There is nothing to compare to it.

So I am trying even harder to show and give love to all, and I see more of the guys here doing the same. It is not always easy, Pierre, and I guess that is what makes it worthwhile.

"God has sustained me thus far.

He has never given up on me, and I will never give up on Him. I was not convicted by God's law. It was man's laws that unjustly convicted me, and they hold no sway over me. They are executing a friend of mine tonight, and they have another of my friends scheduled to be executed tomorrow. These are men's decisions, not God's."

(Roger McGowen, February 11, 2004)

"In his State of the Judiciary address to the Legislature this year [2007], *Texas Supreme Court Justice Wallace Jefferson spoke about 'the unfortunate reality that our criminal justice system, on rare occasions, convicts the innocent. I recognize that the convicted often falsely claim to be innocent, but we know, right here in Texas, that some of our inmates have been exonerated by DNA testing. I cannot imagine wasting away in a prison for a crime I did not commit. Can you? The Legislature should establish a commission to study ways to free the innocent.'"* (Dallas Morning News, April 19, 2007)

A friend of mine who lives in the cell next to me told me after my radio broke down last week that he wanted me to take his. I refused because I know how he loves to listen to the news. He said, *"Roger, take my radio till you get a new one. You help every one around here, man. It's time someone helped you for a change."* I still did not take his radio, but I explained that I did not help people so that I could later claim their help. But I know what he meant. Everything we do will eventually be done to us.

Please thank your friend Antonio for the [quotations from] the Scriptures. I have always known that not only my judgment, but all our judgments rest in God's hand, and no matter what judgments man may render, God's judgment is last and final. I guess that's why I never envisioned myself being taken to Walls unit [in Huntsville] where executions are carried out. I hear guys saying all the time: *"I'll be dead next year,"* or, *"I know they are going to execute me."* I wonder what makes them say things like that. I have never entertained such a thought and never will. God has sustained me thus far. He has never given up on me, and I will never give up on Him. I was not convicted by God's law. It was man's laws that unjustly convicted me, and they hold no sway over me. They are executing a friend of mine tonight, and they have another of my friends scheduled to be executed tomorrow. These are men's decisions, not God's.

Yes, now is the day of salvation. There is no yesterday, and there is no tomorrow. Today is now, and our salvation is now. Any other time may be too late.

You asked me which books most influenced my life. I have, over the years here, read many books, and each in its own way gave me a piece to add to a larger puzzle. It was not necessarily books that influenced me. I lived around people who walked and talked love their entire lives, never wavering once, not even on their death beds.

However, I have read Neale Donald Walsh's *Friendship with God* and Eckhart Tolle's *The Power of Now* – and of course your book, *The Gentle Art of Blessing*. And the Bible has influenced me deeply. But what really influenced me was a speech given by Dr. Martin Luther King, Jr., entitled: *"Dr. King tried to love somebody."*

However, with me, it is mainly people who are my examples of love made manifest in their living.

Guess what? I am a grandfather! My son Roderick and his soon to be wife had a baby boy. I knew his girlfriend was pregnant last year, but we lost touch. Although I continued to write to him, I did not hear anything until December 23, when I received a birthday and grandpa card from Roderick, with pictures. I'm sending you and Elly a picture of my grandson, whose name is Roderick Jr.

I'm going to close now. It's cold here, as usual, it has been raining for days, and I have to fix something to eat. Never forget my love. Thank you for making the end of 2003 the best year in my life.[26] *(February 11, 2004)*

---

26   Roger is referring to the incredible impact of his book on the lives of so many people. His joy comes from having been able to help so many - while being on Death Row!

Getting the clearer vision

Barzan, a Zen monk, had not found enlightenment, even after many years of study and meditation. Then one day at the market, he heard a client say to a butcher: "Give me the best piece of meat you have."

"Every piece of meat here is the best piece," replied the butcher. "There is no piece of meat that is not the best."

With that, Barzan found enlightenment and went on to become a great teacher.

When you have accepted every moment as the best, that is enlightenment.

(Numerous sources)

Our book has given my life not only meaning but more hope for humanity, not because of anything I wrote or said, but because of what all the readers have written and said in their letters. I have never cried so much. I was so touched and filled with joy that I could not read most of the letters in one go. My love for humanity has never been stronger. So many beautiful souls! My only regret is that I was not able to answer every single letter.

I have to pray and meditate just about hourly, because it is almost impossible to follow any kind of schedule here. Every minute is a new reality that must be dealt with and prayed about. One learns to sort of pray on one's feet, so to speak. I am mostly praying for the same things: more love to be shared among mankind. I ask God to grant wisdom and insight to us all so that we may have a clearer vision to see beyond the illusion. I pray so much through the day that I do it unconsciously. I study my [daily] lessons from [the Bible and] Science and Health regularly now. I had been dropping back, then trying to keep up, because I had so much to do, but I'm back on track now. I try to keep from reading too much structured and organized religious material, because I feel in my heart I know what is expected of me by the Creator. *(February 17, 2004)*

I have still been getting letters from new friends who just discovered the book and wish to thank us both. I will send you letters from two ladies who take me for such beautiful nature walks.

I put in a request for a typewriter because there are many things happening here that need to be reported. For instance the water in the showers is so hot you cannot hold your hand under it. But they try to force us to shower in it. Whenever we say something about it, they say we are complaining. All we want is for the water to be at a reasonable temperature. Yesterday, when my neighbor got into the shower, the water was so hot, he was burned on his face, hands, and feet. We tried in vain to get him medical attention.

There are so many incidents of this nature happening now, it is almost impossible to report on them all. But they need to be documented, because cruelty of this magnitude should not go unchecked. The food seems to have gotten worse since our last visit. We laughed so hard at the food on our trays today that I had tears running down my cheeks.

They have been playing all sorts of little games with us to harass us, like telling us we are not going to be able to go to the store the next day. Then they wake us at 5 a.m., telling us they have changed their minds and that we can go, but that we only have fifteen minutes to make a [shopping] list. I just smile and do the best I can. I try to always prepare myself for their cunning. In the evening, I always pray asking God to give me the strength, courage, understanding, and patience to confront whatever the next day may bring. *(April 7, 2004)*

"*Even though the place where I am*
is called "Death Row"
I only think of life.
Death never crosses my mind."

(Roger McGowen, April, 2004)

To Eve

Thank you for your words of freedom for me. I am almost certain that one day it will come. Even though the place where I am is called "Death Row," I only think of life. Death never crosses my mind. So let us hope that, like you finding my book in a small shop, my never thinking of death is a good omen.

There is so much injustice in this world that it is a wonder more people have not lost hope. But many people believe in good, and hope for a better tomorrow. Unfortunately, it cannot be realized without action. If we do not do something to stop our elected officials, we are all doomed. But I am an optimist. I believe that the time is coming when every citizen of the world will stand up in the name of justice and hold their elected officials accountable.

Your letters bring me much sunshine. Thank you for taking the time and writing to me. You can never know what you give to a person who sits in a small cell 23 hours out of 24. Letters are like rain on a hot, dry day. Many of my ideas are considered utopian, and why shouldn't they be? Don't we all basically want the same thing? And as long as you believe, you can make a difference. Your warm words of love and freedom are soothing. Like yourself, I believe that if enough people dream and hope and visualize, then anything can become a reality.

I rarely think of man's justice, because in the end, only cosmic and divine justice will stand the test of truth and time.

Eve, I must close this letter but never my friendship. I have been deeply touched by your very beautiful words. I will keep you in my heart, mind and prayers. You are a gem in this world and the sun shines bright because you are in it. Have peace, my friend. *(April, 2004)*

We are on another lockdown, eating cold peanut butter sandwiches and whatever they can't feed [general] population. Things have gotten worse, if you can believe that. Our property has been restricted even farther. They have been tearing the cells up daily, and we have been almost banned from commissary.

A song to love

The following passage is one of the most famous texts on love in the world of spiritual literature.

"If I speak with the eloquence of men and of angels but have no love, I become no more than blaring brass or crashing cymbal. If I have the gift of foretelling the future and hold in my mind not only all human knowledge but the very secrets of God, and if I also have that absolute faith which can move mountains but have no love, I amount to nothing at all. If I dispose of all that I possess, yes, even if I give my own body to be burned but have no love, I achieve precisely nothing.

This love of which I speak is slow to lose patience — it looks for a way to be constructive. It is not possessive. It is neither anxious to impress nor does it cherish inflated ideas of its own importance.

Love has good manners and does not pursue selfish advantage. It is not touchy. It does not keep account of evil nor gloat over the wickedness of other people. On the contrary, it is glad with all good men when truth prevails.

Love knows no limits to its endurance, no end to its trust, no fading of its hope; it can outlast anything. It is, in fact, the one thing that still stands when all else has fallen.

All gifts except love will be superseded one day.

For if there are prophecies, they will be fulfilled and done with, if there are "tongues" the need for them will disappear, if there is knowledge it will be swallowed up in truth. For our knowledge is always incomplete and our prophecy is always incomplete, and when the complete comes, that is the end of the incomplete.

When I was a little child, I talked and felt and thought like a little child. Now that I am a man, my childish speech and feeling and thought have no further significance for me.

At present we are men looking at puzzling reflections in a mirror. The time will come when we shall see reality whole and face to face! At present all I know is a little fraction of the truth, but the time will come when I shall know it fully as God knows me!

*In this life we have three great lasting qualities — faith, hope and love. But **the greatest of them is love**"* (I Corinthians 13, J.B. Phillips translation, emphasis added).

It has gotten so bad that officers are talking about quitting. What they are doing is human rights abuse. No one here cares, Pierre. The inmates are getting angry and restless, and something has got to give. They have taken everything. They won't let us use clotheslines, and they are taking all of our drinking containers without providing any others. Everything they give death row is filthy – sheets, towels, underwear, it all looks as if it had been dragged through the mud. We show it to them and they laugh at us and then come and confiscate our cleaning supplies!

For Memorial Day, they cooked barbecued ribs for everyone in the prison, including officers. But death row got boiled chicken that was literally ground up in a grinder with all the bones still in it! When we showed it to the officers and told them it was uneatable, they laughed and said, "Write the kitchen." How can people be so cruel? Why can't people be civil to each other?

I don't hate them, because for them to do what they are doing, it is clear that they hate themselves more than I ever could. And besides I don't have the energy to hate. *(May 9, 2004)*

I received two more letters [from readers of the book] last night. Both are beautiful and warm. I will never lose my faith in the beauty and compassion of the spirit. We inspire one another to walk a little farther, smile a lot longer, and love just a little easier.

Yes, I truly feel something spectacular is happening with our book. So many wonderful and courageous people have been writing to me, telling me how the book has helped them heal wounds from years and years ago. God is moving this book, Pierre. I have received many cards with no address on them from nuns and priests explaining that they are saying mass for me. I feel blessed, and I feel happier than I ever was. I feel so much energy and love. Have you ever felt love so strongly that you just wanted to hug someone? I often do.

Yes. Thank you for the blessings and love you sent me from [spiritual healer] Jill G. I have never forgotten her since you mentioned her to me. She is constantly in my prayers, and her prayers have been felt and acted upon. I can't tell you the feeling of knowing someone, somewhere, is calling on God, not for themselves or for some selfish need, but to deliver us *[death row inmates]*.

Yes. I truly believe everything she says. Love is opening prison doors. Love is the key that will unlock the door to the coldest, cruelest heart. Love is more alive here than any other place on earth. The guys here simply show it in peculiar ways. Love has indeed given me wings so that I can fly spiritually over these walls. Love is indeed the key to opening spiritual doors.

A grandmother's letter about Roger's impact on her life (written to Pierre)

"I am a simple grandmother who appreciates you a great deal for all you are undertaking. So I am writing to encourage you to continue. I have most of your books, which I read and reread to open my consciousness to the love of others.

Messages de vie du couloir de la mort [this book's French title] *especially moved me to the depths of my being. Every day, I send Roger a good thought. On Easter Sunday, I was deeply moved when I saw the newspaper article [on your visit to death row]*. The world has to know what is happening, but few people are concerned with the sufferings of others, and they forget rapidly. However, one can be grateful that some at least persist in their search for justice, truth and love, which enables the world to continue.*

Roger is like a brother for me, and I believe that the only way of helping him is to pray for a change of consciousness of those who condemned him. Roger is spiritually very advanced. I have his picture in my room, and sometimes, when I am burdened by some trivial event of everyday life, I ask him how he manages. I look at his wonder-filled smile — what greatness. One says that all suffering generates growth — how true that is.

Here is my modest message of peace:

If you think that a smile is more powerful than a weapon,
If you believe in the power of an extended hand,
If you can look at your brother with a touch of love,
If you prefer hope to suspicion,
If you can rejoice in your neighbor's joy,
If the stranger is for you a brother in disguise,
If you can give of your free time out of love,
If when you share your bread, you can add to it a part of your heart,
If you believe that forgiveness goes further than vengeance,
If you can listen to some unfortunate one who is taking your time and keep smiling at him,
If your neighbor is first and foremost a brother for you,
If you believe that peace is possible -
Then peace will come.

With my most sincere regards, I send you all the peace in the world."

J.F.

*) In a Geneva, French-speaking newspaper.

Yes. I too believe that we are all where we are needed at this moment. The universe allows us to choose our own paths, knowing that the only true path is love, and that all paths ultimately lead back to Divine Love.

I'm happy to hear about your American publisher showing interest in [an American edition of] our book. Americans are beautiful people, open to most methods of spiritual healing.

Sorry not to have answered you sooner, but I have no stamps. We have not been able to make store in three weeks. We are all out of stamps. My neighbor gave me what was left of his. I would have thought they would have by now run out of ideas on how to harass us. But to their credit, they are relentless. They even sell us items, which we keep for a month, sometimes a year, and then they tell us we are not allowed to use them anymore!

Thank you for sharing the letter of the grandmother with me. I'm so very touched by the letters from readers. Sometimes I can't read them in one go. This grandmother is my inspiration, the way she explains we cannot give without leaving something behind.

How is Elly? Please give her a hug and kiss from me and tell her she is my hero. *(May 11, 2004)*

Yes, I certainly do believe that God is moving our book. It has taken on a life of its own, and with God's guidance, it is finding its way where it is needed. We were both vessels for a message of love, peace, and renewal. People want to know that love is still alive and breathing, that miracles exist, and that we are all blessed, whether we realize it or not. The world is in a very confused state right now and people are searching for answers. They know the answers are there and they are determined to find them.

Often I receive cards and short notes saying: "We are praying for you, and don't give up," so I am constantly floating on prayers. Every letter I receive from a reader of the book floats my being. The world is populated with so many beautiful people, isn't it?

The treatment of the prisoners has gotten so bad that someone is going to have to intervene before this prison explodes. You can't constantly keep taking and taking without eventually giving something back. When you do, you create an imbalance. Imbalance is a sign of imperfection, and imperfection does not last long. Balance will, given time, reassert itself.

> *"Everything can be taken from a man*
> *but one thing:*
> *the last of the human freedoms —*
> *to choose one's attitude,*
> *to choose one's way."*
>
> (Victor Frankl, *Man's Search for Meaning*)

> *"Though the good man may fall seven times,*
> *he is soon up again"*
>
> (Proverbs 24:16)

> *"My grace is sufficient for thee:*
> *for my strength is made perfect*
> *in thy weakness"*
>
> (2 Corinthians 12:9, L. Second translation)

They have taken everything. On top of that, we have to near cause a riot just to go to commissary. They have literally begun to systematically starve us. It has been very difficult these last two years, and it does not seem to get any better with the passing of time. At times, I find myself staring out into space, thinking, wondering, and amazed at how vigilant these people are at keeping the hate permeating through this environment. Because they do a good job of it. We went through a terrible lockdown. Prayer is my only weapon, but after a while I feel even prayer has lost its luster. *But I continue.*

I love you dearly, my brother. Do not waste your time being concerned about me. I'll manage. God hasn't let me down yet. Sometimes I'm just impatient. My love flows to you from the only eternal source. *(July 27, 2004)*

To Eve

Every time there is a lockdown we all suffer. I guess anything, even the most unpleasant situation, can be made somewhat tolerable, if it is done in a more or less civil manner or without malice and ill intentions. But the officers treat you and your meager belongings as if you and your property were garbage. We are not considered people. I told one of the female sergeants: *"We do not have to treat one another as if we were animals. Let us be civil to one another throughout this ordeal."* She just looked at me as if I had spoken Klingon (a language from Star Trek). She took all of my food, eight of my books, and many other items that she could have left. She tried to make the entire experience as unpleasant as possible. So, I lost a lot that day, but I smiled at her throughout the entire ordeal. I won't allow them to break me. *(August 28, 2004)*

Yes, "they" (the prison officials) had begun to starve us by continuing to cut back the caloric intake from our daily meals. Pierre, I believe that we are below 1600 calories. If we are lucky, we get meat twice a month, and they have emptied commissary of just about all the meat. All they sell is tuna and chicken Vienna, which are rarely in stock. I got my lunch tray a moment ago. It contained one spoon of spinach, a couple of ranch style beans, a few green peas mixed with carrots, a bean burrito, and some plain white rice. They put very little on the dinner trays, and they have stopped selling any healthy foods in the commissary.

It's very hard to explain to you what they are doing. While they were deliberately keeping us hungry, the officers had a barbecue pit set up outside on the lawn next to our building, and for the last two weeks they have been barbecuing and eating in front of the inmates! Most people wouldn't believe that.

You get what you pay for: Texas prison guards among the worst paid in the United States

Pay starts at $1,870 per month and reaches a maximum of $2,773 after eight years. Officers get just a five and a half-week on-the-job training – and that for an extremely challenging job that requires a real knowledge of human psychology and behavior.

At the end of March, 2007, for the 153,000 inmate population of Texas, the number of prison personnel was twelve percent short of normal requirements. For years prisons have been chronically short of correctional officers, and turnover rates are very high, which is a bad sign in any system. In 2004, over twenty percent of the correctional officer workforce quit, an extremely high turnover.

The result is disastrous. It means one has to constantly train a new workforce. This is costly, inefficient, and dangerous. Having a critical mass of qualified staff is essential, given the nature of prison work. With new and inexperienced personnel always on the job, safety suffers.

The virtual elimination of overtime pay in recent years has only made things worse. Without the allure of a better paycheck through overtime, many officers are not volunteering extra hours, so prison authorities must force staff to work longer hours.

Another serious syndrome of the Texas prison system is the very high rate of arrests among prison guards. The number of arrests has increased steadily for much of the past decade, peaking at 781 in 2003 (latest statistics available as of end 2007). In 2005, 761 were arrested. Guards are routinely arrested for sexual harassment or rape of inmates, and for providing weapons, drugs, intelligence, and other contraband (in exchange for money). In the fall of 2008, portable telephones were discovered in inmate cells at the Allan Polunsky death row.

State Sen. John Whitmire (D-Houston, Chairman of the Senate Criminal Justice Committee, which monitors Texas' corrections system) made the following revealing comment: *"Maybe it's bad luck, and maybe it's because we pay too little because we're 2500 correctional officers short all the time. I guess we can't be too choosy about who we hire. Maybe the problem is where we built all these prisons. Maybe there isn't anything else to do out there but get in trouble."*

The State of Texas as victim of its own prison system?

(Source: www.brokenchains.us/tdcj/txguards.html and www.gritsforbreakfast.blogs-pot.com/2006/04/prison-guards-arrested-at-record-pace.html)

Whom could we complain to when all the ranking officers are eating and fraternizing with the regular officers? One of the sergeants told us that it came from the very top, to treat us as badly and cruelly as they could. Every day here, the situation rises to a new level of cruelty.

They have recently changed the rules governing recreation. I explained to you the recreation schedule and how [on specific days] we are allowed to go outside in a concrete pen without a ceiling and with no shade, even when it gets really hot. On the other days, we recreate in the day rooms. But now, the person in charge is making the officers force us out on days that are not our scheduled days. If you do not want to, you get no recreation. For example, I was forced to go out for two weeks straight in the hot sun, without shade or cold water, stuck in this concrete pen with nothing but the hot sun for company. I told the sergeant, *"Every day on the radio they are giving ozone alerts, warning people to stay out of the sun, and only go out when and if necessary. And you are forcing me to stay out in the sun for sometimes two hours at a time with no shade?"* He shrugged his shoulders and said it was out of his hands, that he was made to do it. I pointed out to him that there were two empty day rooms right inside the door! He said the ranking officers told them not to put death row inmates in the day rooms any more, unless the room was in our section.

The sheets, towels, and jumpsuits we are forced to use are filthy, Pierre. You would not believe how filthy these things are. And when we complain they say that we "cry" too much. The water in the showers is so hot we cannot shower. There are so many atrocities that are being inflicted on us – I could go on and on. But why should I? As long as there is no oversight committee to keep them in check, they know they can do what they want and get away with it. They have to answer to no one.

And I can't speak rationally about the conditions we are subjected to because I'm caught in the middle. I just can't believe people will spend all of their time thinking of ways to further the suffering of people who have spent their whole life suffering. People are appalled by what is going on in the American prisons in Iraq, but there are worse atrocities being committed right here in Texas. Last week, two inmates attempted suicide the same day. And another inmate stabbed an officer in the neck several times because he had reached the end of his patience at having his cell torn apart every day. Twelve days later, in general population, an inmate killed another inmate in a knife fight. As I write this, they are under lockdown for this killing. No one is asking about the conditions that generate such inhuman actions. All people are saying is, "What animals." But the real question is: Who are the animals running these places and allowing such conditions? Every day the abuses mount.

When only love survived: A true story from Africa

In 1994, one of the worst massacres in African history took place in the civil war between Tutsis and Hutus in Rwanda. An estimated 800,000 people died, many killed in the most gruesome manner. School teachers massacred their students, and priests decimated their parishioners. Babies were murdered as mercilessly as adults. Gangs of ethnic killers roamed the streets day and night, entering homes and slaughtering whole families. An African spiritual healer, Ma Pululu Makengo, a very dear friend of a close friend of mine, experienced such an invasion. However, because of his keen sense of infinite Love's omnipotence, which he sees as the fundamental law governing reality, the outcome was different. In his words:

"One night, around two in the morning, an armed band entered my home. I awoke to see what was happening, and we came face to face in the corridor. They were armed with guns and bayonets; I was armed with Truth and Love. As they pointed their weapons to menace me, a thought came to me in a flash, immediately dispelling the fear that was attempting to invade my thought: Love and Life are indestructible and permanent. I am the idea of Life, God, indestructible in Life, permanent in my being. There is only one Life, God, which remains undivided, not two or more lives. This infinite Life is the life of these so-called killers, my life and that of my family."

Moment upon moment, this man continued to make spiritual affirmations based on his unwavering conviction that spiritual laws exist that enable one to meet and heal all situations. Quite a few times, disaster seemed imminent. At one moment, one of his daughters started crying, and the head of the band gave the order to kill her. Without saying a single word out loud, the healer immediately affirmed that the man who had received the order to kill was the perfect child of divine Love: *"The law of Love which is present here controls this situation and governs each and everyone."* Immediately the assailant, who had already raised his bayonet to pierce the girl, interrupted his gesture. Again, in the words of the spiritual healer:

"Each moment of this trial was precious for me. I did not allow myself the slightest mental distraction, to see the problem from a material angle. I constantly maintained my thought on the level of true spiritual reality. [...] After we had worked spiritually for about thirty minutes, those men became very calm, as if feeling the love we reflected. Their chief called them and they left our room. This gave me time to affirm still more forcefully the absolute truths about the perfect man of God's creation. When they came back into the room, these men were transformed. They had become new persons. Even their language had completely changed. They were disarmed and friendly, and started confessing the crimes they had committed. They stayed at our home for two hours. No one was hurt. Everyone was safe and sound."

(Source: P. Pradervand, *The Gentle Art of Blessing*, p.126-128)

These people force us outdoors, and when I say "force," I mean that after being locked in a room no bigger than the normal household bathroom, you're going to use any opportunity to move around and stretch your legs, as you only get that chance once a day. So we go out in the sun without a drop of cold water. Even animals are given cold water by their owners when left in the sun for too long.

I believe that in the end, all the suffering that we are going through will cease. Evil cannot last long before it begins to destroy itself. I keep repeating my mantra, "Only love survives," because in the end only love WILL survive. I do not hate the officers for what they do. I just can't understand how or why they do it, because if they knew the cosmic debt they are incurring, they would not do what they are doing. *(August 28, 2004)*

I asked Roger if he would be willing to pray for some Swiss school children who were undertaking an Easter preparation. His reply:

Of course I will be more than willing to carry these students in prayer. Prayer should be as natural as breathing, and to pray for others is automatic. I will be very happy to pray for the young people. I have so many people praying for me that I can actually feel the power. How can I not share something that belongs to us all?

Our book has been moving and doing remarkable things, transforming hate into love. I can't tell you how deeply touched I was to read your last letter with the article about the book, and all those inspiring and warm letters from readers. I was left speechless and could not even finish reading the letter. I had to take a moment to compose myself. God's hand was in this project since the beginning. There are so many people out there in this world waiting for someone, anyone, to speak the truth about Love. When was the last time you had a world leader speak of Love without expecting something back from it? People from all countries, ethnic backgrounds, and gender, are looking for a truth, the truth, the One. And they do not care who leads them to it, and that is where you come in. You have been given that job, and so have I - for the small part I played – to bring back Love, to bring them back to the only "One."[27]

I agree with having it [my book] published [in English], if God is behind it, and I'm sure He is. In this case nothing is going to stop it anyway.

---

27 This is just one example among many of Roger's amazing humility. The impact of this book is due 100 percent to the power of his non-violent demonstration of love and forgiveness – which is why people are so deeply moved. My role has essentially been one of a scribe – and selecting a few other elements of information to set his letters in a context that speaks to readers.

Leading Texas newspaper opposes death penalty

April 15, 2007, *The Dallas Morning* News ran the following editorial:

"Ernest Ray Willis set a fire that killed two women in Pecos County. So said Texas prosecutors who obtained a conviction in 1987 and sent Mr. Willis to death row. But it wasn't true. Seventeen years later, a federal judge overturned the conviction, finding that prosecutors had drugged Mr. Willis with powerful anti-psychotic medication during his trial and then used his glazed appearance to characterize him as 'cold-hearted.' They also suppressed evidence and introduced neither physical proof nor eyewitnesses in the trial, and his court-appointed lawyers mounted a lousy defense. Besides, another death row inmate confessed to the killings.

The state dropped all charges. Ernest Ray Willis emerged from prison a pauper. But he was lucky: he had his life. Not so Carlos De Luna, who was executed in 1989 for the stabbing death of a single mother who worked at a gas station. For years, another man with a history of violent crimes bragged that he had committed the crime. The case against Mr. De Luna, in many eyes, does not stand up to closer examination. There are signs he was innocent. We don't know for sure, but we do know that if the state made a mistake, nothing can rectify it.

And that uncomfortable truth has led this editorial board to re-examine its century-old stance on the death penalty. This board has lost confidence that the state of Texas can guarantee that every inmate it executes is truly guilty of murder. We do not believe that any legal system devised by inherently flawed human beings can determine with moral certainty the guilt of every defendant convicted of murder.

That is why we believe the state of Texas should abandon the death penalty because we cannot reconcile the fact that it is both imperfect and irreversible.

Flaws in the capital criminal justice system have troubled us for some years. We have editorialized in favor of clearer instructions to juries, better counsel for defendants, the overhaul of forensic labs and restrictions on the execution of certain classes of defendants. We have urged lawmakers to at least put in place a moratorium, as other states have, to closely examine the system. And yet, despite tightening judicial restrictions and growing concern, the exonerations keep coming, and the doubts keep piling up without any reaction from Austin.

From our vantage point in Dallas County, the possibility of tragic, fatal error in the death chamber appears undeniable. We have seen a parade of 13 men walk out of the prison system after years even decades of imprisonment for crimes they didn't commit. Though not death penalty cases, these examples, including an exoneration just last week, reveal how shaky investigative techniques and reliance on eyewitnesses can derail the lives of the innocent.

(continued p.212)

Tuesday, Texas released a guy named Ernest Willis from death row. I know him but have not seen him since about 89 or 90. Now, after spending 17 years on Death Row, the state is saying it is not sure a crime ever took place! So there is hope. God never sleeps. *(September 2004)*

[I shared with Roger the story of a friend, a spiritual healer, who was healed instantaneously of a rattlesnake bite, after all the usual symptoms of oncoming death had manifested themselves, through understanding one powerful spiritual truth really clearly]

The story about the friend of yours who was bitten by a rattlesnake is amazing. I have always believed in the power of healing. Healing is real because God is real, and when we become one with God, one with the spiritual mind, we can do incredible things. Thank you for sharing with me your spiritual treatment to help me find my way out of this delusion. All we do is in spirit. We just don't recognize it. God is Spirit, and we are in God, so all we do and attempt to do is spiritual. Faith certainly does move mountains and our combined faith can move this one. I'm at peace with the whole world and with God. *(October 9, 2004)*

The judge who presided over Roger's case until the summer of 2005 kept it inactive for eight years – possibly to protect Roger. Commenting on this judge, Roger said, "She seems to be a good person. I met her once. I do not want to try and outthink God. I believe she may not know why she is holding my case, but God certainly does."

Soon after his book came out in French, Roger was flooded with letters from readers, writing up to ten to twelve letters every night for days on end.

You have worked long and hard on the book. I really wish I could give you a hug. So many people have been reading and responding to it. I'm always touched to hear people express how the book changed their lives. Thank you for the pages from the website [letters from readers]. I have to stop reading them, because I get too emotional. Smile.

I'm on Level 2 right now. It means I'm restricted from making commissary for three months. I can't have any special visits.[28] I can only have two regular visits a month. I can buy only $10.00 worth of stamps every other week. So letters may be a bit slow. All of the officers are surprised I'm here on Level 2. But I do get the chance to see and talk to people I have not seen in years, and to meet new people. I have been stuck on the same pod around the same people for over four years. I needed a break, and I'm happy and I'm blessed. God is indeed a wonderful God. *(December 2, 2004)*

---

28   Special visits are visits from further than 300 miles. Regular visits are in a radius of 300 miles. All visitors must be on a list which is changed every six months.

Dallas Morning News editorial opposing deeth penalty (continued)

The Tulia and the fake-drug scandals have also eroded public confidence in the justice system. These travesties illustrate how greed and bigotry can poison the process.   It's hard to believe that such pervasive human failings have never resulted in the death of an innocent man. In 2001, Supreme Court Justice Sandra Day O'Connor said, **'If statistics are any indication, the system may well be allowing some innocent defendants to be executed.'**

Some death penalty supporters acknowledge that innocents may have been and may yet be executed, but they argue that serving the greater good is worth risking that unfortunate outcome. Supreme Court Justice Antonin Scalia argues that the Byzantine appeals process effectively sifts innocent convicts from the great mass of guilty, and killing the small number who fall through is a risk he's willing to live with. According to polls, most Texans are, too. But this editorial board is not.

Justice Scalia calls these innocents 'an insignificant minimum.' But that minimum is not insignificant to the unjustly convicted death row inmate. It is not insignificant to his or her family. The jurist's verbiage conceals. This marks a transgression against the Western moral tradition, which establishes both the value of the individual and the wrongness of making an innocent suffer for the supposed good of the whole. Shedding innocent blood has been a scandal since Cain slew Abel, a crime for which, the Bible says, God spared the murderer, who remained under harsh judgment.

This newspaper's death penalty position is based not on sympathy for vile murderers who, many most agree, deserve to die for their crimes but rather in the conviction that not even the just dispatch of 10, 100, or 1,000 of these wretches can remove the stain of innocent blood from our common moral fabric.

This is especially true given that our society can be adequately guarded from killers using bloodless means. In 2005, the Legislature gave juries the option of sentencing killers to life without parole.

The state holds in its hands the power of life and death. It is an awesome power, one that citizens of a democracy must approach in fear and trembling, and in full knowledge that the state's justice system, like everything humanity touches, is fated to fall short of perfection. If we are doomed to err in matters of life and death, it is far better to err on the side of mercy and caution. It is far better to err on the side of life. The state cannot impose death - an irrevocable sentence - with absolute certainty in all cases. Therefore the state should not impose it at all."

> *"What part of 'Thou shalt not kill'*
> *don't you understand?"*
> (God)

(From a letter to the editor, published in response to the above editorial in the *Dallas Morning News*, April 18, 2007)

To Eve (a young photographer who was so moved by Roger's book she organized a exhibition of her photos and donated all the proceeds for his defense).

Hello, how are you and your family? I hope you are well and living every moment that life blesses you with.

I really loved that photo of the beautiful purple mountains. I was wondering where you were standing when you took the photograph. Maybe I haven't received the photo you were talking about. I'm sorry to say I do not have that particular photo any more. It was destroyed November 25 during a shakedown and a move of my property. It may have been done on purpose, but since I was not there I can't be sure. But believe me when I say I looked at it as much as I could, picturing myself one day looking across at those same mountains.

Sometimes our callings in life are clear from the beginning, and sometimes we just awake one day and realize that our cause is to a higher calling, and what is higher than to be of service to those less fortunate? I'm happy you are sharing your photos with me because I love seeing them and knowing that, no matter what we are going through, there is still much beauty to behold. [We need to] open our eyes, not just look, but really see. Your photos bring all that beauty right here to me. I have never seen a real mountain, never held a snowball or looked down on a cloud. Your pictures allow me to do that, Eve. *(December 4, 2004)*

2005

To Monica

I hope you enjoyed your trip to Africa to visit your extended family. Sometimes we find the greatest riches in the poorest places. Riches do not bring happiness, only happiness brings riches. I am sure your extended family knows the difference. I would really love to meet them one day. People are not content in our consumer world because they look outside themselves to find completeness. They carry themselves to places outside the heart to find what makes the heart content, and when they cannot find what they seek, misery comes. It is a sad thing to behold.

Thank you and your extended family for singing Happy Birthday to me! I did imagine myself with you there. You describe a peaceful and tranquil place in the middle of so much violence. I am sure you have seen your share of the world's cruelties. I sometimes wonder how men can be so cruel to themselves. Whenever we harm one another, we harm ourselves.

George Bernard Shaw on being used for a purpose

(Something Roger attempts to live and calls on the younger generation to achieve)

"This is the true joy of life, the being used for a purpose recognized by yourself as a mighty one, the being a force of nature instead of a feverish selfish little clod of ailments and grievances complaining that the world will not devote itself to making you happy.

I am of the opinion that my life belongs to the whole community and so long as I live it is my privilege to do for it whatever I can.

I want to be thoroughly used up when I die, for the harder I work the more I live. I rejoice in life for its own sake. Life is no 'brief candle' to me. It is a sort of splendid torch which I have got hold of for the moment, and I want to make it burn as brightly as possible before handing it on to future generations."

Your faith and love give me faith to keep believing. Your love and support have kept me standing longer than you know. My prayers are always with you, Monica, whatever you do. You have a very beautiful heart. I wish I could embrace you and maybe I will one day. But until then I embrace you in mind and heart. *(January 9, 2005)*

In February 2005, I was asked to speak about Roger to an international youth meeting of young Christians known as Agape, held in Geneva. I asked Roger for a message for these young people:

It is an honor and a privilege to be able to speak to you. As I speak to you today, the world is in need of a love transfusion. The world is in turmoil. Wars are being fought in the name of religion. Children, the elderly, and disabled people are being forced out of their homes and made to sleep in the streets. Many go to sleep hungry. [...]

Do not be discouraged. God will never give us a weight to carry without first giving us the strength to carry it.

I have been on Texas death row for seventeen years. Oh, don't be sorry for me. God gave me the strength to carry my burden. I have lived and thrived on death row. Learning, growing and, most importantly, learning to love. Sometimes falling short, but never giving up – and neither should any of you. Love will never abandon you, and you should never abandon love.

You are love's only chance to bridge the gap between man and man, and between man and God. You are the vanguards of love. You must know that now is your time. You can be better and greater than any who came before you. Arm yourselves with God's Love and prepare to battle hate on every street corner in every country. We must never stop until we have eradicated hate. Hate knows no boundaries and we must show that Love doesn't either.

As our future leaders, it is you who will fight the good fight and you who must balance the scales and set right what is wrong. You must be courageous in spreading God's Love. You must show the world that we are better, kinder, and more merciful than we believe we are. We must remember to pass the love on.

To see as God sees

Science and Health refers to higher seeing in this way: *"The fading forms of matter, the mortal body and material earth, are the fleeting concepts of the human mind. They have their day before the permanent facts and their perfection in Spirit appear. The crude creations of mortal thought must finally give place to the glorious forms which we sometimes behold in the camera of divine Mind, when the mental picture is spiritual and eternal. Mortals must look beyond fading finite forms if they would gain the true sense of things. . . ."*

Shouldn't we always strive to be looking through *"the camera of divine Mind"* - the Mind that is God? This demands a change of standpoint, or rather thought-point. Instead of looking up to God as though He were distant and separate from us, earnestly petitioning Him to change or heal something, our need is to look out, in prayer, through that camera lens of the divine Mind. Then we'll see something of what God is seeing. And isn't God seeing only the expression of Himself - perfection, harmony and limitless good? The very first chapter of the Bible says, *"And God saw everything that He had made and behold, it was very good"* (Gen.1:31)...

So how is this made practical? Here's an illustration. A call came to a Christian Science practitioner from a woman in a public phone booth. She and her husband had been involved in a car crash. She was uninjured, but her husband was very seriously injured, and she asked the practitioner to pray for him. She then went on to describe the scene in front of her - the ambulance, broken limbs, blood, chaos, and pain. After the call, all the practitioner could think about was the terrible picture. It was very hard to pray, because those graphic images kept vividly recurring. Finally, in desperation, the practitioner prayed to God: *"Father, you are there. What are You seeing?"* Then, the most beautiful ideas about God's power and action came to him. He was certain that nothing was actually going on anywhere but God and His perfection. God was seeing *"everything that he had made, and, behold, it was very good."* Nothing could take place in the kingdom of heaven but harmony, peace, and orderly action.

As the practitioner stayed with these divine facts, and began knowing and seeing through "the camera of divine Mind," the disturbing images totally disappeared from his thought. Within twenty minutes, the woman called to say that her husband had been taken to the emergency ward of the hospital, but they could find nothing wrong with him and he had been discharged. They were on their way home" *(To See as God Sees* by Jill Gooding, *The Christian Science Journal*, February, 2001, pp. 12-13).

We must never be afraid to challenge hate! The nature of love is to be passed on. It has to grow – it can never be contained. Love is our only hope, love is our only way. We must never hate. Hate is not a natural emotion, only love is. Hate is not in me. I will never allow hate to win, and neither should you. Everyone of you should take Love to the streets, carry it at all times. We must begin now.

I love each one of you. Through you, Love lives, Love is alive in each of you. Always stand on Love's foundation. It's something we know will never shake or crumble.

Love is your right – claim it. Remember God lives in us all. Hate cannot exist where God abides. When you chose Love, you chose God. (*Roger McGowen's message to Agape, January 3, 2005*)

I'm out of solitary and back on Level 1. Sorry for the inconvenience, Pierre. I have so much to thank you for, my brother. The other day, I received the beautiful text *"Be Ye Thankful"* and *"To see as God sees,"* by our good friend Jill. Both are extraordinary testimonials. I enjoyed reading and reflecting on them.

Thank you for taking the message of my life and using it to help others. Our book has taken on an urgency and a life of its own.

I pride myself on being a humble but strong person. Sometimes it is hard to actually realize what one has been through - and one still is going through - unless one focuses on the negativity and unpleasantness of the experiences. I choose to focus on the blessings and the good that I know is here also.

There were two [suicide] hangings and an attempted hanging, all in the past two weeks. There is something terribly wrong in this place and no one seems to care. Many people can't take the isolation, they can't stand the silence, the total lack of respect shown here for the inmates. We just came off lockdown four days ago. We were locked down for thirteen days. During lockdowns, they show up with this little box and put all of your property into it. What doesn't fit, they destroy. They take lots of food from guys and throw it away. They take radios, coffee pots, and, can you believe it – this time they took tennis shoes from people! Its very bad and getting worse. They feed us as if we were animals. They serve us a little punch or tea, they won't even put sugar in anything. The food is always cold, and they serve just enough to keep the body functioning. So you can imagine how they feed us on level 2 or 3. It is almost certain we will see some more suicide attempts. I only hope someone will want to know what would make three young men take their lives in less than two months, and start an investigation. (*March 6, 2005*)

Blessing heals

My West African friend Mahmoudou, who runs a small NGO (non-government organization) near Mopti, Mali, had his life completely transformed by the practice of blessing. He shared numerous examples of its efficacy, such as the following story about two brothers:

Ahmed had developed the most incredible grudge against his younger brother Karim because he had refused to sell eight bags of rice to his elder brother for his third marriage. Over the years, Ahmed expressed growing hostility toward his younger brother, attacking him physically, even with a knife. The situation became so tense the family asked Karim to leave the village where he lived with his elder brother; he came to the small town of Mopti, where Mahmoudou lives. On September 2, 2005, Ahmed came to Mopti and shot Karim while he was eating. Karim was hit in the shoulder. Ahmed was arrested by the police, and Karim did all he could to free him, even selling his T.V. set so his elder brother could be released on bail. When Ahmed was freed, he swore he would kill his younger brother.

Karim met Mahmoudou in December and asked him what he could do. Mahmoudou suggested he simply bless his brother three or four times a day. He added that Karim might at the same time bless all those who were filled with hate like Ahmed.

Mahmoudou then left for a trip to Switzerland. On his return, in February, Karim came to his home at 2 a.m. because he was so eager to share what had happened. Only ten days after Karim had started blessing, a delegation of four people from the brothers' native village came to present Ahmed's excuses for the way he had treated his brother in the past years. Karim returned to their village, and now Ahmed does not miss a single opportunity to be of service to him. People could hardly believe such a long-standing feud could end so abruptly. Such is the power of blessing.

Personally, since I started blessing twenty years ago, I haven't had a single relationship problem which has not *sooner or later* been healed by this practice. If we create our own reality by our way of looking at the world, and attract events according to the energy we radiate, this law truly can be called scientific, in the sense that results are predictable, and that anyone applying the law of blessing sincerely and with perseverance will achieve the desired results if her or his intention is clear and honest. (These are the two fundamental characteristics of the scientific method: predictability of results if the scientist follows what is called a "protocol," i.e. a specific way of handling an experiment; and universality, i.e. anyone can reach these results, anywhere).

(From the postscript to the British version of *The Gentle Art of Blessing*. Note: For an exceptionally beautiful and inspired website on blessing, see: www.bettertobless.com).

I told Roger of an experience I had giving a talk in London on the power of blessing. Afterwards, a woman participant went home on the subway and started chatting with a young man. They got on so well they continued talking on the platform when they got out. The man saw a friend of his and called him over. The three continued talking, then the woman left. After just a few steps, she realized the second young man had stolen her purse. Rather than shouting and making a scandal, she thought, "Well, if this blessing thing works, I just need to bless him." After blessing the young pickpocket silently, she turned round and saw him coming toward her with her purse in his extended hand.

Blessing works, Pierre! It changes lives. There is a face of goodness, of divine energy, that is immediately manifested in the person being blessed, and it is felt. It was not guilt that made the young man return the purse, it was the healing effect of divine love.

Thank you for your beautiful prayer/meditation for me. The Lord is our judge, our one and only true judge, and He is the only true lawgiver. I have never thought otherwise, Pierre. I have been waiting very patiently for the Lord to send me His justice, against which there is no appeal. *(March 6, 2005)*

To Ginger, Australia.
If you remove just one of your experiences, you would not be who you are today. All your power lies within you because that is where your true strength lies.

Life is about simple things. We have forgotten them, and we have replaced them with complications. That is why we have ulcers and stress and cancers and killings. We listen to people tell us that if things are easy they are not worth having, so we break our backs to make sure that everything is hard and complicated, and we die early trying to do everything the hard way, never realizing that the easiest thing in the world is to take a breath, and many people can do that without complications.

We no longer remember who we are, and when we hear a bird sing we throw rocks at it because it is disturbing our sleep or our peace, never listening to the song it sings. *(April 2005)*

I did not believe that God would allow me to walk the road that I have, that He showed me, for nothing. I was only one piece of a very large puzzle, and you were part of the plan before either one of us ever realized it. You were the piece needed to complete the puzzle, and here we are.

I have gotten some very good responses from readers. I never imagined things would take on this kind of life. This is exactly what we wished for, for my book, i.e. to bring people together. So many people write and tell me that they bought the book and gave it to someone else, gave it to a friend, a family member, an office worker. It is being passed on through love. *(April 10, 2005)*

> *"I truly try to treat people
> as I would want them to treat me"*
>
> (Roger McGowen, August 21, 2005)

The Golden Rule, which Roger formulates above in his own manner, exists, under different formulations, in all the major world religions. If it has reached such universality throughout history, it is surely because this is the simplest, surest path to win-win human relationships yet devised by society.

Christianity
So, in everything, do to others what you would have them do to you, for this sums up the Law and the Prophets. (Matth.7:12)

Islam (the Sunna)
None of you is a believer, if he does not desire for his brother that which he desires for himself.

Judaism
That which you hold as detestable, do not do to your neighbor. That is the whole Torah [law]. The rest is commentary. (Talmud, Shabbat 31a)

Brahmanism (orthodox Hinduism)
Such is the sum of duty, do not do to others that which would do harm to yourself. (Mahabharata, V-15:17)

Buddhism
Do not hurt others in ways that would find hurtful. (Udana Varga 5:18)

Confucianism
Here certainly is the golden maxim: do not do to others that which you do not want them do to you. (Analects 15:23)

Taoism
Regard your neighbor's gain as your gain, and his loss as your loss.
(Tai Shang Kan Yin P'ien)

Zoroastrianism
That nature alone is good which refrains from doing to others that which is not good for itself.
(Dadistan-I-dinik, 94:5)

To Jonas, Switzerland (Jonas, a young French inmate serving time in the Geneva jail for murder, discovered Roger's book while in prison).

Yes, you are in jail to realize something. Everything that you did in your life was a precursor to where you are. Everything [you did] was taking you in the direction you ended up in. But it can only be your teacher if you allow it to be so. It is shaping who you will become. Now you have to try to understand what to do with the awareness you have come to. Drugs can only take us so far. My brother was addicted to drugs. He used to shoot them into his arm. I tried to help him, but the drugs were stronger than reason. So I know how much you must have struggled to let go of them.

Do you think you will go back to them once you are free? Or will the medication that you are taking now be enough to prevent you? I really wish there was something I could do to help you. But just know this: I am always here to talk to, you can ask me anything and discuss anything with me. I will never judge you. We are equals in our suffering and our quest to understand the meaning of the whole experience. It was part of your experience in this life. It was something you were meant to experience.

No, you are not crazy at all, my friend, and neither am I, and even if we were, that is also a part of who we are. *(April 16, 2005)*

To Mirjam

Actually I believe that you are a very spiritual person. You are simply not a very religious person, neither am I. I believe that being spiritual is being in tune with your surroundings, being in tune with yourself, and feeling the spirit in those who surround you. I was raised in a spiritual, not religious, household. I myself take a common [sense] approach to most things, including spirituality. I do not need a book to tell me that if I see someone hungry and I have food, to offer them some, or if I see someone thirsty, to offer them water. I truly try to treat people as I would want them to treat me. I pray, not so much on my knees, but I am always praying in my heart. *(August 21, 2005)*

My first visit to death row, by Elly

In 2005, Elly visited Roger with me for the first time. Her description follows.

"The Allan Polunsky Unit is a foreboding place even from the outside: long gray buildings with slits in the walls in lieu of windows, thick fences of razor wire designed to inflict maximum wounds on anyone mad or desperate enough to attempt to cross it. At the entrance, one passes through a metal detector; the only things visitors can take inside are an ID, car keys, and $20 in small change for the vending machines inside. Not the slightest piece of paper, not a pen or pencil. Nothing. A visitor who once showed a letter to her inmate friend through the glass pane separating them was immediately thrown out.

But even before passing the control, I notice an African American family and a white family in tears. Only women, no men. A chaplain friend of Pierre's comes up to me and whispers in my ear, pointing to the families: "The father of these children is being put to death today, the son of the other lady tomorrow." It is chastening. After passing the control at the outbuilding, one walks along an alley bordered by barbed wire, enters the building, turns left, passes two more sets of automatically controlled metal doors, and then arrives in the visiting area. This space faces a long row of small cubicles through which the handcuffed inmate enters. The door at the back of the cubicle is then locked and he passes his hands in the opening in the door and is un-cuffed. There is a phone on his side, and two phones on the visitors' side. Between us, a thick bullet-proof window. In the rear of the visiting area, vending machines for the sandwiches and prepackaged industrial food visitors are allowed to purchase for the inmates. Guards keep a sharp watch both on visitors and inmates.

The atmosphere on the visitors' side is, to say the least, heavy. Two families are going to lose their husband, son and father in the coming 36 hours. Then Roger arrives. What a beautiful, serene face. What quiet inner strength. We are entitled to two half-days of discussion, and we make the very best of the time. We will be the only visitors Roger has this month. (Inmates are entitled to one "special visit" per month, and have a visiting list with a maximum of ten names. Most of Roger's visitors come from abroad).

Despite the profound and beautiful contact we have with Roger, I cannot help being aware of what's going on in the room. The children with an air of desperation on their faces to my left. The inmate to our right - taut face, whitish skin, unkempt and unshaven — is a dead man sitting, who will be legally "homicided" by the state tomorrow. The next day I see his mother buy the very last sandwich he will ever enjoy and take photos of her son for the very last time. As a mother myself, with a son I love dearly, I find myself imagining what it is like to walk in her shoes. My heart really goes out to her. Is this the culmination of 2000 years of Christian civilization? That night, when we return to our motel, my heart is in turmoil. Shades of intense light (Roger) mingle with the most intense sadness and a desire to cry.

There must be a better way."

I am like anyone else, Pierre. At times I get depressed, you just don't know the half of it.

This is a fight – never think that it is not. We are under constant attack by forces that are always at work seeking to turn us away from the knowledge of who we really are. And without that knowledge we forget how truly beautiful we all are, i.e. that God made us in His image and after His likeness.

So without that knowledge, we begin to hate and condemn, judge and plot against one another. We become envious and calculating and lose respect for one another. And without respect for one another, what do we have? I see that treachery every day, and I promise you, I try my best to stop it, but sometimes people are so comfortable in their misery that no matter what you say or do, you can't get them to see the hurt they do to themselves.

I can't stand to see people hurt each other every day, I can't bear to see them cheat, lie and steal every day trying to get just a little more than the next man. If you add it all up, it isn't worth the time and pain needed to get it.

When I see things like that, I am bothered and get frustrated, and sometimes I allow my burdens to become a mountain, and before I know it, I am laboring under them and at times the weight becomes a little too heavy to carry. So I have learned not to fight against the depression. I allow it to work itself out in time, because to fight against it creates a violent confrontation between the will and the mind.

Concerning the money issue, I never use all the money I get from you and L. for myself. I put money on other inmates' books so that they will have the money to go to the store. I buy guys shoes and sometimes radios. When I go to the store, I always buy enough food so that I can send some back down the hall. Where I just came from, i.e. Level 2, guys are starving right now. I do that because it needs to be done. No one knows this but me and the guys I do it for. On top of that, I save a portion of every penny I get from you and L. so that I can personally send something to my grandson as [I used to send it] to my son when he was younger and going to school.

Nothing will come between what we have. Our love for one another is a barrier that will prevent anything from coming against the love we share. I will be all right, Pierre. I promise you my good friend. I know that one day we will be able to embrace as brothers were meant to.

Not to force anything

One of the greatest lessons Roger learned in jail is letting go, letting things be. This is exquisitely expressed in the following poem by British writer Edward Carpenter:

The Lake of Beauty

"Let your mind be quiet, realizing the beauty of the world,
　　and the immense, the boundless treasures that it holds in store.
All that you have within you, all that your heart desires,
　　all that your Nature so specially fits you for —
that or the counterpart of it waits embedded in the great Whole, for you.
It will surely come to you.

Yet equally surely not one moment before its appointed time will it come.
All your crying and fever and reaching out of hands will make no difference.
Therefore do not begin that game at all.
Do not recklessly spill the waters of your mind in this direction and in that,
　　lest you become like a spring lost and dissipated in the desert.

But draw them still into a little compass, and hold them still, so still;
And let them become clear, so clear — so limpid, so mirror-like;
　　at last the mountains and the sky shall glass themselves in peaceful beauty,
And the antelope shall descend to drink, and to gaze at her reflected image,
　　and the lion to quench his thirst,
And Love himself shall come and bend over, and catch his own likeness in you."

I am sorry once again that it took so long for me to write but I have learned over the years that one way to cope with everyday stress here is not to force anything. Everything will be revealed in time. When I write to you I want to be all the way there, because if I can't give you my best, I do not want to give you my worst. *(July 30, 2005)*

To Jonas, a young prisoner in jail in Geneva (written in response to Jonas' letter about a serious car accident his brother had while driving to visit him)

You have to live for yourself. You can't live for your brother, nor can you die for him. We are our own redeemers – our salvation lies in our hands, Jonas. I hope with all my heart that your brother will pull through this tragedy, I am almost certain that he will. All things work together for good for those who love God.

Of course you did not need these problems. But problems don't wait on you to ask for them, and they don't wait till you are feeling good before striking. They come at all times of the day and night, whether you are feeling terrible or great. We just have to deal with them, brother. Sometimes we have to laugh in the face of adversity, not because we are heartless or insensitive, but because when tragedy strikes everyone and everything expects us to bow our heads and cry. So, on occasion, we have to do the unexpected – laugh when everyone expects you to cry, and love when they expect you to hate. No matter what you do at this present moment, you cannot change your brother's condition, but God can!

So, pray and ask Him to do so, and I will do the same, and be happy to know He is on our side. God won't take you in your brother's place. I tried it! Remember, that is why I am here, Jonas. I tried to give my life for my brother whom I felt the same about as you do concerning your brother. Instead of taking my life, He gave it back to me. There is a lesson in everything that happens in our life, Jonas. Stop for a moment and just clear your mind. Stop thinking for a moment and find the lesson. As your friend, your problems are my problems. I am here to listen if ever you need an ear.

I am alright, Jonas my friend. I take life as it comes. If it gives me lemons, I find sugar from somewhere and make lemonade. I can't fight against it, and I won't let it fight against me. So, we sort of move together in a kind of dance where we each get the chance to lead. I have very few complaints. I do not need anything.

Thank you, my friend, for asking. *(September 10, 2005)*

Legal representation the critical factor

The quality of representation is unquestionably *the key factor in determining wheth-er an accused will be condemned to death or not.* In one of the best books on the death penalty, *Executed on a Technicality*, author Professor David Dow states: *"Race matters in the death penalty system, but socioeconomic status matters even more. Wealth matters because in many cases trial outcomes depend less on what really happened than on the advocate's skill. . . . In the area of death penalty prosecutions, a lawyer's skill is the most important factor determining whether a defendant is sentenced to death or to life in prison."* (p.7). Dr. Dow further writes:

"Lawyers who show up drunk, who have sexual affairs with the spouse of the defendant they rep-resent, who go through entire trials without raising a single objection, and who file one-page appellate briefs from city drunk tanks have all been deemed constitutionally competent. . . . In the USA, 20,000 homicides occur every year. In a busy year for executioners, one fourth of one percent of murderers will be executed. . . . The tiny handful that we execute is almost never the worst of the worst. Instead, people are executed because eyewitnesses make mistakes, police lie, defense lawyers sleep, and judges do not care" (pp.8-9, xv).

In Roger's case as in many, many others, the level of representation was below anything one could reasonably expect. As already noted, his first lawyer only met him once very briefly before the trial, prepared the plea on the basis of the police report, and did not make a single phone call to check his alibi.

In their book *Actual Innocence*, Barry Scheck, Peter Neufeld, and Jim Dwyer mention the case of a Kentucky attorney who was assigned to a capital case, and *"gave his business address as 'Kelly's Keg,' the local watering hole. . . . He had no experience. His home was decorated with a big neon beer sign. He missed the testimony of important witnesses because he was out of the courtroom. He came to the trial drunk. When police searched his home, they found garbage bags hidden under a floor containing stolen property. The court said his behavior did not adversely affect his client"* (p.244, emphasis added).

Edward Honaker was convicted for rape and kidnapping, and served ten years of a life sentence. The "expert" criminalist stated he had been able to detect sperm on the slides of the rapist's semen. Honaker's court-appointed lawyer never even mentioned that his client had had a vasectomy years before and was therefore biologically incapable of producing one single sperm! Without the help of the Innocence Project, specialized in DNA testing, Honaker would still be rotting in jail today, 23 years later.

These are not a few rare cases hunted down in some obscure court documents. Such cases appear in the courts daily. The life and death of Roger McGowens all around the country depend on the skills, competence, and integrity of their defense lawyers, but all too often these so-called advocates are asleep, drunk, incompetent, terribly underpaid or simply don't really care.

To Monica

I am sorry to read that you have been feeling sad lately. At times we all feel that way – I do myself. I guess sadness lets us appreciate our happiness more. I look at the state of the world, and I am often saddened by it. But I do not feel bad about it, because I know that something can be done to change that state, and that good people are fighting daily to make that happen, so sadness is just one piece of a larger emotional puzzle that we were given to navigate these troubled waters we have been thrust upon. A little rain is good for the soul. It makes our roots grow stronger and our leaves greener.

We do what we can, Monica. Just be sincere in whatever you do. God wants sincerity more than He wants sacrifice. It makes no difference whether you succeed or not. You are everything you need to be. Recognize it. *(June 4, 2005)*

The summer and fall of 2005 were extremely tough on Roger, with a state-appointed lawyer who had no respect for him and who did not even believe him. Despite this long, dark valley, there were some green pastures, for example when a new correspondent, Marion, sent him a book by German mystic Meister Eckhart. After receiving it, Roger responded with this statement:

We are what we are looking for
We seek what has not been lost.
When we look too hard, we miss what we seek.
God is all around us.
Why must we seek Him?
We are what we seek.
(September 2005)

To Ginger, in Australia, in answer to her question whether Roger thought he might have chosen his life before coming here on earth.

This may have been a path I chose before coming here. I believe that it is a role that I must play out and I will do it with all the dignity and love that I can muster. But if I had to choose this path again, I don't believe that I would. Smile.

I believe that my purpose in life is to be where I am for the moment, and to do what I am doing for the time being. I believe that everything happens for some reason. I may be here simply to give one person who feels like giving up a word of encouragement, so that that person may go on to greater things. Sometimes we must accept our fate and bow our heads and push on into the wind. I believe that my journey is to plant seeds of love and understanding in the soil of the heart of all those I meet along this path.

Deterrence

Truth is a very rare kind of commodity, for however small the supply, it always exceeds the demand.
(Anonymous)

One of the fundamental issues in the death penalty debate is whether or not it actually acts as a deterrent to crime. Although statistics suggest that it does not, this doesn't seem to disturb the proponents of the penalty. A *Chicago Sun-Times* column (November 20, 2007) on the subject notes recent studies by economists Roy D. Adler and Michael Summers, who claimed the death penalty had a very high deterrence impact. Commenting on the study, sociologist and author Amitai Etzioni states: *"The data on which this model is based are extremely thin.[. . .] All that the economists demonstrate is some (deeply questionable) correlation between capital punishment and murder.[. . .] It doesn't take a doctorate in economics to know that correlation does not prove causality."* He warns against society taking comfort in *"pseudo-scientific mumbo-jumbo"* (*Lifespark Weekly News*, No. 47-2007).

The home-page banner on www.prodeathpenalty.com features this statement by John McAdams, of Marquette University's Department of Political Science: *"If we execute murderers and there is in fact no deterrent effect, we have killed a bunch of murderers. If we fail to execute murderers, and doing so would in fact have deterred other murders, we have allowed the killing of a bunch of innocent victims. I would much rather risk the former. This, to me, is not a tough call."*

The basic flaw in this and similar statements, however, is that it is estimated that seven to nine percent (possibly more) of those on death row are innocent. Over 130 people have been released from death row since the reestablishment of the death penalty. Some proponents of the death penalty go as far as saying that even if innocents have been executed, that is just too bad and they are a "negligible minimum." If they, or one of their loved ones, belonged to that minimum, one suspects they might have a different viewpoint.

One hard statistical fact is that states with the death penalty systematically have higher crime rates than those without. In recent years, *"not only has the consolidated murder rate in states without the death penalty remained consistently lower than in the states that have had executions, but the gap has grown wider. As a result, some sociologists have suggested that **executions actually inspire murder**, a so-called brutalization effect"* (Scott Turner, *Ultimate Punishment*, Picador, N.Y., 2003, p.58, our emphasis).

A study by Sorenson, Wrinkle, Brewer, and Marquart on executions in Texas between 1984 and 1997 hypothesized that if a deterrent effect were to exist, it should be found in Texas, which executed a third of the people put to death in the USA during that period (around forty percent since 1998). Yet, they found no deterrent effect there whatsoever. One of the most thorough studies on the subject ever done, by Harries and Cheatwood, investigated differences in homicides and violent crime in 293 counties.

(continued p.230)

Don't get me wrong, I do not consider myself to be some holy person. I am not a religious person, but I do consider myself to be a spiritual person because we all are. I just embrace what I know to be the truth and use it accordingly. We can learn from anything if we are willing to open ourselves up to it. We are all being, but what are you being at the moment? Are you being helpful or hurtful? And while we are being, we are also constantly becoming. Are we becoming more or less than what we are? Everything you do and have been doing was to awake you to whom and what you truly are. Most people go [through] a lifetime and never think about it or never understand. *(October, 2005)*

Pierre, I sometimes stop and look around at where I am – I look at the walls that confine me to this place physically, and I look at the bars and razor wire and guard towers that are put in place to ensure that we are kept here. And I laugh at the foolish efforts of the powers that be to oppress and suppress our every move, our very freedom, our very happiness, and I laugh even harder. Because the more they try and stop the love, the more love we receive. The more they try and suppress our happiness, the more happiness comes. And it is because of you and those like you who are not afraid to reach out to those who have been forgotten, who have been marked as undesirable and say: "I love you, I am here for you, I do not care what you did or have been accused of doing – I love you anyway."

And I realize that nothing outside of me can take the joy you give me, it is rooted too deep. Thank you and those like you who bring light and give hope to men and women all round the world that find themselves in conditions where they believe all hope has abandoned them. You are the light that shines to the far corners of the world, that illuminates the horrors and sufferings that are kept in the dark. Thank you my friends, thank you. *(Undated, 2005)*

To a class of high school students, France

Your first question is "How did I feel after being sentenced to death?" When I first heard the verdict I felt nothing. My mind and body were in a kind of shock. At first, it is hard to believe, until the judge asks you to stand and then he recites to you that you have been found guilty and are hereby remanded to the custody of the state until a date is set for the day of your execution. At that point, I looked around at the jurors, the court, and back at the judge, and I honestly did not care anymore. I had lost everything anyway.

Deterrence (continued)

Counties were matched in pairs based on geographic location, regional context, historical development, and a series of demographic and economic variables. The pairs shared a continuous border but differed on use of capital punishment. The authors found no support of any kind for a deterrent effect of capital punishment. However, they did find higher violent crime rates in the death penalty counties. (*The Geography of Execution: The Capital Punishment Quagmire in America*, 1997)

According to FBI statistics, eighty percent of executions take place in the South, the region with the highest homicide rate. The Northeast, which has the lowest homicide rate, has less than one percent of executions. The average murder rate among death penalty states is much higher than among non-death penalty States.

A study by UCLA statistics professor Richard Berk on the methodology of pro-death penalty research (*New Claims about Executions and General Deterrence : Déjà Vu All Over Again?*) shows that recent studies claiming to demonstrate a deterrent effect of the death penalty were based on a major flaw in statistical methodology.

Among professional criminologists, eighty-four percent do not believe in any deterrence effect of the death penalty. Most important of all, police chiefs, the first to be concerned, believe the death penalty to be the least effective approach for reducing crime, as the following graph shows clearly.

Police Chiefs Place Death Penalty Last in Reducing Violent Crime

Law enforcement officers do not view the death penalty as an effective deterrent to violent crime. A 1995 Hart Research Associates Poll of police chiefs in the U.S. found that the majority of police chiefs (67%) do not believe that the death penalty significantly reduces the number of homicides. In fact, the police chiefs polled ranked the death penalty last among effective ways of reducing violent crime.

(Source: www.deathpenaltyinfo.org/law-enforcement-views-deterrence)

International comparisons are even more striking. The USA – one of the three industrialized countries to still maintain the death penalty – has a homicide rate of over 6 per 100,000 inhabitants, compared to less than 2 for Sweden, 1.45 for Britain, and a modest 1.28 for Germany. In Canada, which abolished the death penalty in 1976, the homicide rate has dropped by well over a fifth since the abolition.

(Source: www.deathpenaltyinfo.org/search/node/deterrence)

Two months prior to my being sentenced, my brother was shot down in the middle of the street by Houston police officers in the commission of a robbery. One year earlier, I had lost my mother. Deep down I knew I was innocent, but still I did not care. I came from a poor family. We did not have money to hire an attorney, and as far as I knew, my life was over. So I felt nothing.

Your next question was whether I believed in God before coming here. I have always believed in God. My mother, grandmother, and great grandmother were very religious people. They had come from the country[side]. Before that, they were descendants of slaves, and slaves were very religious because they needed something to hold on to during those very brutal times. I went to church every Sunday with my grandmother, but as I grew older I became too busy to attend church every Sunday, but I never stopped believing.

I do not subscribe to any particular religion. I have often believed that all of them have some truth to them. I do not believe in speaking ill of any religion, and I refuse to judge any person. That is God's job. I have met atheists who were some of the most generous and loving people in this world, and I have met devout Christians who were very mean and nasty.

You asked what is God for me. To me, God is all things. God is every lesson you ever learned, every heartache you ever felt, every smile you showed and every tear you cried. I believe that God is the voice in you that says "don't" when you know you should not and "yes" when you should. God is a fountain that never stops giving. When you are trapped in your car and there is no way out and you think you are going to die, that person, that firefighter, that rescue-worker that comes to your aid is God, because they are acting for God and God is acting through them to show you His glory.

When I first took the case for my brother [i.e. Roger confessed to the crime he believed at the time had been committed by his brother], he deliberately got into trouble so that he could get arrested and come to jail and talk me out of my decision. We never really got the chance to speak because they kept us separate from one another, but the last time I saw him before he was released from jail, we were standing in the cafeteria of the jail. He worked in the kitchen and crept out to talk to me. He told me he was leaving that very night and he asked me: "Roger, why?" We were embracing one another and I had a cross around my neck that I had made from knitted socks and bread wrappers. It was black and red, and I took it off and gave it to him. . . . I would never see or speak to him again.

I survive because I have no choice. I do not believe that God has brought me this far to abandon me.

Reuben Cantu – The Texan smoking-gun case
(Editorial in the *Houston Chronicle*)

"Up until his death by lethal injection in the summer of 1993, San Antonian Reuben Cantu steadfastly claimed that he had been framed at the age of 17 for shooting two men during a robbery. One of them died, and the other lived to bear witness against him. An investigation of Cantu's conviction by the Chronicle's Lise Olsen provides persuasive evidence that his execution by the state was a mistake.

Opponents of capital punishment point to the fact that the Texas criminal justice *system is far from fool-proof. Inevitably, they argue, death sentences will cause innocent people to suffer the ultimate, irreversible miscarriage of justice. The poor are at greatest risk of falling victim to a wrongful death sentence, as they must rely on an appointed lawyer who might not give the case his full attention. Every step of the way, from arrest to conviction, Cantu's history matches that scenario.*

The 15-year-old who participated in the crime, David Garza, has signed an affidavit claiming **Cantu was not the gunman and was not at the scene of the shooting.** *Garza, incarcerated for unrelated burglary, says both he and Cantu took a vow of secrecy not to identify the killer. He says he's speaking out now because he continues to be tormented by his failure to prevent the execution of his friend.*

The surviving witness, Juan Moreno, testified at the trial that Cantu was the killer. Moreno claims police pressured him to ID Cantu after showing him Cantu's picture numerous times. **He now says he is sure Cantu was not the man who shot him.**

. . . . **There was no evidence tying the defendant to the crime.** *The jury did not believe Cantu's claim that he was in Waco stealing pick-up trucks when the shooting took place, despite the fact that his sister corroborated the alibi. . . .*

As the forewoman of the jury told a Chronicle *reporter, the jury did the best they could with the information they were given, but* "the bottom line is **an innocent person was put to death** and we all have our finger in that." *The district attorney at the time, Sam Millsap, Jr.* **says he made a mistake trying Cantu for capital murder.** *Today's criminal justice system, he said, allows people to be convicted based on mistaken or corrupted evidence. . . .*

The execution of one innocent person in Texas is too many at the hands of the state. The Chronicle's investigation of Reuben Cantu's life and death strongly argues for both his innocence and the need for new safeguards to prevent mistakes or malice from sending others to his fate" (Houston Chronicle, November 23, 2005, emphasis added).

I refuse to buy into the hate that surrounds me because I know that the heart of man is naturally good. We just sometimes forget that and have to be reminded. I spend my time trying to remind my friends and the officers alike that they are better than what they believe they are. There is injustice and torture all over the world. We can't fight it everywhere, but we have to fight it where we encounter it.

One of the things about supporting the death penalty is that it is an act that once committed cannot be undone.

Just last week there has been an uproar in the news because it has just been proved that Texas executed an innocent man named Reuben Cantu. He was 18 years old when he was arrested. The witnesses that testified against him are now saying that they were forced to say he did it. It is too late now. He is dead and cannot be brought back. And nothing is done to the prosecutor and the judge who conspired to send him to death row. Isn't that murder in itself? *(December 3, 2005)*

To Marion, Germany

We thought the officials would allow the volunteer ministers to come inside the building where we are kept to hold services at least for the holidays, but they did not, although they had festivities for the general population inmates, like gospel singers and volunteer bands to entertain them. They feel that since we have been deemed unredeemable, we do not warrant prayers. But we manage to enjoy each other's company, so the holidays were not bad at all. Christmas used to be difficult when we first came to this particular prison, but it did not take long before we all realized that Christmas was not something that you do or see, but that you feel and know. It's about love and sacrifice. So when excluded from participating, we came to appreciate even more and discovered the love that existed within us all and each made an effort to spread more love among ourselves. I believe that someday I will be free of this place and able to share my experience with others. Heaven is the state or realizing that we cannot think of ourselves without thinking of God and knowing that where there is God, there is also heaven. And so when I look at you and recognize God in you, then there is no you. *(Christmas, 2005)*

Former police chief: Death penalty fails to reduce crime and wastes money

In an article written for California's *San Jose Mercury News*, former Seattle police chief Norm Stamper, a 29-year veteran of the San Diego police department, recalled *"more than a few occasions during my career as a police officer when, in opposition to my conscience, I wished for someone's sudden death. Cop killers, child killers, cold-blooded murderers come to mind."* He went on to say:

"Despite my visceral reactions to violent offenders, while working as a police officer I discovered that the death penalty is inefficient and extravagantly expensive. Prosecuting and publicly defending a capital case - through up to eleven years of appeals - can cost taxpayers millions of dollars more than simply locking someone else for the rest of his or her life. The Los Angeles Times reports that the death penalty system in California alone costs $114 million per year over the costs of locking up prisoners for life.

Spending all this money on the death penalty might be worth it - if it actually made our communities safer. But it doesn't. If capital punishment were a deterrent, you'd think our murder rate (20,000 killings a year) would be among the lowest in the civilized world. But in fact, it's close to topping the list. According to The New York Times, *the twelve states that have abolished the death penalty boast average homicide rates consistently lower than those states that kill their killers. . . .*

Our communities would be exponentially better off by reinvesting the time, money and resources we spend on trying to get a few people executed into crime prevention measures that work. Spending scarce public resources on after-school programs, mental health care, drug and alcohol treatment, education, more crime labs and new technologies, or on hiring more police officers, would truly help create safer communities. . . .

This is why I have joined the Walk to Stop Executions, and why you should consider joining too."

(Source: *San Jose Mercury News*, Nov. 19, 2007, quoted in *Lifespark Weekly-News*, No. 47, 2007)

2006

There are few letters from the 2005/2006 winter because Roger went through an incredibly trying time, legally speaking. His difficulties were due to major differences between him and his state-appointed lawyer, who finally left Texas in the summer of 2006, just a year after his former attorney had also left the state. The upside of this was that it cleared the field, enabling Roger's international support committee, at his request, to finally hire a private lawyer.

To Marion (written after looking at Japanese American photographer John Maeda's book on the Japanese Alps. Marion sent it to Roger via one of the few bookstores – online or other – authorized to send books to death row inmates.)

I could not stop turning the pages. Each one was a meditation. I got lost in the beauty of each photo. Looking at such beauty allows man to understand his place in the divine wheel that turns in the life of each of us, at the same time giving us the opportunity to realize how blessed we truly are. I do not believe that one can take such beautiful pictures without first touching the beauty that lies within oneself. What we see on the outside only reflects what we feel on the inside, which is why people say that beauty is in the eyes of the beholder. I had no idea there were places so beautiful they could take one's breath away.

One can never really know the true way until one gets there. And once we get where we think we should be, *we realize we were there all the time. (January 9, 2006)*

Time does not exist here, Marion. I have been living one long day that has lasted for a little over 20 years. When your letter reaches my hand, then that is the day I was meant to receive it.

Actually, the way they treat us is criminal, period! Now is the coldest week of the winter in Texas. The last few months have not been so cold, but they had the heater on all the time. It was so hot that at times it was suffocating. But as soon as it got really cold, they turned the heater off! And let me tell you, it is freezing in here – my feet and hands are frozen. I have on everything I own, and I am still freezing. My fingers are numb beating on this machine, I have to stop and blow on my hands every few minutes. They are telling us that the heater broke and they won't be able to fix it. They give us coats to wear but we can't wear them when we go to the day room to recreate! *(February 17, 2006)*

"Love allows us to make mistakes
because love does not judge us when we are wrong.
It simply waits that we correct ourselves
while it keeps on loving.
Even in the darkest hours,
there are lessons to be learned."

(Roger McGowen, May 2, 2006)

To Ginger

I used to be very sad not to be there for my son, I wanted more than anything in this world to be a father to him and later become his friend as he grew older. However the cards we were both dealt had other plans. But through it all I never forgot my responsibility as a father to him and through the pain and anguish, steel bars and concrete walls, guard towers and beat downs and gassings, I tried my very best to do what I could do from where I was. I saved every penny I had and got so that I could send it to him, I wrote letters and tried to stay in touch in every way that I could, to let him know that he had a father and that he cared. *(February, 2006)*

To Marion

Now the officials have told the officers that they cannot wake people up and ask them anymore if they are going to eat. Once they get to the person's door, if he's not already up they are just to walk by and not feed him! I am a diabetic and I have to eat. The other morning they did not wake me up and give me my breakfast tray, and for the first time in a very long period I slept through breakfast. Well, when I got up I wasn't feeling too well because I had not eaten. When I told the sergeant that he could not give the officers permission to pass me up on my breakfast because I was diabetic and had to eat for medical reasons, he told me it was not his problem!

Every morning they pass 20-30 guys up on breakfast, and you can see the officers standing in front of the trash can slamming the breakfast trays with all that food on them into the trash can! Every morning, I can hear them throwing the food away that they have just denied one of the inmates. It's madness. But I realize that the average officer can't do anything but follow orders, so if there is a victim in this, then there are two of them. I realize that this is just a play, and that we all have our parts to play. I try not to get too angry at what goes on here. Most times I will laugh, but on rare occasions my heart really feels sad watching them throw so much food away knowing that so many are starving in the world. Out of spite and pure meanness they would rather throw the food away than wake the inmates and feed them. I can go on and on about the abuses that we are made to suffer here, but it makes no difference. Nothing is ever done about it. It is a learning experience. *(February 17, 2006)*

A Brazilian tale (also known under the name "Footprints")

Once, a man arrived in paradise. He asked God if he could be shown his whole life in review – the difficult moments as well as the joys. And God willingly acquiesced. He showed him his whole life as if it were on a beach, so that he could see his own footprints.

The man saw that throughout his entire life there were two pairs of footprints: his own and God's. But then he noticed that in the most difficult moments, during the greatest trials and even in life-threatening situations, there was suddenly only one pair of footprints.

This deeply troubled him, and he asked God: "How, in the most difficult moments of all, could You possibly have left me alone?"

"My beloved child," God replied, "the reason why there was only one pair of marks, is because, in those moments, I was carrying you" (Numerous sources).

To Ron and Robin

I hope your skies are beautiful and blue.

I have been doing a lot of praying the last couple of hours. On the news for the last few hours, [they have been talking of a] plane circling George Bush Intercontinental Airport with 48 passengers on board trying to let the plane run out of fuel before landing because one or both of the tires on the landing gear had blown off, and they feared that the plane could not land without crashing and burning. When I heard this, I started asking God to create a safe landing for the passengers and bring the plane in safely. It circled for a few hours before the pilot finally decided to attempt his landing. There was not even a spark from the plane. They said the pilot landed the plane like it had its wheels.

The moment we think God is not there is the moment He proves us wrong. God is the prize fighter that can never be counted out. We get angry about something and doubt sets in and we cry because we fear we have been abandoned and we do not know where to turn. So we blame God for not being there. And then we see a miracle such as this one and we know in our hearts that God is in control.

I had been down on myself, Ron, because I feared that I had not acted soon enough to save my life. I would never blame others for my mistakes, but we all need help. I really did not know what I was doing, Ron. I needed help and was too ashamed to simply ask X for it. So when things went wrong, it was hard for me to face X because he thinks so highly of me and I love him to death. I just could not have him think that I was mistaken. But love allows us to make mistakes because love does not judge us when we are wrong, it simply waits that we correct ourselves while it keeps on loving. Even in the darkest hours, there are lessons to be learned.

Take care of yourselves and remember to smile and enjoy the colors in your life, they fade sometimes before we have the time to appreciate them. *(May 2, 2006)*

To Ulrike

What a fantastic letter I received from you. It made my heart soar and sing. Thank you for reading my book. I am glad that you were able to take something from it. That is all any of us can really ask from life: that someone, anyone, may get some lesson from our suffering and turn it into love and joy.

It was my experience in this life to face what I face now. I do so with as much dignity and courage as I can muster, because some days are so difficult to wake up to that at times one wishes one had died in one's sleep.

But rise and face it I do, and I can do it filled with bitterness or I can do it filled with Love.

30 years on death row

Many people are understandably amazed that a person can stay well over 30 years on death row. There is little doubt that inmates receive two distinct punishments: death – and many years awaiting their execution. In recent years, the time inmates spend on death row has steadily increased. The US Supreme Court has yet to hear a case based on the length of an inmate's death row tenure, but Supreme Court justices Stephen Breyer and John Paul Stevens have questioned the constitutionality of long delays.

In other western countries, courts have not been as conservative. The British Privy Council, the highest appeals court for the Caribbean Commonwealth countries, ruled in 1993 that hanging anyone who had spent over five years on death row was "inhumane and degrading" and amounted to double punishment. In the so-called Pratt and Morgan ruling, the Judicial Committee of the Privy Council commuted the sentences of all those with five years or more on death row to life in prison. In the United States, a death penalty case goes through three phases:

Phase 1 - Trial *"A death penalty lawyer who is a trial lawyer has three principal tasks. The first two involve investigation. The third is picking the jury. If the lawyer does not pay attention, the case is already lost. But no matter how good the jury, the case is lost if the lawyer has not performed an investigation."* The lawyer is supposed to challenge the state's claim that his client is a criminal, which can include hiring experts to challenge the prosecution's arguments and presenting arguments from the background of the accused that help explain why he behaved in a given way (these are the so-called mitigating circumstances). This is especially important: most of the accused have committed the crime they are charged with, so the lawyer will attempt to avoid the death penalty, and to do that he will need to convince the jury of his client's humanity. The first stage has two distinct phases:

- Determining guilt or innocence - Is the accused guilty of the crime?
- Sentencing - What punishment should the accused receive?

(In Roger's case, the lawyer did not perform the slightest investigation and made no effort to present background information on Roger's life. Moreover, he let a former policeman sit on the jury, which dramatically changed the outcome, as he bullied hesitant jury members into accepting the death penalty for Roger by incorrectly introducing evidence not presented to the jury about crime and recidivism in general in Houston. This convinced the jury that Roger could be a potential future danger to society - such so-called "future dangerousness" being a requirement for giving the death sentence).

(continued p.242)

I am glad you were able to make a decision on your job and I hope it was a fruitful one. In the meantime, you take care of yourself and see God in all things because nothing exists without Him/Her and everything exists within God. Thank you for your prayers. *(May 26, 2006)*

To Clotilde
Thank you very much for all the beautiful letters, cards, prayers, and mental energy you have been sending me. I know that it is the things that we cannot see that provide us with the greatest strength and inspiration. There are times when we feel that we cannot go one step further, that we are at the ebb of our strength. We just don't find the strength to even lift our foot and take one more step or hold on just a little tighter. And then inspiration comes to us from the prayers and mental energy sent to us by others. So I know that the positive energy we direct towards one another does indeed have an effect.

Thank you for that beautiful card, the water color painting done by a handicapped person with her foot. It is amazing how the universe at the same time takes and gives back. It is hard to believe that someone painted that with their feet.

Your words have been like balm on a wound. They are filled with healing power and strength. Forgive me for not writing back sooner, but as I stated in an earlier letter, there will be times when I can't reply because of the stamp problem.

Yes, I am in good health – thank-you for asking. Even when I am not feeling my best, I realize that it could be worse, so I am thankful for just that moment. Each and every moment, I try my very best to be the best that I can be every moment of every day of my life. Life never stops its lessons. As long as there is life, there will be lessons to learn, experiences to draw from and love to share. Yes, everything is filled with something, even despair is filled with hope. We must learn to perceive life differently than we have been taught to believe, because there is so much more to it than we see. Being here in this prison has also taught me that nothing stands alone and that every space is filled with something.

I bow my head in your presence. Have many colors in your world. *(June 10, 2006)*

30 years on death row (continued)

Phase 2 – Appeal Most of the accused in capital cases are sentenced to death. However, in every US state, there is an automatic appeal, which takes place on the state level. *"At the end of the direct appeal, the death row inmate can ask the U.S. Supreme Court to review the case, but the Court rarely does so. At this point, the case is said to be 'final' and death row inmates no longer have a constitutional right to counsel."*

Phase 3 - *Habeas corpus* appeals It is a federal right for the accused to have one *habeas* appeal in a federal court, but the claims they can make are severely limited and almost nil if the lawyer performed badly on the state level. (Once more, this is Roger's situation). At the end of this stage, *"his case is, for all intents and purposes, over. He may ask a state or federal court to address a new issue he has thought of, [. . .] [but] even if the inmate's lawyer asks, the courts will almost never listen. Hence, once the death row inmate has completed the third stage, the execution is almost inevitable."*

(Sources: D. Dow, op.cit. p.4-6, and DPIC, *Time on Death Row*)

Poor lack access to courts

"One of the most fundamental aspects of any normally functioning democracy is equal access to law. However, even in the West, few if any countries can really claim such equal access. In the USA, the disparity is possibly greater than in any other Western country. If you are white and rich you can hire the very best lawyers and often walk out of court a free man, even if you have committed a serious crime, not to mention defrauding billions of dollars as in some well-known cases. If you are poor and African-American or Latino, your chances of getting fair justice are frequently almost inexistent. If you are poor, African-American, and living in Texas, you can almost forget it. There are about 330 potential clients for every lawyer in Texas, but the ratio is closer to 18'000 for low income people according to David Hall, executive Director of Rio Grande Legal aid. Texas ranks 42nd in the country in per capita spending on legal services to the poor" (El Paso Times, September 9, 2004).

ccording to the *National Catholic Reporter*, in a country of one million attorneys, there are approximately fifty who work for private, non profit agencies specializing in capital representation work. Stephen Bright, one of the most brilliant lawyers in the USA defending the poor, has said of Texas that it has *"the worst public legal system of any state. It has just the appearance of a process."* Frederico Martinez-Macias *"was represented at his capital trial in Texas by a court appointed attorney paid $ 11.84 an hour. His counsel failed to present any available alibi-witnesses, failed to interview and present witnesses who could have rebutted the prosecutor's case and failed to thoroughly examine key evidence."* Lawyers defending the rich can earn hundreds of dollars an hour, and, according to *The New York Times, "a Florida firm reported it spent 10 years and $ 10 million worth of lawyering hours representing one death row client'"* (National Catholic Reporter, October 5, 2001).

In June 2006, I attended the first World Conference on the Ecological Footprint in Sienna, Italy, and wrote to Roger about it. The ecological footprint is a scientific tool for measuring the impact individuals and nations have on the world environment. To maintain an environmentally sustainable world, individuals should not have a footprint of more than 1.8 hectares (4.45 acres). In many European nations, each person has a "footprint" of five to six hectares (12.35 to 14.83 acres), in the US, close to ten (about 2 acres). And here comes Roger, whose personal consumption must not go beyond that of the poor in the Third World, explaining the efforts he makes to live in a more environmentally conscious manner!

This is the first time I've heard that particular term "ecological footprint," Pierre. Yes, I would imagine that the USA probably has the largest footprint of all developed nations. I was washing my sheets the other day and pondered what you said about the use of water and how far women in Africa had to walk to fetch water. I was conscious of how much water I used. I have always tried to be environmentally conscious. That is why I no longer have any magazine or newspaper subscriptions. I see so much waste daily when the trash is swept up. You would be amazed. I have always believed that we are all given a certain amount of space in this world and this life, and it is up to us to maintain that space and make certain that space is always clean and ready for the next soul that will occupy it after we have gone. I think that "ecological footprint" is a good concept if we could get everyone to agree and follow it. *(June 18, 2006)*

To Marion

I am fine at the moment. I try not to look too far beyond the now and focus on what is, and enjoy the blessings that come one moment at a time. There have been and still continue to be so many executions going on weekly that it makes one wonder what use it is to do things. Many of the people who were killed were people I had grown up with in here. I was very young when I came here, and so were many others, and we kind of found our callings inside this prison. So it is very hard to watch them walk to their death. So, physically I am fine, but I can't say that I am fine mentally. I don't think anyone can go through a thing like this and come out sane. But we don't have the luxury to go insane. So, I won't lose my hope, nor will I ever give up my quest for truth and justice in the midst of insanity. *(July 9, 2006)*

Most of Roger's letters during the summer and fall of 2006 dealt with legal issues concerning his case, including the many challenges posed by the way an earlier state-appointed lawyer had handled it. They are of lesser interest to readers.

Well, I have a bit of good news. Two of my friends have been released from death row over the last few months and are free now. Isn't that great? Neither of them achieved it with a court-appointed lawyer. Why does money always impede earthly justice? Why do people who hire [private] lawyers get the best representation and go free more often? Shouldn't the poor and unfortunate be given the better treatment?

Can one define God?

Ask ten people to define God and you will almost certainly get ten different replies. Ask ten members of a sect for a definition of their God, and you might well get ten stereotyped replies. Some early Christian mystics stated that God could only be defined negatively, by what he was not (why He and not She or It?)

As Eckhart Tolle states in his landmark book, *The Power of Now*, *"The word God has become a closed concept. The moment the word is uttered, a mental image is created, no longer, perhaps, of an old man with a white beard, but still a mental representation of someone or something outside you, and, yes, almost inevitably a male someone or something."*

No word can adequately define the Divine, because all words are historically limited, culturally defined constructs, and because each person ultimately gives her or his own meaning to every single word. Say "pasta" to an inhabitant of Naples who just enjoyed his mamma's home made *linguini caprese*, and you will see a huge smile spreading across his illumined face. Say "spaghetti" to the hurried Manchester businessman who just ate an almost cold plate of poorly cooked pasta in a fast food joint, and you will certainly not witness the same response. If that is true of pasta, how much more of "God."

If "God" is an *experience*, as so many great mystics and luminaries have suggested, then any attempt to define this reality in words is hopeless. If "God" is Love, as the apostle John, one of the greatest seers of all times, stated, then maybe the only way to approach that awesome reality is to live it every moment - with all your heart, mind, and strength. Then the experience will become so real and powerful, words will become useless and unimportant.

You remember my friend Ronald Chambers? He has an execution date and has exhausted all of his appeals. He believes it is over for him and my heart aches for him. He has been here thirty (30) years, Pierre! Shouldn't that count for something?[29] *(September 23, 2006)*

I am sorry Pierre for the delay in writing, but you are aware that there exists no time in our concept of reality, just as love has no boundaries. The difficulties of the past few months have been somewhat refreshing because I was able to meditate more and experience a new source of happiness. It came to me that, regardless of how much we talk or how much we think we know, we will never be able to define God or bring it down to fit our distorted image of what we have been taught to believe is God. We define our image of God from the thoughts formed from the words we were taught to shape our concept of reality. We cannot define God using words. In the first chapter of [the Gospel according to] John, it says: "In the beginning was the word and the word was God." I came to the understanding that no matter what we did, God was always going to be God! And that we will never know God because God is unknowable – and that the moment we [believe we] know God, it ceases to be God and simply becomes another word.

We must claim the happiness that comes with life. If life came without happiness it would be incomplete, like love without compassion. Only the everyday difficulties brought on by the adversities of life have blinded us to true happiness, because we use the same words to capture and hold the very things that create the feeling of being unhappy. We name them depression, hate, dislike, broke, poverty and so on. I started to become depressed when in solitary confinement, but after meditating I refused to identify with these feelings, I ignored them, it was easy to do so.

It has been awhile, Pierre, since I was able to write to you that I was happy. It is still the little things that we take for granted, even in here, that prove us human. They just turned on the heaters yesterday, Monday 20th. I think they had to somehow show that they do have some decency, at least for the holidays. They froze our butts off the last month and a half. They do it every year, but what made this year even worse than last year was that they did not give us coats in October as they are supposed to. Guys were setting fires in the front of their cells and others were flooding the runs which made things worse because now we are cold and water has flooded our cells and we have to get down and clean it out. The officers are not going to do so. But the new person in charge refused to turn on the heat or simply turn the air-conditioning off.

---

29   His execution date was set for January 25, 2007. On January 22, the Supreme Court of the United States canceled the date of execution, without a new date being set. Ron Chambers is now (June, 2009) in his 34th year on death row.

What is death?

I am standing on the sea shore. A ship spreads her white sails on the morning breeze and starts for the ocean.

She is an object of beauty and I stand watching her till at last she fades on the horizon, and then someone at my side says, "She is gone."

Gone where? Gone from my sight, that is all.

She is just as large at the masts, hull and spars as she was when I first saw her, and just as able to bear her load of living freight to its destination.

The diminished size and total loss of sight is in me, not in her.

And just at the moment when someone at my side says:

"She is gone,"

There are others who are watching her coming and voices take up a glad shout: "There she comes."

That is dying.

(Anon).

"Verily, verily I say unto you, If a man keep my saying, he shall never see death."

(John 8:51)

"To love abundantly is to live abundantly, and to love forever is to live forever."

(Henry Drummond)

Everyone stayed under their blankets most of the day. There were times when I found myself knotted into a ball on my bunk because I could not get warm. I tried to explain to this person that as a diabetic it wasn't good for me or any diabetics to be exposed to those kinds of temperatures for very long because it damages the blood circulation. He looked at me as if I were asking him for a pardon.

Then, right in the middle of going through all this they put us on lockdown, and now not only are we freezing, but we are being fed cold food: sometimes only a cheese sandwich and peanut butter, sometimes a very dry and hard meat loaf or a piece of chicken, but it would all be frozen! And being on level 2 we do not have coffee pots so we can't heat the food or drink warm beverages.

But don't get me wrong. I am not complaining. Every adversity in life is given to bring us a lesson. *(November 21, 2006)*

To Marion

You asked me what death meant to me. You would think that being here on death row, growing up watching friends die would have caused me to spend countless hours thinking of death. But that is not the case. I think very little of death. We cannot go forwards and backwards at the same time. I do not know anything about death. I only know about life, and to speak of something I have no experience of goes against me.

But you asked what death meant personally to me, so I can give you an answer from my perspective. To me death is an enemy, but it has functions as everything does. A knife can be a weapon only if it is used in that capacity. I have seen men who dropped their appeals because they were sick and could not stand the pain of wasting away. So death became a way out for them, it became a comforter, something to ease the pain. I have seen men fight against it, not wanting to be embraced by it, fearing the unknown. But I have seen others accept death with smiles on their faces as they opened their arms.

I believe that life is something special, that once it is given it cannot be taken back, that once it is formed, the energy that becomes you in the flesh will always exist, and since energy dos not disappear, it has to reappear some place. Death makes us realize how wonderful life truly is.

Most of my life I went through life never feeling really loved by anyone. The only person in my life who was positive [towards me] was my great-grandmother. I loved my older brother, but I knew that he was loved more [than I] by my mother and sisters. I spent all my life never having one single person to look out for me. When I was a kid, if I needed new shoes, I would not wait for anyone to get them. I would go and find a job at the supermarket tearing up boxes, or I would collect cans or bottles. I even bought my baby sister clothes and shoes.

Trusting Divine Love

"Fear not, for I have redeemed thee,
I have called thee by thy name, THOU ART MINE.[. . .]
Since thou wast precious in my sight,
thou hast been honorable and I have loved thee."

(Isaiah 43:1, 4)

"Are not two little sparrows sold for a penny?
And yet not one of them will fall to the ground
without your Father's leave and notice.
But even the very hairs of your head are all numbered. Fear not then, you are of more value
than sparrows."

(Jesus, The Amplified Bible)

"The steps of a good man are ordered by the Lord
and he delighteth in his way.[. . .]
The law of God is in his heart,
none of his steps shall slide."

(Psalm 37: 23, 31)

"He sent from above, He took me, He drew me out of many waters.[. . .] He brought me forth
into a large place, He delivered me because He delighted in me."

(Psalm 18:16, 19)

When I spoke to my mother before she died, she explained that the reason she never worried about me or paid much attention to me was because she knew I did not need it, that I was the strongest and hence should look out for my brothers and sisters. *(November 24, 2006)*

To Clotilde (who personally gave a photo of Roger to Amma, the great Indian spiritual leader, during one of her "hugging marathons" – she has hugged over 23 million people worldwide – requesting that she pray for him. Roger was put on level 2 [solitary] because he refused to enter a new cell (prisoners are shuffled around constantly) that was so filthy basic decency prevents us from describing it).

I am sorry for the delay in writing but I was in solitary confinement for three months. I received most of your letters there, but I was not able to answer them until now because I was unable to make commissary and did not have any stamps. I am out of con-finement now and trying to catch up on correspondence and simply get back to where I was at first. I am healthy and smiling and feeling blessed as I do every day.

Many people give thanks to God when they are happy but very few remember to give thanks to God when they are sad. God is the same whether you are happy or sad. We will never be able to understand God or His plan for our lives, but if we believe in God then we must trust Him and allow Her to be in control. Thank you for the energies that you never forget to send my way.

No, I am not able to see the moon. In the cell I had before I went into solitary, I was able to stand in the center of the floor and look straight up through the small window and there would be the moon looking back at me. It was so beautiful to behold. The light would fill the room with this soft yellow-orange glow. I used to look forward to it every single night. Some nights it would appear later than others and sometimes earlier, but it would always show up. I miss it. *(December 4, 2006)*

"I have learned
to carry my altar
in my heart"

(Roger McGowen, January 14, 2007)

2007

To Marion

I have learned to carry my altar in my heart because that is the only place where it is safe here. I have had pictures ripped from the walls and torn to shreds and I have had little altars set up in the corner of my cell destroyed accidentally by the officers – and I have no doubt that they were accidents. But I realized that the greatest altar of all I carried with me all the time and that it could never be destroyed.

It is very difficult to find quiet time here because it is always noisy. They only give us the opportunity to get five hours sleep and that is from 10 p.m. to 3 a.m., so one has to learn to meditate when possible. But I have learned to wait till it is the noisiest time of the day. I have a star on my wall facing east. I sit on the floor of the cell and I focus on the star until I block out all the noise and my vision goes black and I give my prayers in the quiet of that blackness. I do not attempt to block any thoughts out. I allow them to manifest as they will and as they come to me. I watch as they pass and I bless each one as they come and go. Then when I am out of meditation, I reflect on the thoughts and search my feelings to find out where they originated from, because somewhere during the day or night someone said or did something that made those thoughts form and thus helped shape my reality whether I wanted them to or not. Smile.

I guess I say death is my enemy because it holds its secrets so close to its chest and refuses to give them up. I have witnessed many deaths, and I have seen the fear in the eyes of those who were facing it, but maybe you have seen what I have not and your understanding of it surpasses mine. We are all teachers and students. We must never be afraid to teach and we must never be afraid to learn. I truly believe that there is a life after death. I also believe there are realms we must obtain before we can move on to our destination, but we must continue to die in order to obtain them. Each death is like the layers of an onion that we peel off until we get to the core of our true being. Even Jesus feared death because he did not know it. Yet he conquered it because it was his destiny. I said that death was my enemy. I do not fear an enemy, I simply respect it more because I cannot understand it. I must admit that I am sure that most of my perceptions about death were passed down to me from parents and the churches that I attended as a child. Maybe, before this ordeal is over, I will see death as being more of a portal that opens and allows me to move from one realm into the next. Many cultures have many different beliefs about life and death and we should explore each to get a thorough understanding of both.

Without love there is no life, there is only existing. I believe that is why this place is so cold, so void of emotion, because they have taken human contact out of the prison. Everyone exists in their own sanctum. Many have gone mad, and others have chosen suicide. But I choose to draw from the love that was given to me and is still given to me by my friends through prayer. Thank you for coming into my life and thank you for allowing me to be me. Feel my arms embracing you, feel my warmth. I hope your days are filled with color and light. *(January 7, 2007)*

> "Love ever gives
> forgives
> outlives
> and ever stands
> with open hands.
> For this is love's prerogative:
> to give and to give and to give."
>
> (A short verse the author's grandmother once shared with him)

To Ulrike

Yes, I started reading The Art of Being but had to stop to do some work for my lawyer. It is funny in a way: I have been here for almost twenty years. I have had six lawyers and I have never been questioned by any of them as to what actually happened and my whereabouts on the night [of the crime]. Actually, I only met two of the six lawyers I had, and they wouldn't answer the letters I wrote them. But my new lawyer has been to see me more times than all of the others added together, and he and his staff have discovered information that was not very hard to find out that the others never bothered to concern themselves with.[30] So, I am having to go over a lot of the things that took place over twenty years ago, write them down, and read a lot of the court documents I never had access to before.

Thank you so much for all your contributions and your friends' contributions. It is sad that one has to raise money to afford justice in a country that claims to be the leader of the free world, whatever that means. I still believe that regardless of money, without prayers we cannot expect miracles. I need your prayers more than I need your money, because through prayer God will deliver the necessary funds. All my friends in Europe have become more than friends. They are my family and that is how I see them all. I wish I could thank everyone in Europe for all the love and kindness they have shown me over the years. I can't help but feel special and at the same time humbled.

Of course I will pray for you, but I do not have to pray that the right person will come along. I am sure that that person is looking for you as well. Sometimes we have to stop looking for the things we seek, then they will come to us. We seek what we are. Love attracts love, hate attracts hate, happiness attracts happiness. Be happy in spite of your situation, so when that someone comes along into your life they will only add to your happiness. Don't be too hard on yourself. Give yourself a break. Sometimes we waste time looking for what is right in front of us.

Remember, love will find its own way if we give it the chance.

Thank you for all your blessings and prayers and love. Enjoy the light of the year and never be afraid to laugh at yourself. *(January 14, 2007)*

---

30   One of the members of the international support group behind Roger, a student living in Switzerland, by simply searching on the internet in 2006, managed to locate two of the key witnesses, one of whom she was able to reach by phone and who said he would be most willing to testify in favor of Roger. A professional investigator working out of Texas, who was paid thousands of dollars, did not get half the valuable information this student reached with a few clicks on her computer.

One lethal bullet, but two executed
(*Houston Chronicle* editorial about Joseph Nichols)

"Capital punishment is always a controversial issue, a fair trial should not be. Joseph Nichols' execution should be halted. The murder of Claude Shaffer, Jr. . . . was a heinous crime by any measure, but if Joseph Nichols is executed by the State as planned on Wednesday, it will also be a terrible injustice. Nichols has been on death row since 1982, convicted of firing the single bullet that killed Claude Shaffer.

At Nichols' trial, the State knew that Nichols did not shoot the single bullet that killed Claude Shaffer, because the State had previously tried and convicted Willie Ray Williams for firing the single bullet. In January, 1981, Williams, who had confessed to the shooting, was tried, convicted and sentenced to death as the shooter. Williams has since been executed. According to the trial transcripts, the State argued: 'Willie Williams is the individual who killed Claude Shaffer. That's all there is to it. It is scientific. It is complete. It is final and it is evidence.' *Six months after Williams' conviction, Joseph Nichols' first trial began. Nichols was tried as an accomplice under the law of parties, through which a person can be held criminally responsible for an offense committed by the conduct of another under certain circumstances.*

The jury found him guilty, but hung in the punishment phase. After the trial, the prosecutor questioned some of the jurors at a local bar. They stated they were reluctant to impose the death penalty because, as the prosecutors had admitted, Nichols was not the shooter.

Six months later, in February 1982, Nichols' second trial began. This time the State changed the story, and Nichols was tried as the shooter and not the accomplice. He was convicted and sentenced to death. In complete contradiction to the State's previous argument, the trial transcripts reveal that the State contended: 'Willie Ray Williams could not have shot [Shaffer]. And I submit to you from this evidence [Nichols] fired the fatal bullet that killed the man in cold blood and he should answer for that.' *The prosecution further argued:* 'You should think about justice when you think about this case. Is it fair and equal for Williams to sit up there on death row when this man [Nichols] planned the whole thing and fired the fatal shot?'

It is an undisputed fact that a single shot killed Shaffer. For their convenience, Harris County prosecutors changed the facts from day to day and from case to case, making a mockery of the justice system. This apparently does not matter to the State of Texas, as it refuses to give Nichols a new trial.

(continued p.258)

Last Wednesday they killed a friend of mine named Joseph Nichols. He is the guy who was sitting two seats from us on your last visit, Pierre. He was visiting with his mother, and on the way out he stopped and we touched fingers through the mesh wires surrounding the cages. He was put to death on the seventh of March. He fought them every step of the way. I believe they had to execute him in his underwear because he would not put on a jumper or any clothes and stayed strapped down the entire time. The sad part about it all is that he was innocent. His partner confessed to being the trigger man. Joe did not kill the store clerk – Willie Williams did and admitted it! They executed Willie Williams in 1995. They used the same evidence to convict both guys of the same murder. In a murder case, unless a person is shot more than once by different guns, there is only one murderer. For moralists who like to quote from the Bible and quote "An eye for an eye, and tooth for a tooth," why do two people have to die for one death? If the law was fair, once Williams was executed, Joseph should have gotten a life sentence. He will be missed. He was a peacemaker here behind these walls, and his quiet wisdom and soft voice will be missed. *(March 11, 2007)*

To Marion

I assume most visitors would never be the same after visiting Polunsky Unit's Death Row. It has a life altering effect on some people. It bares the soul for all to see and leaves wounds in the heart that can never be healed. Mothers are crying for their sons, crying for themselves, crying for all the mothers that cried before them and that will cry after them. Crying tears that African American mothers have been crying for over 400 years, crying for the lost life of a son. Sons trying to be strong and not allow their mothers to see them cry, all the time crying an eternal river inside. I have never witnessed love being expressed so mightily, so profoundly, so hard as in Polunsky Unit's death row visiting room. So it does not surprise me that you felt it there. We only feel what is inside us.

You asked me to describe how I am so free? Some things that you try to put in words take the magic from it. You can see the beauty of a sunset all your life, and no matter how you try, you simply never will be able to describe that kind of beauty. I feel free because I refuse to bow down to someone else's reality. I did not see this for me, I will never accept it Marion, and by not accepting it I live my life the only way that I can, and that is moment by simple moment. When I find myself dragging my feet and feeling sorry for myself, I shake myself and wake myself up, because we all fall asleep sometimes with work still to be done.

I am free, Marion, because I refuse not to be.
Simply that.

(March 11, 2007)

Editorial about Joseph Nichols' execution (continued)

The State also suppressed evidence favorable to Nichols' defense. There were two witnesses to the crime, Cindy Johnson and Teresa Ishman. Johnson was the State's star witness because she testified to witnessing the entire murder. However, Ishman informed the police that Johnson 'could not have seen the fatal shot being fired, because she (Johnson) was hidden in the bathroom when the shooting started.' *The State suppressed the identity and location of Ishman from the defense so that she could not testify at the trial.*

The State of Texas now claims her testimony would not have made a difference and does not matter. If the state doesn't think Ishman's testimony would have altered the outcome of the trial, one has to wonder why they hid her true identity and whereabouts from the defense, and further, why they refuse to grant Nichols a new trial, one in which the jury hears both witnesses, instead of just one.

Joseph Nichols' court-appointed attorney was shamefully negligent. After having been granted eleven extensions in two years for filing an appellate brief, Nichols' attorney ignored the orders of the Texas Court of Criminal Appeals. He was held in contempt, arrested, and put in jail. Nichols' appellate brief was written by his attorney while he was in jail. The attorney was so inept that he was ultimately disbarred, but the damage to Nichols' case was done. The State doesn't think this matters either, even though the American Constitution guarantees its citizens effective counsel" (Editorial, *Houston Chronicle*, March 4, 2007).

Joseph Nichols was put to death for the crime Williams admitted committing and for which Williams had been put to death earlier.

A paradigm shift in the United States?

Very recent developments in the United States have contributed to a gradual shift in the ongoing public debate about the death penalty. The growing realization that innocent men and women have been sentenced to death and have actually been executed is changing the focus of attention from the question of the moral right to execute the guilty to that of the unacceptable and irreversible injustice of killing the innocent. The August 17, 2009 decision of the US Supreme Court to order a federal District Court in Georgia to review the now world-famous case of Troy Davis in a hearing on his claim of innocence was historic, the first such decision in 50 years, and it could have far reaching implications for the workings of appellate courts in capital cases in the whole country.

The New Yorker magazine reported on September 7, 2009 that Texas could become the first state to acknowledge officially that it has carried out the "execution of a legally and factually innocent person" when it executed Cameron Todd Willingham on February 17, 2004.

2009

Since his letters were selected and assembled for this book in 2007, Roger's correspondence with me and with all his other friends has continued and deepened. The original 2003 French version of the book has been completely revised, adapted, and expanded also to include letters of the last six years for the English edition. Roger is still on death row in Texas and his case is slowly making progress.

In the last few months, I have sensed a very subtle change of feel in our correspondence. Something is shifting and it's noticeable. We more and more believe that Roger will make it, or better said, our conviction that he will regain his freedom is stronger than ever.

In his most recent letter to me, Roger wrote:

Pierre, I believe we did a beautiful thing [publishing the book]. If I never do a single thing worth mentioning in my life ever again, I can go to my grave knowing that if one person gained strength from my suffering and learned to live and enjoy life again, I will be happy. (August 16, 2009)

Postscript

Roger was arrested in 1986 and sentenced to death a year later, after a first trial that was a farce as this book describes.

I first started corresponding with him in 1997, when an execution date had been scheduled. A long-time correspondent of Roger's alerted a number of people in Switzerland and we pooled our resources together to hire a first private lawyer who submitted what is known as a Writ of Habeas Corpus. This automatically annulled the execution date (the case stayed on the judge's desk for well over seven years with no further action being taken).

Around 2000 I realized Roger's letters were so amazing that I could not keep them to myself; those letters belonged to humanity and had to be shared, so I decided, with Roger's approval of course, to publish a book of them in French. The book (later published in a Dutch translation as well) came out in 2003 and changed absolutely everything in Roger's life. He started receiving letters from all over the world, from people telling him how his letters had changed their lives. You can well imagine the impact this had on Roger. There he was, living an apparently useless life in hell, with no future, when all of a sudden total strangers start thanking him and telling him his book has had such a deep impact, changing everything for them!

In 2005, Gary Taylor, Roger's first private lawyer, left Texas, the judge withdrew from the case and a state-appointed lawyer was assigned. This man turned out to be the very last Roger would have wanted, since, as he did not even believe in Roger's innocence, execution was a certainty. Fortunately, that attorney also left Texas in 2006. I had then just formed an international support and defense committee mostly made up of readers who had written to me. We created a first website (2006) and decided to hire a new private lawyer, Anthony Haughton. Another lawyer was also appointed by the state - this time an excellent man, Paul Mansur, who had already got someone else off death row. Together, they make a very strong team.

In the summer of 2009, our lawyers filed a brief presenting our side of the case. At Easter of 2010, the judge on the case, one of the most conservative in Houston, did not recognize Roger's innocence but acknowledged that a number of grave errors in procedure had been made and that he should not have been condemned to death. So the death penalty was lifted, which is a huge relief for our lawyers who are under less pressure now. The state district attorney, as is usual in Texas, appealed this ruling, and the case is now moving to a federal court in New Orleans, where a judgment might take place toward the end of the year.

In this case the death penalty could be transformed into prison for life. But when Roger was judged in 1987, life meant 25 years, and he has already done 23 of them, which means he could theoretically be freed in two years.

APPENDIX: LIST OF ADDITIONAL
DOCUMENTS AND TEXTS

BIBLIOGRAPHY

Arriens, Jan, editor, Sister Helen **Prejean** and Clive Stafford **Smith**. *Welcome to Hell: Letters and Writings from Death Row*. Northeastern University Press, 2004. A case history and collection of letters written on death row collected by the founder of *LifeLines* (Great Britain).

Atwood, David. *Detour to Death Row*. Peace Center Books, San Antonio, TX, 2008. The founder of the Texas Coalition to Abolish the Death Penalty describes the challenges of campaigning for human rights in the number one state for executions in the USA.

Baird, Robert M., and Stuart E. **Rosenbaum**, editors. *Punishment and the Death Penalty: The Current Debate*. Prometheus Books, 1995. Twenty outstanding essays for and against the death penalty by philosophers, sociologists, legal scholars and ethicists.

Banner, Stuart. *The Death Penalty, an American History*. Harvard University Press, 2003. A comprehensive history of the death penalty in the USA over the past four centuries.

Bedau, Hugo Adam, and Paul G. **Cassell**. *Debating the Death Penalty: Should America Have Capital Punishment*. Oxford University Press, 2004. The experts on both sides make their case. For: District Judge Paul Cassell, Judge Alexander Kozinski, District Attorney Joshua Marquis, philosopher Louis Pojman. Against: philosopher Hugo Bedau, defense attorney Stephen Bright, Bryan Stevensen (Equal Justice Initiative), former Illinois Governor George Ryan.

Burton-Rose, Daniel, editor (with editors of *Prison Legal News* Dan Pens and Paul Wright). *The Celling of America*. Common Courage Press, 1998.

Cahill, Thomas. *A Saint on Death Row: The Story of Dominic Green*. Nan A. Talese/Doubleday, 2008. One of the greatest writers on the history of civilization tells the story of Dominique Jerome Green, probably an innocent man, executed in Texas in 2004.

Dow, David. *Executed on a Technicality: Lethal Injustice on America's Death Row.* Beacon Press, 2005. One of the most brilliant legal minds of the country describes the intractable mazes of the American, and especially Texan, legal system that enables the triumph of form over substance, of technicality over justice and humanity. Absolute "must" reading for anyone who wants to get a real grasp on the real reasons for which the death penalty system resembles more a lottery than true justice.

Fuhrman, Mark. *Death and Justice. An Expose of Oklahoma's Death Row Machine.* Harper-Collins, 2004. America's most famous detective examines death row in the American State with the highest per capita rate of executions (even more than Texas). Fuhrman focuses his skills on a dozen of the most controversial cases. When he started his research, he was a firm believer in the death penalty. What he saw in Oklahoma changed his mind.

Grisham, John. *The Innocent Man – Murder and Injustice in a Small Town.* Doubleday, 2006. One of America's most successful novelists turns his talents to the exploration of justice gone awry. An extraordinary nonfiction legal thriller and a terrible indictment.

Hirsch, James S. *Hurricane: The Life of Rubin Carter, Fighter.* Fourth Estate, 2000. A well-known boxer finds himself wrongfully convicted of murder and is rehabilitated thanks to a group of idealists. (Also a film with Denzel Washington, *Hurricane*).

King, Rachel. *Don't Kill in our Names: Families of Murder Victims Speak Out Against the Death Penalty.* Rutgers University Press, 2003.

Latzer, Barry. *Death Penalty Cases: Leading U.S. Supreme Court Cases on Capital Punishment*, 2nd edition. Butterworth-Heinemann, 2002. An unbiased collection of 25 seminal death penalty cases presented to the Supreme Court. Without taking sides, the author offers a keen selection of material. The quality of the commentary makes this a superb resource and educational tool for the concerned citizen.

Lewis, Reginald S. *Where I'm Writing from: Essays from Pennsylvania's Death Row.* PublishAmerica, 2005. A fascinating collection of essays about life behind bars and corruption by a talented death row poet.

Light, Ken and Suzanne **Donovan**. *Texas Death Row.* University Press of Mississippi, 1997. Ken Light and his camera were permitted unparalleled access to Texas death row. His stark, powerful images unveil more than reams of written pages. Suzanne Donovan's essay draws upon her interviews with the inmates, prison authorities, family members and members of victims' families.

Mello, Michael. *The Wrong Man: A True Story of Innocence on Death Row*. University of Minnesota Press, 2001. The dramatic story of Mello's 25 year fight to save "Crazy Joe" Spaziano from being executed for a murder he did not commit. The inevitable conclusion is that wrongful convictions can easily occur, and innocent people are sentenced to death and executed in America.

Palmer, Louis J., Jr. *The Death Penalty: An American Citizen's Guide to Understanding Federal and State Laws*. McFarland & Company, 1998. In a country where even lawyers are challenged by the complexity of the system, the primary focus of this book written in plain language is on the death penalty phase of criminal prosecution. Important reading for anyone following a death row inmate or who simply wants to understand why and how innocents are put to death.

Prejean, Sister Helen. *Dead Man Walking – An Eyewitness Account Of the Death Penalty in the United States*. Vintage Books, 1994. This international bestseller takes an unprecedented look at the human consequences of the death penalty on both sides (the victims and the accused). (Also a film with Susan Sarandon and Sean Penn, *Dead Man Walking*).

Prejean, Sister Helen. *The Death of Innocents – An Eyewitness Account of Wrongful Executions*. Vintage Books, 2005. Describes with both passion and sharp intelligence the "awful truth" about capital punishment in the USA where "procedure arbitrarily trumps substance, maddening incompetence undermines best intentions, racism shames everyone and innocents are executed" (B. Scheck).

Schabas, William A. *The Abolition of the Death Penalty in International Law*, 3rd edition. Cambridge University Press, 2002. This highly praised study details the progress of the international community away from the use of capital punishment.

Sharp, Susan F. *Hidden Victims: The Effects of the Death Penalty on Families of the Accused* (Critical Issues in Crime and Society). Rutgers University Press, 2005. Many people consider murderers to be subhuman. Sociologist Susan Sharp interviewed many families of people on death row.

Scheck, Barry, Peter **Neufeld**, and Jim **Dwyer**: *Actual Innocence: Five Days to Execution, and Other Dispatches from the Wrongly Convicted*. Doubleday, 2000. In what may well be the most important book on the US criminal justice published in a decade, the founders of The Innocence Project tell the harrowing account of ten innocent men wrongfully convicted by a justice system that often simply does not work. The number one "must" reading for anyone concerned with the issue of justice in the USA.

Sorensen, Jonathan R., and Rocky LeAnn **Pilgrim**. *Lethal Injection: Capital Punishment in Texas During the Modern Era*. University of Texas Press, 2006. This book is the first comprehensive empirical study of the system of capital punishment of Texas in the modern era.

Schmid-Eastwood, Wendy. *Twisted Truth*. Athena Press, 2004. The correspondent of a death row inmate who was probably innocent documents his struggle for justice until the very last minute and his execution in 2000.

Sundry, Scott E. *A Life and Death Decision: A Jury Weighs the Death Penalty*. Palgrave Macmillan, 2005. A sharp look into jury deliberation rooms, where jurors often don't even really understand the rules supposed to govern their decisions.

Turow, Scott. *Ultimate Punishment – A Lawyer's Reflections on Dealing with the Death Penalty*. Farrar, Straus & Giroux, 2003. A brilliant and respected criminal lawyer tells the human stories behind the statistics and engages in a profound and solidly grounded examination of the functioning of the present legal system.

Willett, Jim, and Ron **Rozelle**. *Warden: Texas Prison Life and Death from the Inside Out*. Bright Sky Press, Texas, 2005. The man who probably accompanied more men to their grave than any other in Texas tells of his 30-years career in Texas prisons, first as a guard, then as a warden.

FINANCIAL SUPPORT FOR ROGER MCGOWEN

Should you wish to make a financial contribution to Roger McGowen's defence fund, you can use the PayPal link at www.rogermcgowen.org. (Note: you do not need a Pay-Pal account. PayPal will process your credit card without you joining their system).

For details about making donations by cheque, money order, credit card, or wire transfer, please call Ronald Radford at 1-800-291-7050 (USA).
Or send an email to ron@ronaldradford.com

Or send a note to:
  Ronald Radford
  734, Henry Rd
  Ballwin
  MO 63011
  U.S.A.

Outside the United States:
Please contact Pierre Pradervand at pierre@vivreautrement.ch

  Pierre Pradervand,
  Bd. James Fazy 3 ,
  1201 Genève,
  Switzerland

We also have an account at a British bank where people can send funds:
Natwest Bank, sort code 60-10-34, account number 12625868,
account name P Pradervand, Legal defense RMCG
IBAN: GB31 NWBK 6010 3412 6258 68
BIC: NWBK GB 2L

If received funds exceed the sum needed, they will be given to the Texas Defender Service, which does an outstanding job defending indigent inmates in Texas and has authored some of the best research on the much needed reforms of the Texas legal system.

Corresponding with Roger

Should you wish to express your appreciation to Roger, you can send a typewritten letter in English to the following address:

Mr. Roger McGowen
c/o G.C. Jaquet
132 Turk Street # 102908
San Fransisco, CA 94102
U.S.A.

Do not forget to mention your name and address on the letter itself. Mail will be forwarded to Roger on a regular basis, but it may not be possible for him to answer each letter and card personally due to shortage of stamps. You can also ask Roger a question on-line. Go to the website his friends have created for him: www.rogermcgowen.org